MARGARET FULLER

PARKLAND COLLEGE LRC

MARGARET FULLER

A BIOGRAPHY BY
☆ MARGARET BELL ☆

WITH AN INTRODUCTION BY
MRS. FRANKLIN D. ROOSEVELT

BOOKS FOR LIBRARIES PRESS
FREEPORT, NEW YORK

First Published 1930
Reprinted 1971

INTERNATIONAL STANDARD BOOK NUMBER:
0-8369-5871-3

LIBRARY OF CONGRESS CATALOG CARD NUMBER:
72-164587

PRINTED IN THE UNITED STATES OF AMERICA

TO
MY MOTHER

CONTENTS

PART I: PREPARATION
PAGE 17

PART II: EXPERIMENTATION
PAGE 88

PART III: FULFILLMENT
PAGE 196

Special acknowledgments and thanks are due to Mrs. Arthur Nicholls, of Cambridge, Massachusetts, niece of Margaret Fuller, for allowing me to use many unpublished manuscripts and letters; to Mr. Edward Locke Gookin, Registrar of Harvard College Library, for his courtesy in giving me the freedom of the archives of the library; and to Mrs. Anna Felton Dakin, for her invaluable assistance therein.

INTRODUCTION

It is good for us to-day to reread the life of a woman like Margaret Fuller and remind ourselves of the trail which she and many other women, her contemporaries and followers, blazed. It is a trail in which the present generation is now following with some difficulties still, but when we read of the early days we can certainly feel that we owe much to the pioneers.

Margaret Fuller may be said to have had no childhood. Her father forced a very brilliant mind far beyond the ordinary development of a child and this early forcing shows in her mental attitudes all through her life. In the thirties she was still longing for some of the things that early youth should have given her. She was a loving and devoted daughter, sister, friend, wife and mother. She happened to live in New England but her nature was not stamped with the mark of any locality. It had the warmth of the South and the breadth of the whole world. Her reading had been wide and, as one would expect of those days, she was tremendously influenced by the classics.

To us to-day much of what she said and wrote seems pedantic and the language, which was that of the scholar of her day, smacks somewhat of the Blue Stocking to-day, but back of it we still sense the enthusiasm for greatness of mind and soul; the humility which was prepared to sit at the feet of any great men or women; the self-sacrifice which gave always in every way possible, first to her father and mother and brothers and sisters and, finally, when real love came to her, to her husband and child. It was a day when women were of little account in the intellectual field. There were few women of note in this country in the world of letters and she stands out as teacher and writer.

Her book, *Woman in the Nineteenth Century*, was an epoch-making book and her power to impress her personality and her greatness of soul on those around her did more than anything else to bring the acknowledgment and the recognition that women had an intellectual and spiritual contribution to make, as great as that of men. She blazed new trails; she made many friends, both men and women, in this country and in Europe; she left a trail wherever she went which stimulated thought. It is not what she wrote which makes her life for us a vivid influence to-day, but what she was, and in this book, from a rather tragic childhood to the heroic and tragic end, you feel the sweep of a great personality. She sometimes touched the depths of human sorrow; she sometimes touched the heights of joy and exaltation, but all through there is the strain of indomitable courage and fineness of spirit, which is as exhilarating and valuable to us to-day as it was to those who actually met and knew her.

You feel when you have closed this book that you have known and lived with a real person. You might not always have been sympathetic with her but you could not help recognizing the bigness and high striving that sometimes lay behind the sharp tongue and the bitter words. To the weak and the suffering she was always gentle; those she loved she never failed—what more can be asked of any human being?

I hope that to all who read this book will come a realization of one quality which stands out in Margaret Fuller, namely, the belief and trust that human beings were marching on through wider sympathy and tolerance and understanding to a higher and finer destiny.

Mrs. Franklin D. Roosevelt

MARGARET FULLER

PART I
PREPARATION

I
THE FIGHTING FULLERS

She came from a race called The Fighting Fullers. Had she disembarked at Salem in 1638 with her forbear Thomas Fuller, she doubtless would have been burned as a witch, for she believed in signs and omens, in the magic of certain precious stones, in charms and talismans. Fortunately, they had given up burning witches long before she was born.

That first Fuller, Thomas, came over from England out of curiosity. He was a blacksmith by trade, but at odd moments he turned to the goose-quill and expressed himself in verse. He was a man of few words but of ardent feelings. A streak of mysticism ran through him; he was awed by the splendor of the wilderness in whose long shadows strange animals moved, across whose crests strange birds flew southward with the autumn winds. He was a church-going man but he did not care for Hugh Peters. So, one day, he went over to Cambridge to hear the Reverend Thomas Shephard, that "gracious, sweet, heavenly-minded and soul-ravishing minister," who, for his liberal opinions, had been unfrocked by William Laud, Bishop of London, and hounded out of England.

Shephard's preaching satisfied Thomas Fuller so entirely that he decided to remain in New England where he might come regularly under such influence. And back he went to Salem, took up his goose-quill and paid tribute to Mr. Shephard's eloquence and spiritual zeal. His meter limped, his words were commonplace. What matter? Language is at times a cracked cymbal when it attempts to measure human longing or despair or exaltation.

He looked around for a business site. The country was a primitive wilderness, but there were some open stretches from which the aboriginal tribes had removed the trees, and there were salt marshes and boggy lowlands. There was in particular the lowland of that section of Salem called Middleton. Iron had been found there. This was propitious. Thomas Fuller chose that site for his blacksmith shop and "ironworking establishment."

He became an influential citizen and before very long married Miss Elizabeth Tidd of Woburn and built a house for her on the bank of a small brook which emptied itself into Middleton Pond, half a mile away. They had six sons and one daughter. And thus began the long line of American Fullers, of whom the most illustrious was Sarah Margaret, Marchioness of Ossoli.

Before her came many aggressive men with substantial names suggesting the Bible: John, Joseph, Stephen, Jacob, Jonathan, Timothy. They were carpenters, shipjoiners, soldiers, tinsmiths, printers. The women had substantial names too: Hannah, Sarah, Abigail, Margaret, Ruth. They were large-boned and healthy, and they brought forth many children. All of them, men and women, were positive and were not afraid to express themselves.

There was Timothy, the great-grandson of the original Thomas. He was a Harvard man of the class of 1760; he became a clergyman but he did not turn his back on politics. He believed that the Revolution was premature and told his congregation so. At the very time when the blunderbusses were all primed to fire their reverberant shots, Timothy stood up before his congregation at Princeton, Massachusetts, and preached an eloquent sermon on passive resistance, taking for his text, "Let not him that girdeth on the harness boast himself as he that putteth it off." He was listened to in silence, was allowed to go home to his Sunday dinner. But he soon learned what his congregation thought of his sermon; was quietly removed from his ministry and refused his year's salary.

He fought for it, but vainly; and eventually decided to commune with his God in the out-of-doors, to seek Him in the fields and woods. He bought a farm which lay in the shadow of Wachusset Mountain, and all the years he lived there, voted steadily against the Constitution because it recognized human slavery. He left five sons, all of whom became lawyers; and five daughters; and he died five years before the birth of his grandchild Margaret Fuller, who would have delighted him.

Margaret's father was Timothy, the eldest son of Timothy the pacifist. He was born in 1778, while the republic was still feeling its way about. He was no advocate of passive resistance, but was arrogant, proud, self-assertive. In his attitude toward England, he was the fiery youth exulting in freedom from maternal tyranny; in his attitude toward France, he was a sentimental schoolboy in love with a fair unknown. He believed in learning for learning's sake and expressed himself always in pedantic language; he believed in a personal God, in Puritanism and in the superiority of the "fighting Fullers." Life to him was a serious business, made up of innumerable individual lives which had to be constantly disciplined. Homes were the natural division of the great kingdom of life and each home was ruled by its father-monarch. A good father was one whose children held him in respect and awe; a good husband was one who provided material necessities and who saw that his wife contributed plentifully to the population of the state. Any demonstration of affection, any display of tenderness was a weakness and belonged to women; to men belonged strength, austerity and the right to rule.

All of this Timothy Fuller believed; he believed, too, in man's duty to the state. He was a fiery patriot and held that governments derived their strength from the will of the governed. He supported Jefferson in the presidential elections of 1801—a year of twofold significance for him, it being the year in which he graduated from Harvard and the year in which he cast his first vote.

He began reading law with the father of Governor Levi Lincoln, a man of democratic views. He worked hard and in eight years had saved enough to establish himself as a householder. He chose for a wife Miss Margaret Crane, the daughter of Major Peter Crane of Canton, Massachusetts, a quiet self-effacing young woman, admirably suited to a man who believed so implicitly in man's right to rule. She was ten years younger than her husband.

Timothy took her to Cambridgeport to live. It was a straggling village of no particular pretensions; its cellars were often flooded by the tidewaters which broke through the dykes. But its orchards bore fruit and its gardens bloomed; it had pleasant wooded spaces which ran back as far as the buildings of Harvard College; it had its own meeting-house and two schools, its music club, "for cultivating sacred music," and its little coteries of friendly citizens.

The Fuller house was a large, rambling, ugly building at the corner of Cherry and Eaton streets. The ceilings were high, the walls austere; but at the back of it was a good-sized garden with several fruit-trees, and at the far end of the garden a wooden gate set in the wall opened into fields where violets grew and where the sun lay lingeringly.

Timothy's young wife loved flowers. She made flower-beds and set out bulbs of tulips, narcissi, hyacinths and daffodils that autumn, and planned what seeds she would sow when spring came.

But when spring came some one else sowed the seeds for her: mignonette and columbine; sweet-scented stock, veronica, forget-me-nots. On warm afternoons she took her sewing and sat in the garden. The birds sang among the fruit-blossoms, petals dropped down into her lap.

II

THE FIRST FIVE YEARS

ON MAY 23RD OF THAT YEAR, 1810, her first child was born,—a daughter. She received the name Sarah Margaret. The birth of his first child affected Timothy deeply; the event was one of mystical significance to him. To celebrate it and to symbolize the bond which was to exist between him and the child, he planted two elm-trees in front of his house. And immediately asserted his authority by giving orders for the babe's upbringing. Before he left for his office in the morning, he gave instructions about this and that— the hours that the child should spend in sleeping, the time she should spend in the sun, what diversions she should have, if any. The Lord had visited him with the responsibilities of fatherhood; he felt that he must lose no time in acknowledging them and in discharging his fatherly duties to the utmost of his ability.

He was a brain-worshiper; and he determined that his firstborn should be given every opportunity for mental development. And while she lay in her cradle, wondering about this strange, new world and looking with pleasure at her long, graceful fingers, he made out a schedule for her, which was to make her a super-woman.

Every evening on coming home from his office, he went to his daughter and noted what development had taken place during his absence. Perhaps she looked at him more knowingly, perhaps she responded to his greeting with greater intelligence. Mrs. Fuller stood aside while these inspections were going on.

Books soon became Sarah Margaret's playthings; soon she went into the garden with her mother, soon learned that the garden was something which gave her feelings different from the feelings given by anything else. And she understood the significance of the word, beautiful.

There were other things in her life which were not exactly beautiful, but which were important. Learning the alphabet was one, and learning how to tell the number of things that were around her was another.

Her mother represented beauty to her. She used to look at her attentively and one day she told her mother that she was like a certain flower in the garden. It was a white amaranth.

Her father represented something entirely different; she felt excited when she heard his footstep, but the excitement was not a happy sensation; there was fear in it, for she knew that she would have to answer a great many questions and that she would have to take a book and read to him about things that did not give her a happy feeling. Sometimes she stumbled over words, for she did not see very well. This was bad; her father frowned and spoke to her in a voice that made her feel shivery.

There was a baby in the house. She was a fragile, little thing with a large name,—Julia Adelaide. Sarah Margaret sat with her a good deal and talked to her, happy in her companionship. Her mother seemed more than ever like a white amaranth; she was very pale; often she lay all afternoon on a sofa in front of the window which looked into the garden....

One day Sarah Margaret saw the nursemaid weeping. Perplexed, she looked up into the ugly, contorted face; and a strange realization came to her: This person *knew* things that she did not know; dark, secret things which she must learn sooner or later. She shrank from such knowledge, because it obviously involved pain. But she was curious.

The nursemaid took her by the hand and led her into a terribly silent room; she drew aside a curtain. There lay little Julia Adelaide, white and still and unsmiling.

Strange persons came to the house and spoke in whispers; they were dressed in black; the father did not go to the office that day, nor did he ask Sarah Margaret to read him anything. A solemn-looking man in a long, black coat stood up and said things she did not understand. His voice made her feel all creepy inside. After a while, every one moved in silence out of the house and got into carriages which waited in the street. Throughout the dreary drive, Sarah Margaret sat perplexed between her father and mother, trying vainly to understand what all the mournful parade had to do with the pretty, playful baby, who must be terribly sad about it all.

At the cemetery, her numb perplexity broke. She could not bear the idea that Julia Adelaide was to be put under the ground. She insisted that this should not be; she cried aloud, she stormed, she tried to snatch up the small, white coffin and take it away from the hideous, mocking hole. At length she was led gently back to the carriage and taken home.

This was Margaret Fuller's first memory. "My first experience of life was one of death." She was but three years old, but she felt that the experience was in some vague way prophetic, that her life would be made up of a great many experiences she did not understand experiences which would cause her pain.

The death of his second child affected Timothy Fuller in this way: all his feelings, all his ambitions were more than ever centered in Sarah Margaret. He began at once a rigid outline of study for her, impressed upon her the fact that he expected unusual things from her. From then on, he became not only her father, but her preceptor and her mother as well. He said what clothes she should wear, and himself bought little dresses for her—plain little dresses, of good materials. Sometimes he took her for walks as far as Craigie Bridge and back again. Sarah Margaret would have liked to cross the bridge.

It was not long till she began to study Latin. The words had a pleasant sound to her; she liked to say them over and over aloud: *æternitas, magister, regina*. There was about them a grandeur which responded to some questioning within her. She liked the story of Romulus having been suckled by a wolf; she liked to read of the gallantry of Cæsar, who, against the custom of his country, pronounced a panegyric over the dead body of his young wife. The Romans, being men of action, appealed to this child of thought; she saw demonstrated in them the power of indomitable will, the virtue of self-discipline, the ability to turn thoughts into deeds. "I loved this ideal in my childhood, and this is the cause, probably, why I have always felt that man must know how to stand firm on the ground before he can fly."

Yet she longed to fly; and many times bruised her wings in premature attempts.

Next she met Ovid, and a new world opened to her, the opposite of the rugged, forceful, Roman world. She looked into the "enchanted gardens" of Greek mythology and found there not only something which answered a questioning within her, but something which created new questionings and made her seek the answers for herself.

She sat in the garden behind the ugly house; she liked especially the roses and the lilies and the pinks which smelled like cloves. She lay beside the wall against the clematis vine; she was a conqueror from Rome and on the other side of the wall her enemies were gathered. She saw herself returning in great honor to Rome and heard proud clamor in the market-place.

Greece to her meant triumphs of another kind: the mailed fist gave place to the open palm, the helmet to the wreath of laurel. In Greece she walked leisurely in the shadow of purple-hooded hills, and through groves of cypresses and olive-trees. White temples with porphyry-studded pillars stood in the groves and white statues gleamed against the dark leaves.

She found more reality in her worlds of ancient Greece and Rome than in the tangible, everyday world where children played hide-and-seek and tag and ring-around-a-rosy. She felt strange with other children and was more lonely with them than with the roses and the lilies and the pinks which smelled like cloves. Yet she was hungry for companionship and for some demonstration of love; so hungry that she pressed the flowers passionately to her lips and to her breast and tried to imagine that they gave her all she needed.

Living was a lonely and rather a difficult business. The child prayed for a sign which would guide her, in some inexplicable way, through her days. She had no doubt that she would recognize such a sign, and hopefully, in the morning, when her father had gone to work, she opened the door which led to the garden, walked along the path and looked very carefully.

But there was no sign. Sighingly, she returned to the house and to her studies.

III

FANTASIES

THERE WERE THINGS going on in the world which affected Timothy Fuller very much. One was a war quite close at hand, which had recently been ended by something called the Treaty of Ghent. One cold day in February, all the church bells began to ring and flags began to fly from all the houses. The schools were closed and children ran about in the snow, shouting and hurrahing.

Timothy came home earlier than usual that day, and in the evening, took Margaret to see the illuminations. All the college buildings and many others as well looked like Christmas Eve on Beacon Hill. A great many persons were in the streets, most of them going toward Boston where emblazoned mottoes were shown up and down the seven stories of the Exchange Coffee House. Margaret could not go to Boston, because she had to recite her lessons when she got home.

On the way home, her father talked to her about the war. He did not like England nearly as much as he liked France. But a person can have only one country, he said. To that country he must be loyal. Being loyal meant being patriotic; being patriotic meant making speeches at certain times, and hanging flags on houses and shooting off a gun. The Fourth of July was the greatest day of all for this. There was a very great man connected with this day; Margaret's father spoke of him almost as reverently as he spoke of God. The man's name was Thomas Jefferson.

Timothy was a member of the State Legislature now and was working very hard; often he was not home till after dark. Most children were in bed then, but Margaret's day was not finished; she still had to recite her lessons. This took two or three hours and was very exhausting. When at length she was allowed to go to bed, she was in a state of such nervous excitement that sleep was practically impossible. When sleep finally came, it was accompanied by hideous dreams: She was on a wild heath where untamed horses raced; in vain she tried to escape from them; she stumbled and fell; their hoofs trampled over her. Or, she was lost in a forest where the trees dripped blood. It rose higher and higher; it came up past her knees. She ran through it till she stumbled and fell into a deep, red pool; she called out.

Her father, hearing her, went to her and shook her out of the dreams. She woke trembling and tried to tell him of her terror. He silenced her, ordered her to "go to sleep at once and leave off thinking of such nonsense." It never occurred to him that he was the cause of all her suffering, or that her overstimulated brain might bring on grave illness when she was older.

The child longed for a tender touch. Sometimes she dreamed that her mother was dead. She followed her to the grave as she had followed Julia Adelaide, she saw her shut away and tried to cry out, but could not. When she woke, her pillow was tear-drenched.

Life was a strange, unfathomable complexity, made up of daytime tasks and nighttime fantasies. The child felt the lack of beauty in her surroundings; the house was stoically furnished, the street was drab. She felt the lack of companionship; her mother was fully occupied, for another baby had arrived,—the first son, who was called Eugene. The world was vast and lonely. If there had been a dog in the house, it would have been less gloomy; if there had been a silly singing-bird, the hours would have been lightened. There was "no graceful, animated form of existence."

Margaret imagined things about herself: She was a princess, the daughter of a king; by some mistake she had been left on the doorstep of an ugly house in Cambridgeport and the child who should have been there was living in a palace. One day her real father would call for her, would drive up the pokey street in a gold-mounted carriage drawn by beautiful, black horses with shining coats. Flunkeys in wigs and sumptuous liveries would sit up as stiff as ramrods on the box, a great train would follow on horseback. The king would demand the return of his rightful child, who would rush into his arms and leave the ugly house and its horrible nightmares forever and ever.

She was a passionate child, and could have given much love, had love been asked of her. But it was not; no mention was ever made of it; the Puritan mind shrank from any demonstration of tenderness; there was no expression of warmth, there were no subtleties of living. Nothing but "that coarse but wearable stuff woven by the ages—Common Sense."

Margaret submitted to her father's discipline; she studied her Horace and her Ovid; she gave her father all that he apparently wanted of her. But all the time her real world "sank deep within, away from the surface of my life." Timothy, not realizing that he was admitted only to the threshold, was satisfied.

There were family gatherings on Sundays, at which Timothy usually made a point of drawing Margaret into the conversation. Even at that age, the child talked very well and was inclined to display a precociousness of which her aunts did not approve. She had been trained to speak positively on any subject she undertook; for her father did not tolerate uncertain waverings. Such modifying clauses as "if I am not mistaken," or "it may possibly be so," were unknown to him. In conversation, as in life, there were but two realms, that of fact and that of not-fact. One did not enter the latter realm, for reason did not dwell in it. There was no pleasant halfway kingdom, where imagination played. How sadly out of place would Timothy have been among the French whom he admired!

He sat at the head of his table and catechized his daughter on subjects his sisters had scarcely ever heard of; and Margaret answered him as he had taught her to answer—so positively that she sounded pert.

Her aunts were shocked. They had no patience with childish precocity, and thought a daughter's place was in the kitchen, or, if not there, in the living-room before an embroidery-frame or a triangle of knitting-needles. They wondered at their brother's lack of perception which prevented him from seeing how out of place the girl was with her Latin phrases and her constant classical references.

Margaret, on the whole, liked Sunday, although it was a solemn day, when one wore different clothes and ate different food; although it meant family prayers, for which there was no time on ordinary days; although it meant church, which was a bore. But one did not have to give an account of one's thoughts and while one sat apparently absorbed in all that the minister was saying, one might think of all manner of things.

Sometimes the minister was so thunderous that thinking was rather difficult. There was in particular one minister, who painted the most dreadful pictures: of God as a wrathful ogre riding on a black cloud and waving a flaming torch in his right hand; of some one called Satan, a being who smiled in a wheedling but highly dangerous way and who had a long, scaly tail, and hoofs instead of feet. One of Satan's favorite occupations was poking a fire, the fuel of which was human beings who had listened to his wheedlings while they were on earth. Afterwards, when they died, Satan threw them into his everlasting fire—a course of action which seemed a very unfair return for their loyalty, Margaret thought. Those who managed to avoid Satan during their lives on earth usually had a pretty hard time of it, but that did not matter, for the harder the time on earth, the easier the time in heaven, which was the name of the place they went to when they died. There they spent their time playing on harps and running up and down stairs that were made of gold, and going through a great many gates, which were made of pearls. They had large wings growing out of their shoulders and they always dressed in white. Both men and women wore the same kind of clothes—loose and flowing, and of extremely light material. Margaret supposed that some of the warmth from Satan's fire must drift up to heaven sometimes; otherwise the angels would get awfully cold.

The man who told all these wonderful and terrible things was the Reverend Abiel Holmes. He had a beautiful face and a distinguished manner. It seemed strange that he could talk about such terrible things. After the service, a small boy with funny lights in his eyes hung around the door till the hand-shaking was over, when he would slip his hand into that of the reverend gentleman and walk home with him. He was the minister's son, young Oliver Wendell Holmes.

Every one did much the same as every one else on Sunday; ate a heavy dinner after church; sat around in best clothes talking about things not usually talked about on ordinary days. On Sunday night, no one slept as well as on other nights, because of the lassitude of the day.

In the Fuller home, Sunday was very strictly observed as a day of rest. Margaret was not allowed to read novels or plays on Sunday. One winter afternoon there were several visitors in the parlor, the men in a group on one side of the room, the women in another. Timothy and his group began talking about the Missouri Compromise; the women yawned surreptitiously and remarked on the difficulty of getting supplies in winter. Margaret was sitting in a corner reading. For over two hours she remained motionless with her book.

Her father became suspicious; it must be a very engrossing tale that could keep her so occupied. He spoke her name; she did not answer. He spoke more sharply; she looked up.

"What are you reading, Margaret?"

"Shakespeare." Back went her eyes to the open page.

"Shakespeare! That won't do; that's no book for Sunday. Go, put it away immediately and find another."

The child rose obediently, put the book back in its place and returned to her corner as before.

But things were not as before. Through Margaret's mind

·(31)·

trooped a company of new acquaintances: Beautiful Juliet, so swayed by passion that she forgot her natural modesty; ardent Romeo, swearing great oaths of fidelity and love; Mercutio, the wit, who fell to cursing both Montagues and Capulets; the elders of the two houses tyrannizing over the younger generation.

These persons were real to her, so much more real than those tiresome aunts and uncles who cluttered the parlor, that she could not bear to be separated from them. So she got up quietly and once more took the book from its place.

It is early morning; a mist hangs over the Capulet orchard. At a window looking over a balcony Juliet appears; her hair is tumbled and her voice throbs, "It was the nightingale and not the lark...believe me, love, it was the nightingale." A bird's call comes through the blue mist; light spreads. Now Romeo emerges from the shadows; they cling to each other....A voice from within calls softly, "Juliet!"

A shrill voice asked querulously, "What is the child about, that she doesn't hear a word that's said to her?" One of the aunts.

Timothy spoke sharply. "What are you reading, Margaret?"

The intrusion irked the child. "Shakespeare," she answered, with impatience, and without looking up.

That was too much for Timothy, whose face suddenly went all red. He got up quickly, went to her. An awful silence hung over the room.

"How!" Timothy began, then stopped. He bit his lip to keep back some of the things that rushed to be said. He held out his hand. "Give me the book and go directly to bed."

Margaret's room was friendly. Was it not peopled by the only companions that she knew, and did it not now welcome a whole new company? They moved gracefully before her—

those Capulets and those Montagues—and she tried to solve satisfactorily the tangle of their lives. But she could scarcely wait to see how Shakespeare had solved it. Through her window the stars looked at her from a sullen sky, the scrawny branches left their shadows on the window-panes, the wind made a low shriek in the eaves.

Firm footsteps sounded in the hall. Margaret's door opened and her father came and stood beside the bed. The full flame of his anger had died down; now he could speak more calmly. He lectured her at length on the sin of her disobedience and on her manner, which had been extremely insolent. She lay looking up at the darkening ceiling, waiting for him to finish so that she go on with her dreams.

Timothy felt that she was not fully attending him, but because of her silence and docility he could do nothing about it but feel aggrieved. He left her to her dreams and went downstairs wondering vaguely what had escaped him.

There was no library in the Fuller home, but there was a closetful of books off Timothy's room. Margaret was allowed to browse among these when her studying was done. She liked her father's room; it was on the second floor and its windows were on a level with the treetops. One looked across the treetops to rolling fields which went on and on until they were lost in a blue range of hills. She spent a great deal of time in that room, especially in winter.

Sometimes she went for solitary walks. But she did not like Cambridgeport whose houses were all of uniform ugliness and whose streets were too painfully self-respecting. Sometimes thrilling things took place around the college— Commencement Day, for example, which was held at the end of August. The governor always attended. He drove through the streets in an open carriage and was followed by a troop of soldiers on horseback. The graduates went around in long gowns and funny-looking caps and afforded a great deal of amusement to the street urchins, who would have thrown stones and dirt at them if they had dared. Margaret liked the gowns, and thought that she would like to wear one when she was a little older. But only men students wore gowns, it seemed. She thought how strange it was that men and boys might do so many things that women and girls were not allowed to do. And she resolved that she would do whatever she pleased when she grew up.

IV

CONFLICTS

WHEN MARGARET was seven years old her father was elected to Congress. This meant that he was now the Honorable Timothy Fuller and that he had to leave home. A tutor was found for Margaret and her lessons continued. But she missed her father, whose knowledge of the classics she quickly found was much greater than that of his successor. She did not enjoy the task of writing and asking permission for everything she wanted to do, but this was one of the first laws.

Her particular friends at this time were Shakespeare, Molière and Cervantes. Shakespeare came first; he understood the Roman nature and he understood equally well the opposite of the Roman, such as he expressed in Hamlet. Cervantes emphasized the truth which had already fastened itself in her mind,—that life is divided into the leaders, who are few, and the followers, who are many. Molière was the witty duelist who ran his rapier through shams.

Her father assigned special tasks to her: "I wish you would give me sometimes a short passage of Latin of your own composition or at best translated from some very plain and easy passage in English. Take for instance the ten or twelve first verses of the first chapter of St. John's Gospel, which is very easy."

He began by addressing her by her full name, but after a time omitted the Sarah, and from now on she is simply Margaret.

When her letters to him were not as affectionate as he wished, or when she took longer than he thought necessary over an assignment, he questioned his wife about her. "What has become of Margaret's letter, and what of her Deserted Village in Latin? The latter seems deserted indeed."

Margaret had other letters to write. Oftener than not, they never reached their destinations, because, oftener than not, their destinations were in that vast country which is not divided into definite areas—a child's imagination. There was one written to an imaginary friend in Liverpool; a very important document this, for it had to do with the betrothal of the writer's younger brother who was three, to a distant charmer called Elise K. Greene. "Do you think it would do any harm to let them be married at 13? I have heard of a French princess who was married at 10 and a prince betrothed at 6 months.... As to nobility of blood, our family needs no ennobling. I, as you well know, am a queen. William Henry unites a prince and a king in his single person and Eugene is prince of Savoy. I am besides being a queen, the Duchess of Marlborough. But I remember I told you all our titles in a former letter...."

Timothy came home frequently. He was bothered by Margaret's increasing shortsightedness and brooded over it a good deal. And he brooded over other things: the effect of his continued absence on the child. Would it teach her to be more self-sufficing, more detached? Of late he had detected slight indifference in her attitude when he went home; this was not pleasing.

He decided that Margaret should go to school. Association with other children of the right kind should improve her manners, make her less brusque and more mindful of the respect due her elders. There was a very good school in Boston which was kept by Dr. Park. Timothy applied to this school and one day a new pupil put in an appearance. She was ten years old but looked thirteen; she had soft, brown hair which was brushed straight back from her high forehead, wide-set brown eyes which squinted a good deal, a longish nose and a large mouth. Beside the self-possessed young misses from Boston, she appeared countrified; but she had points which they had not: beautiful hands and the art of using them beautifully, a proud lift to her head which at times gave her a merely arrogant air, at others the superiority of a duchess.

She held herself aloof from other children because she felt ill at ease with them. She did not know how to play and considered their childish chatterings silly. She talked of things that they had never heard about; they thought she gave herself too many airs.

In class she always answered correctly, and in spite of themselves, the other children found themselves secretly admiring her. After a while they agreed to accept her.

Margaret sought in vain among them for a companion, and finding none, plunged deeper into her world of fancy. But she did not quite give up hope of eventually finding some one who combined at least some of the qualities of her imaginary heroes and heroines. Naturally, she had many disappointments; for instead of Cæsars and Hamlets she saw ordinary Johns and Henrys, instead of Beatrice and Juliet and Calpurnia, thrifty New England housewives whose horizons stretched no further than the horsehair sofas which stood against their walls.

There was a family that she could not tolerate. She sat next to them in church. There were five daughters in the family and they were evidently the only indulgence the parents had ever allowed themselves; but even they had a "hard, dry, dwarfed look" as if they were begotten grudgingly, as if, in the process of their creation some intrinsic quality had been left out. The mother was a wisp of womanhood from whom all vigor had been wrung, the father had the shrewd and canny eye which sees church as a good business venture, and the weekly public assembling of his brood as outward evidence of an inward state of grace.

This family was a contradiction of all that Margaret thought and felt; it was a denial of her convictions, it got between her and her illusions. She could not bear to look at the row of them seated so complacently in church, yet she could not forbear to look at them.

The only satisfaction she received from church was the hope that, one day, her eye might light on some one who was "different," and during the singing and the sermon, she looked frankly around.

One day the long-hoped-for happened; she caught sight of some one who seemed to have stepped straight out of her own imagination. She was beautiful and was dressed beautifully. But that was not all. There was about her a poise and ease of bearing, a *je ne sais quoi* not usual in Cambridge. Margaret knew at once that here was some one to whom she could talk openly and freely. She was at an impressionable age. She fell in love.

The stranger was an Englishwoman, cultivated and charming, who was spending some months in Cambridge. Had Pallas Athene suddenly appeared, had Venus been discovered walking in the Fuller garden, neither could have received more homage than did this English visitor, who, being intelligent, quickly saw the potentialities of Margaret's mind, and being sensitive, felt the eager searchings of her spirit.

And now Margaret was supremely happy. All her pent-up ardor found an outlet; she worshiped frankly.

The stranger, who had plenty of leisure hours, gave them to her young worshiper. They walked together through the fields and woods, and the fields and woods became enchanted gardens to Margaret, who now found that everything around her was clothed in new beauty and that she herself abounded in new life. She understood many things that she had often wondered about—mountains clapping their hands and giving thanks to God; she had her first inkling of the meaning of Paradise. She realized that Paradise belonged to the mind and to the heart and that was why it was so large. She had often wondered about the vast geographical extent of the place as presented to her in church. The Bible took on a new meaning for her, she began to see a meaning back of the first meaning. She thrilled with understanding of the words, "He that hath ears to hear, let him hear."

Her goddess played on the harp; Margaret sat languorously listening. Now she knew why the harp was called the instrument of the angels.

She painted in oils. All the old masters came to life for Margaret.

She moved gracefully. Margaret thought anew of the Greek worship of beauty and of the divinity in every human life.

Her happiness made her wonder about those she loved. Her mother, for example: Was she happy with her babies and her busy life? Four babies had arrived since Julia Adelaide died—Eugene, William Henry, Ellen and Arthur. Ellen was a beautiful child a little over two years old, Arthur was the youngest, a red-faced, pugnacious infant who stuck his fists into his eyes and screwed his cheeks up in a supercilious way.

The mother was becoming more and more shadowy. When neighbors came in and told her that they had heard very complimentary things about Margaret's progress at school, she smiled happily and always made a point of telling them that Margaret never neglected her share of the housework, was always ready to rock the cradle or set the table or make the beds; and that she knitted no end of woolen jackets for the little ones. The mother was afraid that the neighbors might think that because Margaret was so clever, she was spoiled.

Cambridge was a small town, ready enough to gossip. Quite a good deal of the old Tory spirit still remained; indeed there were some houses in Tory Row which were suspected of having secret, underground passages from one to the other. Several of these houses being isolated, the children played in the tangled gardens, under the yew-trees and the elms. The ivy-covered walls made splendid hiding-places, the adjoining fishponds were all-the-year-around delights. In the summer there were minnows in them, in the winter they were the skaters' paradise. Tom Higginson was one of the boys who played there. He called at the Fuller house for Eugene and the two of them went off on their adventures. Often Tom saw Margaret whom he considered rather staid.

One day the boys saw a strange spectacle—an old man in a cocked hat carrying a circular canopy over his head. This was Dr. Popkin, introducing the first umbrella to Cambridge. It was not long till the tax collector had one, then Professor Hedge was seen carrying one back and forth from lectures.

Every seventeenth of June, the boys dressed up like soldiers and played the battle of Bunker Hill. For these occasions Margaret sewed on buttons and made sashes. There were three or four wounded veterans of the revolution in Cambridge. They inspired all the boys with considerable awe, for on every holiday they got out their uniforms, put on their medals and allowed themselves to be put on parade.

A quiet, unprepossessing backwater of a town. But it was made up of honest citizens who paid their debts and who did not worry if there was not a large balance at the bank after the debts were paid. There was nothing dashing about it, there was more sincerity than gallantry, more talk of Plutarch and Socrates than of the Missouri Compromise. If the countenance of the place was provincial, the soul was not. The revolution in Europe was sending splendid men across the seas—Pietro Bachi from Italy and Frederich Grater and Charles Follen from Germany. Harvard welcomed them. It welcomed too that delightful Englishman, Thomas Nuttall, the botanist, who organized the Botanic Garden and gave a strong push to the scientific side of education.

The most picturesque of all the Harvard group was Francis Sales, who taught French and Spanish. He came from the shores of the Mediterranean and he always wore a powdered wig and pigtail. George Ticknor was getting his department of modern languages into shape, Edward Channing was Professor of English. Quite frequently he got into an argument with Edward Everett, who maintained that there was more teaching and more learning in the American Cambridge than in both the great English universities put together. Ticknor preferred the German institutions. Jared Sparks and Richard Dana and Joseph Green Cogswell had their opinions too.

The influence of these men stretched across the river to Boston and was so evident that a visiting New Yorker was moved to remark that music, painting and sculpture in Boston seemed to be regarded merely as branches of literature, that the learned professors knew more about the creators of music, painting and sculpture than they did about their creations.

It was the springtime of American letters, from which seeding was to be gathered a harvest of such names as Emerson, Holmes, Lowell, Thoreau, Longfellow, Hawthorne, Parker, Alcott, Clarke, Ripley, Norton and Margaret Fuller.

When Timothy Fuller came home from Washington, the talk turned frequently to politics. Charles Follen and Frederich Grater wanted to know more about the Monroe Doctrine and what it was going to mean to Europe....

There was occasional gossip: Was it true that Daniel Webster sometimes took a drop too much? Was it true that the judges of the Supreme Court used snuff? And did Andrew Jackson's wife really smoke a pipe? Professor Sales was interested to know whether the fashionable men at the capital ordered their clothes from London or from Paris. . . .

. . . .

TIMOTHY WANTED MARGARET to be a social success. She was now thirteen, but she looked much older than that; she went to parties and gave parties of her own. But she was lacking in social graces. Not even three years at the leading school in Boston had given her charm of manner. She was too frank to be tactful and was intolerant of silly, simpering ways. She knew many young persons who were satisfactory enough as play-fellows, but who were not to be thought of in any other rôle. Sometimes she was like a wild thing when she joined in their games, at others, no amount of wheedling would make her go near the playground.

She had grown rapidly into a "blooming girl of florid complexion," and she was by no means a sylph. This worried her, made her self-conscious. She tried to remedy things by lacing her corsets very tight. In spite of this, the girls in the Park school giggled about her buxom figure. Margaret responded with witty sarcasms about their empty heads. Seeds of bitterness fell into her subconscious mind.

At about this time she gave her most ambitious party, inviting her Cambridge friends and the superior Boston misses from the Park school. The Bostonians kept to themselves. Margaret felt a tension and supposed that it was caused by a feeling of strangeness. So she made an effort to overcome this, and was particularly attentive to the guests from the other side of the river.

Cambridge resented this. "She thinks they're better than we are," said Cambridge, doubtless secretly agreeing that they were. They took on an offended air. The result was disastrous: the tension became greater, the looks leveled at the intruding Bostonians were anything but pleasant; finally the party ended by Cambridge going home in a tiff and Boston smiling and shrugging in a supercilious way at the boorishness of Cambridge.

The moment the door had closed on her last guest, Margaret dashed up to her room, tore off her party dress and her corsets, and threw herself on her bed and wept. What a frightful fiasco the whole thing had been! How mean of her Cambridge friends! She could scarcely believe that they could have acted in such a way....

Tears end eventually. She got up from her bed and went to her dressing-table; she studied herself very carefully in the glass and with the utmost frankness, appraised herself: she was ugly. Her forehead was too high, her nose too long; her mouth drooped at the corners, she had to keep squinting her eyes in order to see anything. What was worse, she was utterly without wiles, hadn't the slightest knowledge of fascinating tricks; coquetry was something absolutely foreign to her nature.... She was nothing but a Puritan after all....

Her brain began to work, began to make deductions: The thing to do under such unfortunate circumstances was to make herself so striking a personality that she could do anything without creating a debacle; to develop herself so that she could turn the most difficult situation into a success, so that her presence would be enough to make impossible such a *contretemps* as she had just experienced. "I have more brains than all the rest of them put together; it is ridiculous that their pique should have dominated my party. What I must learn is graciousness."

With this thought in the foreground of her mind, she prepared for bed.

Her self-analysis was harsher than that of one of her guests, Frederick Henry Hedge, a Harvard student. He watched Margaret closely that night, for he saw how difficult her situation was. He was struck by two things—the graceful poise of her head and the evidence of a very striking personality. "That girl could do anything if she tried," he said to a friend. "Her face fascinates me, and how she can talk!"

And he determined to know her better.

. . . . . .

Life went on unhappily for a time, with shrugs and petty head-tossings from those who had chosen to be offended. For consolation Margaret turned to her English friend. And one day, learned that she was soon to leave.

The day came much too soon. Margaret was inconsolable; she could not eat, she could not read. She stood at her window and looked down at the garden which she had always loved. It was now dull and barren. She walked in the fields and in the woods; the trees reminded her that her friend was gone. She hurried home; her brothers' voices jarred on her. She shut herself up in her room.

She grew thin, there were dark circles under her eyes. Her mother was so much concerned about her that she sent for Timothy. Timothy sent for a doctor. He examined Margaret carefully and prescribed a change of scene. "She needs the companionship of children of her own age; she has been too long with grown-ups."

Timothy accepted the dictum and begain to think about a good boarding-school. After careful consideration, he decided that Margaret should go to Groton, to the school kept by the Misses Prescott, which was supposed to be very good. He went to Margaret to tell her of his decision; he spoke more gently to her than usual: "I am to blame, for I kept you at home because I took such pleasure in teaching you myself. I see that you should be with others of your own age." At this point he was so much overcome with self-consciousness that his cold formality came back. Up went the old barrier again. "I trust that I shall soon hear that you are better." He left her.

Margaret sat for a long time, thinking. She was disgusted with the idea of being sent away to school; for three years she had associated with girls of her own age; they were like babes to her. If they wanted to send her away, why didn't they put her on a boat and send her to England where all her thoughts were? She allowed herself the luxury of speculation, and for a brief quarter of an hour, played with *ifs;* then sank anew into voluptuous melancholy.

Gradually her mind rose above her feelings, and she began to classify the different associations one makes: There were those whom one met casually, with whom one talked only of superficial things. They dwelt on the outer circle and left but little impression. There were others who came closer, who spread warmth because of their kind thoughts and their kind deeds. One was always glad to see them; and they left behind something which was pleasant to think about. Then there was another group, belonging to the innermost circle. This was composed of those from whom there was no separation; their presence held a kind of magic, they kindled something in the soul, they brought new knowledge not easily expressed. "They not only know themselves more, but *are* more, for having met; and regions of their being which else would have lain sealed in cold obstruction burst into leaf and bloom and song."

Such meetings were the rarest that there were. Margaret reflected on her good fortune in having experienced one of them; and she reflected on the fact that one's surroundings seemed to play but little part in these meetings with one's spiritual kindred. It would have been natural, for example, that she find her most congenial friends among those who had been brought up on traditions similar to her own; who had breathed the same air, listened to the same sermons.... Such was not the case.

She was already attacking one of the riddles of the universe....

She wondered what her friend in England would advise her to do. She decided that she would advise a good school. Margaret prepared to go to Groton.

V

REBELLION

THE MISSES PRESCOTT were conscientious women with certain limitations. They believed, for example, that all the natural impulses of youth should be repressed. Their days were divided into hourly duties, any digression from which was unheard of. Life flowed on, week after week, month after month, in a meandering, sluggish stream.

One day a new girl arrived. She seemed different—she walked like a duchess and carried her head high. She was not beautiful but there was about her something which made every one look long at her. She felt the looks and her spirit sank; but she held her head higher than ever.

At recess there were whisperings: She was from Cambridge, where all the learning was; her father was a lawyer and a congressman; his father had been a Somebody too, for his name was chipped into the corner-stone of one of the Harvard dormitories, Stoughton Hall. The girl had been to school in Boston for two or three years, but that was all. Before that, her father had taught her at home. She was said to be terribly clever—a regular bluestocking in fact.

And yet . . . there was something about her which you do not associate with bluestockings; it made you want to get close to her. And there was a look in her eyes which made you wonder if she had had a romance. . . . Maybe that was why she had been sent away to school. . . .

She did the most extraordinary things. One evening, during study hour, she suddenly threw her book into the air, jumped up and began dancing in the wildest way, round and round like one of those dervishes you read of in the East. She made every one's head reel by her mad spinning; yet the girls watched her, fascinated. And when they were all about to fall from giddiness if they watched her any longer, she stopped as suddenly as she had begun and began reciting weird poetry.

She finished her solemn declamation and went back to her chair. No one spoke. She broke into a laugh and said something ridiculous: "Here we all sat like a lot of mummies in a tomb! I had to see whether I was alive or dead."

The discipline of the school was anathema to Margaret. She felt suffocated, as if a blanket were constantly being plopped down over her head. Mealtimes were the worst. There they all sat, like rows of dumb, wax figures above plates of steaming food. The long face of the preceptress at the head of the table was like the face of an approaching doom. Margaret could scarcely control the impulse to throw something at it.

There came a day when she could not bear to sit through the meal. She remained in her room, saying that she had a headache. She planned new entertainment for the girls when they came up from the funereal feast: First, the spinning dance, which always gave her stimulus for other things, especially when she dressed for it. She had made herself a number of sashes of gay colors, had bought long, ornate ear-rings and glittering things for her hair.

The girls trooped in, the entertainment began. Margaret had all her ornaments on; she stood in the center of the room, her eyes half-closed, her head arched back. She whirled around, her ear-rings tinkled. She danced like a mad thing till the girls almost swooned from looking at her. After the dance came a fantastic play. She was a goddess who communed with fire and with water; and with other things not so easily seen.... She was a princess in a foreign land. But she could not remember whence she came.

The girls enjoyed the plays so much that it was not long before Margaret was rehearsing them in minor parts, reserving, of course, the principal characters for herself. She was a good manager and in the dual rôle of manager and star, received considerable homage.

She thought it would liven things up a bit if she appeared in class in her fancy costumes. This was allowed once or twice; then the preceptress put a stop to it. The poor woman was afraid that one day Margaret might disgrace the school by appearing in the street in her ridiculous clothes.

Margaret formed several ardent friendships. But she always felt that her own feelings were deeper and more abiding than those of the other girls, just as her own nature was more ardent, more intense. She had her moods; she would, for a time, join eagerly in all the school activities, then, suddenly, without reason and without excuse, would go off to her room, overcome by her inherent craving for solitude. She always expected her moods to be understood.

They were not understood. There was, in fact, a great deal of talk about them. Finally the girls decided that she was too exacting in her demands and not reliable when demands were made of her. They began to cold-shoulder her.

She was lonely; she began her fantasying again. The theatricals, which were now a regular part of the school curriculum, gave her the opportunity to carry her fantasies into her everyday life. She began to use make-up all the time, and appeared in class with crimson cheekbones and crimson lips. There was a snickering among the girls. At recess they jeered openly at her. She met the jeers frankly, frankly answered them: Since she was not pretty, she felt justified in improving her looks.

After a while she did not bother to explain herself.

The jeers increased, became more pointed and more unkind; there was now evident a feeling of open hostility. This wounded Margaret deeply, but she concealed her feeling under a mask of increased haughtiness, which was very irritating to the girls. Petty retorts they could cope with, angry outbursts they could understand, but this air of superiority was too much for them. One night they held a meeting to decide how they could punish Margaret for her eccentricity and for her pride....

The next day was beautiful. Soft winds set the leaves and the grasses swaying, the sky was cloudless, the sun was bright.

The weather had always been an important factor in Margaret's life; a dull day was likely to bring a dull mood, gray skies meant gray thoughts. A radiant day, on the other hand, brought exalted feelings.

She stood on the balcony looking over the hills. Birds called from the trees, warmth danced on golden waves. She forgot completely the external circumstances of her immediate life.

Suddenly a bell clanged—the dinner-bell. It brought her back to painful awareness of her immediate life; she heard footsteps hurrying along the corridor, heard the guarded hum of voices and sudden shrill breaks of laughter. Reluctantly she went to her room and changed her dress. And this time she neglected to put on her make-up.

She took her place at table still in the half-dreamy state which the beautiful day had produced. A sharp voice addressed her, asked her if she wished to be served. She looked up; and immediately became conscious of something unpleasant. The whole room seemed to be charged with antagonism, with bitter feelings. She noticed that the girl sitting next to her looked unfamiliar. What was there about her which was different? In a moment Margaret saw; the girl's cheeks and lips were deeply rouged. Margaret let her eyes look upon all the faces around the table; she saw that every pair of cheeks bore glaring circles of red.

The discovery was followed by a moment's silence which

was suddenly broken by a trill of a song-sparrow outside the window. Then Margaret began talking in a perfectly natural way to the girl sitting next to her. All through dinner she chatted, as if nothing unusual had happened.

Her composure enraged the girls; the moment they were released from the restraint of the dining-room, they broke into malicious laughter, drew themselves aside and jeered at Margaret.

With head high, she went to her room and locked the door. She knew that something devastating was about to happen to her and had a terrifying memory of something which used to come upon her when she was a child, and which had alarmed her parents very much. . . .

In a moment she was writhing on the floor in convulsions.

When the classes assembled, she was not among them. A teacher sent one of the girls to find her. The girl returned saying she had received no answer when she knocked on Margaret's door. The teacher became alarmed, reported to the head mistress. Together they went upstairs. They tapped on Margaret's door; there was no response. They called to her, but heard no sound. Finally they broke the door down. . . .

They feared that Margaret would not live. For several hours they worked with her and at last, to their great relief, saw her from sheer exhaustion drop into sleep.

She awoke another person. She felt cold and hard and barren; she was conscious of having lost something precious. The buoyancy which had been the expression of an abiding faith in the inherent splendor of mankind, had gone from her. Where she had felt all love she now felt all hate.

The girls were penitent. She listened to them silently, as if she did not understand what they said. What was running through her mind was this: "There was not *one* of you who took my part!"

They asked her to take charge of their theatricals as she had done before. She shrugged. They looked for the gay sashes she used to wear, for the ornate ear-rings and for the glittering things in her hair. They did not see them. They were on the alert for any fanciful suggestion she might make. She made none. They sought her out on the least excuse, they hung around her, not knowing what to say; they missed her ardor, her fiery looks, her sudden bursts of energy.

She went about like some one who has forgotten how to feel....

The girls gossipped to her of one another. As she sat half-listening to them, Margaret detected some force at work in the back of her mind. It was as if some voice whispered evil suggestions to her; she suspected that it was her demon at work. For it whispered ways by which she could repay the treachery of the girls....

She became less passive, but where she had been active in a loving way, she was now a "genius of discord."

For four months she ruled as demon of the school. She was very subtle in her methods; she dropped hints, she made insinuations.

The teachers had their suspicions and began questioning the girls....

One night after prayers, the principal announced that she wished every one to remain in the assembly-room for a few minutes.

The assembly-room became a court of justice. The principal announced that certain unpleasant things had come to her attention and that she would like Margaret Fuller to say whether they were true.

Margaret was asked to stand up. She struck a graceful attitude against the mantelpiece. Witnesses were called, to testify against her. She listened to them with a supercilious expression on her face.

After all the evidence was taken, the principal asked

Margaret what she had to say for herself. She began an eloquent oration, in which she denied all the charges. The girls looked at her in amazement.

Then, all of a sudden, Margaret's bravado left her. She threw herself down and began beating her head against the iron hearth. At length she became unconscious. . . .

The teachers were alarmed. Was she dead? Had they killed her by this second chastisement?

Fearfully they carried her to her room and got her into bed. With great relief they saw her regain consciousness.

She became feverish; for days she could not eat, for days she would not speak. Her demon was conducting her through the intricacies of a purgatorio. She was in the throes of despair; she had allowed herself to become defiled. She might as well die. . . .

One of the teachers who had admired Margaret without understanding her, made her her special charge. She showed unusual tenderness to her, and gradually Margaret took an interest in life again. As soon as she was able, she sent for all the girls and asked their forgiveness. Completely penitent, they eagerly forgave. Once more she took her place as ruler among them. . . .

But not in the old sense. Now her imperiousness was tempered, her arrogance subdued. She had learned the first lesson of humility.

VI

THE FEMINIST

MONROE'S TERM as President was finished, and Timothy Fuller was home again. He saw no reason for Margaret's remaining in school since he was once more in the position to assume charge of her studies. So she left Groton.

She was fifteen—an awkward age. Yet she was not awkward, although her near-sightedness made her appear so at times. She had a natural sense of rhythm; she found joy in watching the slow movements of branches when the wind was in them; the come and go of the tides was soothing to her; she liked to watch children and young animals at their play.

Sometimes her movements suggested the languor of the East. Looking at her, one thought of pillared temples and of tropical gardens with fountains sparkling and peacocks spreading their proud tails. The set of her head was regal, there was about her a magnetism which attracted and a haughtiness which repelled. The humility of spirit which had been so dearly bought was not evident in her gait.

She was now the eldest of six. It took her mother a little while to get used to her tall, imperious daughter, so ardent and so remote. She thought about her a great deal and wondered about her future. She was so different from other girls; she seemed to think that being a wife and a mother was not enough.... And she was a little intolerant of the usual talk that went on between women—of clothes and parties and servants.

Margaret pitied her mother, whose eyes, she thought, had a yearning look. She was gentle, almost too gentle; and she talked less and less. Lines were beginning to appear around her mouth and her eyes, there were streaks of gray in her hair. There were times when Margaret almost burst with the longing to draw close to her mother and try to satisfy that hunger which was in her eyes....

But all she could do was rock the baby's cradle and mend the children's clothes. Soon they began to look on her as a second mother, more vigorous than the first, because she made up games for them on rainy days and planned little treats at unexpected times.

Margaret's study went on. She knew that she would never find satisfaction in a merely social life, yet she did not wish to become a mere bluestocking. She had met a number of them, of both sexes, and she considered them incomplete. There were mental giants with the souls and bodies of dwarfs; there were physical giants with the mentalities of dwarfs. This would not do. She wanted to be capable of enjoying pleasures; she wanted to get excited now and then; she wanted to be gracious and graceful.... And she hungered to learn more and more and more; about life and about lives, through experience and through books....

She scrutinized herself in the glass. What a misfortune that she was so plain! She shrugged and turned away. She made a resolution: "I can't help being ugly, but I can help being dull. So ... I shall be ugly, but *bright*."

On with her studies then! Up at five in the morning, to walk for an hour in the early quiet; then piano-practice while the boys were racketing around before breakfast. After breakfast, French and philosophy till half-past nine, at which hour she set off for school. A different kind of school this. Its head master was Dr. Perkins, a Yale graduate, and it was co-educational. Oliver Wendell Holmes was studying there, preparatory to entering Harvard; Richard Henry Dana was there too.

Margaret was a special pupil and went for Greek recitations only. Every one used to watch for her entrance: that peculiar rhythmic walk, the half-closed eyes which seemed to see into vague distances, the haughty head. All this was fascinating to some, to others it brought smiles.

The girls in the school tried to imitate that walk and that proud carriage of the head. "If we could come into school that way, we'd know as much Greek as she does."

There was a circulating library in one of the shops. Margaret frequented it. At about the same time every day she appeared in a long cloak with a good-sized hood. She went about choosing her books; she took off her cloak, put the books into the hood, threw the cloak over her shoulder and started for home. As she went out of the shop, she saw several girls waiting in the street.

They were waiting as girls wait at stage-doors to see famous actresses. They were infatuated with Margaret's cloak, and with the regal way she carried it slung over her shoulder. And they went home and coaxed their mothers to let them have similar cloaks, so that they too might make magnificent appearances.

In the afternoons, Margaret read Italian and went for a walk and rode on horseback; in the evenings she wrote in her diary. She was determined on distinction. And she wrote: "My powers of intellect are not well disciplined. Yet all such hindrances may be overcome by an ardent spirit." "I am wanting in that intuitive tact and polish which nature has bestowed on some, but which I must acquire."

It was not very long till she realized that there were few who equaled her in quickness of perception and in witty response. Even her father, for whose intellectual attainments she had deep admiration, was heavy and deliberate by comparison.

. . . .

Another baby was on the way. That would make seven. Timothy decided that it was time to move; the Cambridgeport house was becoming rather cramped.

When Margaret was sixteen, the family moved into the Dana house on Dana Hill near Harvard College. This was spacious and dignified and altogether fitting as the home of an ex-congressman, who might entertain the President one day.

A New Englander was in the White House now. He had been professor of rhetoric at Harvard and had all the stiffness and precision of the serious man of letters; he was

American representative in Russia when the Czar broke with
Napoleon; he was one of the signers of the Treaty of Ghent
and had seen Napoleon's abortive return from Elba; he had
served—with no particular distinction—as American Minister to Great Britain. To the people of his own country he
symbolized the old order of government; they awaited the
new. He kept men at arm's length, was cold and conservative. He was a minority president, elected by the vote of the
House. His name was John Quincy Adams.

The Fullers knew him very well; and although Timothy
did not share his political convictions, he did not believe the
stories his opponents told about him: How he had bargained
for the support of Daniel Webster by promising good posts
to Federalists; how his accounts during his term as Secretary
of State could not bear too close inspection; how he had
seduced a beautiful American girl when he was Minister
to Russia....

Timothy awaited the day when the President would come
North to visit his old home at Quincy. At last came the
rumor that he was to come. And Timothy's invitation went
off.... He would make the Presidential visit the occasion of
Margaret's social début.

The invitation was accepted, the President came North....

And, one night, drove through the streets of Cambridge
to the Fuller home on Dana Hill.

All day long people had been coming and going: grocers'
boys and butchers' boys, florists, bakers, caterers. The neighbors shamefully neglected their work that day, and spent
most of the time at the windows. Children loitered in the
street before the Fuller gates. Such an affair had not been
heard of in Cambridge since the days of the Lechmeres and
the Vassals, long before there was any unfriendly talk of
tea. Grand balls there were then!

Margaret was busy all day superintending everything. Her

mother was not able to do much, being in her periodical state of pregnancy. The younger children were kept out of the kitchen, where marvelous concoctions were in the process of creation.

Timothy came home earlier than usual, went dutifully to his wife's room and inquired how she was, then questioned Margaret about everything, not forgetting her dress, which she had to show him. He approved of the dress.

In a very short time she was putting it on. Oh dear, how tight it was! How could she ever get into it? She called a maid to help her. What a pull the maid had to give at Margaret's corsets to make her small enough for the dress! But at last it was on; at last the curl-papers were taken out of her hair and all the little curls were bunched together like birds on a rainy day.

The dress was pink. And what a glaring testimony it was to Timothy's taste! It was atrociously cut, it had no "line," it hung badly. It was so tight that Margaret had to keep her arms close to her sides. She looked excruciatingly uncomfortable, as indeed she was.

She received with her father, and looked forward to the hour for dancing, of which she was passionately fond. But dancing was no joy to her that night. She felt that at any moment she might burst out of her pink enclosure; she longed to burst out of it, to fling her arms about, to take a long breath. But there she stood in the brilliantly lighted room, squinting her eyes at each guest, gingerly giving each guest the tips of her fingers.

And the guests—what did they think of her? One of them, Mrs. John Farrar, the wife of the Harvard professor of astronomy, decided to take Margaret in hand. She was a brilliant conversationalist, Mrs. Farrar thought; she had magnetism; given an opportunity to expand, she could develop into something quite unusual. What she needed especially was freedom from the paternal stranglehold.

It was a delicate task, but Eliza Farrar was equal to it. She called on Margaret soon after the party, she soon gained her confidence. She suggested that Margaret try *her* dressmaker and that she consult a hairdresser....

Now Margaret was constantly at the Farrar home, now heard a new language spoken, which was not merely of great intellectual accomplishments, but of social accomplishments as well. Mrs. Farrar had traveled extensively and the world in which she had moved was more cavalier than Puritan. She was of the opinion that the Puritan world could be made considerably more charming by the infusion of a little of the cavalier spirit.

This association with the older woman opened Margaret's eyes to many things: She saw that the candid expression of tastes and convictions was not always necessary; that argument, nine times out of ten, was a proclamation of vanity; that a quick retort was seldom appreciated and that repartee should be indulged only in the company of those able to return it. In the company of others it was likely to be regarded as the expression of a caustic nature and to make more enemies than friends. Margaret learned that in the cavalier world small lies were sometimes necessary to peace and that truth was generally relative.

Mrs. Farrar had a young cousin staying with her, a Southerner from New Orleans, called Anna Barker. Margaret could scarcely have found a better example of one possessing the kind of charm which she herself was desirous of possessing. They became warm friends.

Margaret confided some of her pagan fantasies to her friend: "I sometimes see myself in a large hall; it is the age of feudalism; a charming company is assembled and a minstrel is playing on a harp. Torches flicker and now and then one hears the clank of armor, as the sentries at the doorways change their places.... The night wears on; servants bring refreshments; there is a flash of golden goblets and the sound of a purse of gold falling at the feet of the minstrel. . . .

"And sometimes I am in another company and the world is not so old. It is the East where the sun is hot and where fragrant fruits hang from the boughs. An altar stands at the end of a grove and down a slope the waters of the lake can be seen between the trees. A group of dancing-girls comes through the grove, carrying baskets of fruits and garlands of flowers; their white bodies glisten like alabaster, for they wear no clothes. They dance around the altar and they chant an old pagan melody. Suddenly they stop, place their offerings before the altar and prostrate themselves; then go dancing back through the trees, down the slope to the lake, to bathe."

Margaret saw no virture in the puritanical denial of the body. "If the body is the temple of the spirit, why should it be regarded as something evil?" She found vulgarity in the prevailing tendency to censure nude statuary; she longed to live where natural things were treated naturally.

She formed ardent friendships, mostly with women older than herself. She sat on a footstool beside them, listening with rapt intensity to all they said. If they were sometimes embarrassed by her ardent demonstrations, they gave no sign of it, for they knew that the early forcing of her intellect and the neglect of her emotional life had left her with a great emotional surplus which needed to be used.

The young men she knew did not supply the necessary outlet. Henry Hedge, who had been so much intrigued that night she gave the disastrous party, talked philosophy with her; others were glad to listen to her talk of Greek mythology, of Madame de Staël, of Maria Edgeworth. Others ran from her and found refuge in the coy smiles of more normal and less scintillating young women.

Margaret's determination to make herself distinguished left little room for romantic dilly-dallying. She read voraciously and formed her own opinions. Over in Russia there was a change of emperors; the "shifty Byzantine" was dead. Margaret, a fervent liberal, now saw signs of freedom for Europe. She wondered about herself and about what she would do with her life. She thought a great deal about the inequalities of men and women. Men were the leaders; a fully developed life was conceded to be their natural right. Women, on the other hand, were conceded only such development as fitted them to be man's companions. This idea puzzled her; it assumed that women as entities were not important; only in their relation to men were they important. The same might be said of animals; a horse was worthless if it were not trained to do man's bidding. The same might be said of a machine; in relation to itself, a machine had no life. Margaret regarded women as more important than horses or machines. She was convinced that women had an obligation to themselves and that was to make themselves as complete human beings as they were capable of becoming....

She studied Greek mythology and saw her idea borne out; the goddesses were self-sufficing. She studied Madame de Staël and was up in arms when it was suggested that she had a masculine mind.... Then she went to a tea party and listened to the chatter of some of the women who were there; and thought more tolerantly about de Staël's masculine mind.

VII

CREED

MARGARET WAS EIGHTEEN NOW. What does one associate with eighteen? Delightful irresponsibility; the foam of life—life's spindrift, lightly coming and going; much use of the first personal pronoun; clothes, cosmetics, coquetry;

the flowering springtime before the ripening of wisdom. But Margaret? At eighteen she was conscious of all the sorrows of the world. There were times when she was oppressed by overwhelming grief; in the middle of the night she woke, cold and apprehensive; a word came to her—*Weltschmerz!* She wrote poems about the "wearied sense," the "vanished dream," and about the swift passing of life's freshness.

She longed to be frivolous, to be interested in jolly nothings, to float, like spindrift, on the surface of things. But she could not. She had received no childish encouragement in the natural interests of children. When she should have been playing with dolls and bouncing a rubber ball, she was straining her eyes over Horace and Ovid; when she should have been sleeping deep in her pillow after a day's hard play, she was telling her father all about the Punic Wars! She had never learned how to play.

And now at eighteen, she did not know how to play. Here is her idea of a thrilling day: "I have passed a luxurious afternoon... reading Rammohun Roy's book, and framing dialogues aloud on every argument beneath the sun."

But who was there to argue with her? Very few, it seemed. And the more she studied, the less she seemed fitted for the life around her. This puzzled her, saddened her. Was it all wrong then—the idea that each individual should seek the highest development? She could not think so; she believed in the divinity of God and was firmly convinced that human beings were created by divine principle. Each human being was a god in embryo; it was his obligation to nourish that embryonic divinity till it came forth a fully developed spiritual entity.

There were so few who were interested in such things. Margaret longed to speak "fully and openly" of them. Of what avail was all her study if she must keep it locked within her like some fragile treasure?

One day, perhaps, it would find an outlet.... She could not turn back now; she had mapped out her course; nothing else would satisfy her.

Meanwhile, there were other things for her to do. The ninth child had been born; her mother was spent. Margaret took charge of the family, and from now on, the children went to her when they wanted anything.

When callers came, it was Margaret who received them. She always had plenty to say. Sometimes she talked over their heads, and they thought she was pedantic; sometimes she gave a thrust at popular hypocrisies, and they thought she was sarcastic. At other times she was gay and her eyes had merry lights in them; then they thought she was a siren.

She knew the things that were said of her and sometimes made light of them: "I have been styled a Syren!! O rapturous sound! I have reached the goal of my ambition. Earth has nothing fairer or brighter to offer. 'Intelligence' was nothing to it. A 'supercilious,' 'satirical,' 'affected,' 'pedantic' Syren!!!"

Her friend Eliza Farrar was abroad. Margaret went traveling in her mind.

. . . .

Timothy was concerned with the way things were going at Washington. The reign of John Quincy Adams had not brought the prosperity that had been hoped for. The wool growers and the manufacturers sent a petition to Congress, asking for a protective tariff. Congress proved most amenable, was lavish in promises, assuring protection for all and sundry who sought it. The Southerners saw disaster ahead; for their prosperity depended on the free movement of trade, especially cotton. They called the new measure the Tariff of Abomination....

They were up in arms; they called on Vice-President Calhoun to be their spokesman. He, a Southerner himself, understood their grievance, and issued a manifesto, "The South Carolina Exposition," a fiery document which proved that the Southerners in choosing him, knew their man. South Carolina adopted this manifesto as its own declaration of rights, then settled back to await events. A presidential election was about to be.

Andrew Jackson, the fighting Irishman from South Carolina, was up again as the democratic candidate. The campaign was largely one of slander. Jackson's early life afforded many choice tid-bits for his opponents; he had killed one man and fought with many; he was an uncouth boor, highly illiterate and utterly lacking in self-control; he had married a woman who was already married and had lived with her two years before she was divorced....

Jackson won the election. A great hurrah went up all over the country; a man of the common people had been chosen for the highest office in the land. And the common people determined to give him a great inauguration. They flocked to Washington, they invaded all the buildings, they swaggered through the streets. It seemed to the gentle Washingtonians as if a menagerie of good-natured animals had been suddenly loosed....

Up in Massachusetts the people read of these crude activities and said that the country was going to the dogs. Timothy Fuller was a Jeffersonian, but he saw no Jeffersonism in this volcanic demonstration. This was hooliganism.

Margaret was more tolerant than her father; she viewed humanity with a kindlier eye and believed in giving the great rank and file a chance to express itself. But she made deductions from such conduct as was reported from Washington: The emotions make better servants than masters; they must not be ignored, but they must be made subservient to the mind.

She was growing in wisdom. She decided henceforth to concentrate on the aspirations of those she met and to ignore their weaknesses. One thing, however, she could not ignore—self-satisfied mediocrity.

Human beings became her hobby. She decided to make a study of character and to fit herself to exert constructive influence on every one she met. She was not interested in the outward show of people; she had an insatiable interest in their "inward springs of thought and action." She knew very well that by the majority she was considered haughty and supercilious; she knew herself to be humble and capable of great love.

She went everywhere and was a distinctive personality. Thanks to Eliza Farrar, she now wore becoming clothes. These, together with her natural proud bearing, gave her a decidedly dashing air. When she entered a room, the room seemed to become charged with electricity.

The year 1829 was a great year for Cambridge. There graduated that year "the most eminent class that ever left Harvard." Margaret danced with all of them and made several friends.

One of these was James Freeman Clarke, who reminded her that they had met before when they were about five years old. Even at five Margaret had made an impression; now at nineteen she exerted an influence which seemed likely to be as lasting as it was profound. She astonished the youth by the breadth of her knowledge, she thrilled him by the depth of her thought. They were together a great deal; they walked and rode; they talked of books and music and of the long road which leads to spiritual supremacy; they discussed the meanings of good and evil and talked of the desires which are natural to youth. Margaret was all fire as she talked; she kindled aspiration in the serious youth, and she kindled a more romantic feeling, which he would have liked to speak of at once. But he knew that talk of love and passion just then would have obstructed the course of their harmonious relationship.

They wrote to each other. Margaret's letters often had a humorous lilt; she could clothe a serious thought in light array; her pen dripped epigrams....

She became a sibyl to this youth, and he depended on her for guidance and advice. She might have married him and become a minister's wife. She did not wish to marry him.

She was building up a stronghold of friendships. Women succumbed to her in legion; they saw in her much of what they aspired to be. Although she was not beautiful, she possessed that strange allurement which occasional women have had since time began. It is something very powerful yet very subtle; it has the fire of the sun and the cold chastity of the moon; it is electric, it is dynamic; and because it is centered in a human being, it draws human beings to it. Cleopatra had it and it destroyed her; Aspasia had it and it made Pericles more than he otherwise would have been. It made Sappho the greatest woman lyricist; it made a Duse, a George Eliot, a Raquel Meller....

Margaret's life so far was not marked by any extraordinary outward event. She went among people and received them in her home; she rode and walked and attended concerts; she took care of the younger children and helped with the housework. Her extraordinary events were subjective. She had high moments when she was filled with abounding joy. At these times she knew more of life's mystery than she could have told; they were transcendent moments. She knew that if she made her life identical with her knowledge of its meaning, there would be no limit to her influence for good.

She learned to welcome everything that life brought to her—all the joy and all the pain. She believed that no one was tested beyond his ability to endure.

She had a passion for everything beautiful; she loved to surround herself with beautiful persons and the superiority in looks of many of her friends excited no jealousy in her.

It is more than probable that she knew she was superior in other ways. She would have been much less intelligent than she was, if she did not know this.

She loved the sunrise and the dew-drenched time of day; she loved the midday lull, the evening songs of birds and the long arms of twilight stretching toward the night. Trees she loved and pastures and purple-shadowed hills; and children's voices raised to shrill heights of happiness.

Friendships were sacred to her; her own natural constancy demanded constancy in return. She did not understand the easy come-and-go of intimacies—sudden withdrawals of interest because of superficial disagreements. Some found her too exacting, found her intensity of feeling too hard to live up to. It is doubtful if many took their friendships as seriously as she.

She knew that she had many obstacles to surmount in her realization of spiritual supremacy: Her manner, which was often brusque and often proud; her caustic tongue which often ran ahead of her judgment. On the other hand, she knew that there were times when frankness could not be sacrificed to tact, and that conformity to a standard she could not accept was a denial of all she hoped eventually to achieve.

People sought her when they were distressed; she found the right word for them; and they left her, heartened. Exhausted from the expenditure of much nervous energy, Margaret sought her own room. These solitudes were necessary to her, but there were times of great loneliness, when she longed for a human touch which would spring the secret lock of her soul ... there were times when she longed to fall in love.

She began to fear that that supreme experience was to be denied her.

And why could she find no one who satisfied the deepest reaches of her spirit? Doubtless because those reaches had their roots in richer soil than that in which most persons dwelt; doubtless because her development had gone too far. Her immediate world contained no one who was her equal.

There were other reasons. For years she had been accustomed to live in imaginative worlds "amid scenes and persons of nobleness and beauty." These scenes and persons were her ideals; by them all others were judged.

She hated the pettiness of everyday life, and longed for grandeur wherein both tragedy and ecstasy played important parts. She was not old enough to know that a life of grandeur can be lived in the humblest of surroundings. Judged by ordinary standards, she was supercritical. But she must not be judged by ordinary standards. She was appreciative of all the talents and all the virtues that she saw, but her standard of judgment was the potential rather than the actual. Her perceptions were swift and sure, and no one was more disappointed than she when a friend failed to maintain the appropriation of gifts with which he gave promise of being endowed.

She had friends who made her merry and friends who made her sad. She liked to be excited to "frequent and boundless gayety," she liked "scintillating, arrowy wit." Usually she read the thoughts of her friends, as if their minds were lying open before her. Sometimes they tried to conceal their thoughts with words. It was no use; Margaret saw through their words.

Her witty friend did not appeal to her heart. He was cold, detached, intangible; he analyzed acts to find sinister motives in them. "He tore the buds open to see if there were no worm sheathed in the heart." Several of much slower perceptions appealed to her heart. If their aspirations were high, she was content. She reined in her mind when she talked to them.... Suddenly, in the midst of a discussion, she would break out with, "Your wintry aspect is quite becoming to you. That is not always so; most often a sad and melancholy mien is oppressive."

Humility in others tore her heart open. If a friend asked her how to overcome some weakness, she overflowed with love.

She built a little oratory in her room and there communed in solitude with God and with many others whom she knew only through their books. The family was living in the Brattle House in Brattle Street, which stood in a large, old-fashioned garden. In the spring the crocuses poked their heads up almost as soon as the snow had gone; little plots later gave forth hyacinths and daffodils and tulips; then came forget-me-nots and candytuft; and night-scented stock which, at sundown, began to spray the air. On toward the end of summer, came the delphiniums and the lupins, waving their blue and purple torches.

The row of linden-trees in front of the house had heard much talk within the last four years. The fighting Irishman from South Carolina had been elected for a second term; he had kept his sword in the right hand and taken a broom in his left. The federal offices were now swept clean of their old associates. Two of the new brigade were Yankees from Massachusetts; Amos Kendall was one, Isaac Hill the other. They were eager to be rid of the old ruling "aristocracy." Kendall became Fourth Auditor of the Treasury. He made himself a man of mystery; he never attended social functions and on occasion showed remarkable talent for silence. On others he made himself heard and understood. He was a little whiffet of a man with a thundering voice; he was round-shouldered and had asthma. He sat behind the scenes during Jackson's administration and manipulated the wires which made every one else jump. He was not entirely scrupulous.

Although born in Massachusetts, Hill represented New Hampshire, where he had been living for some time and where, through his newspaper, *The Patriot,* he had managed to build up quite a formidable Democratic party. Cambridge did not relish the idea of such a man as Hill representing New England in the federal government.

But there were many things about the new administration that Cambridge did not relish. It never forgot the slap that Jackson had given John Quincy Adams, his predecessor, by refusing to call on him after taking office. Jackson had his reasons for this, and many agreed that they were adequate.

The linden-trees heard much talk about the Eaton affair, the pet scandal of Washington. Mrs. Eaton was the wife of the Secretary of War. She was a divorcee; and there were stories afloat that Eaton had been extremely attentive to her while she was still securely united to her first husband. Furthermore, who was she? Peggy O'Neill, the daughter of a Washington tavern-keeper! What kind of woman was that to sit at cabinet dinners and receive respectable cabinet wives?

Other things were talked of, as men went up and down Brattle Street: The unbelievable prosperity of the cotton-mills in Massachusetts, which were taking girls from the farms and sending old-fashioned spinning-wheels up into attics. The large number of men and women who were in jail for debt ... the large numbers who were going West into Ohio, Indiana and Illinois; the ships which were bringing new settlers from all over Europe; the Irish, who did not venture any further West than New York and Massachusetts.

Over in England there was talk of a young man called Faraday, who was going to do great things with electricity; and of a dandified young Jew, who had written a bold book and who was received at all the big houses. Italy had a prophet. He was organizing the movement of *Young Italy,* through whose endeavors he hoped soon to see a united and independent country. His name was Mazzini.

VIII

THE "PROSE OF LIFE"

AGITATIONS, HOPES, creations—the ceaseless process of life's long unfoldment went on, destroying new forms, creating new. Margaret, walking alone up and down the garden paths behind the big, old house, thought of the inexorable march of destiny. She longed to participate in eventful movements, to feel herself an important unit in the whirl and throb of universal life; she longed to do noble deeds. But her world revolved around the trivial, monotonous domesticity of a Cambridge home.

She was concentrating on German; French, Italian and Spanish she already knew. Her companion in study was Henry Hedge, who had lately returned from a German university.

She went riding with James Freeman Clarke. In the morning when the sun was high, he rode up and led another horse by the bridle. "It's a day for a gallop," he called. Margaret gave orders to the servant, had a few words with her mother and ran upstairs for her hat.

The town, she thought, had an old-world look. The ivy-covered buildings were calm and placid. Students hurried along or sauntered under the trees. She caught sight of Judge Story walking, in deep thought, and called good morning to some one she knew.

They trotted along by the river, where the willows kept moving their feathery branches, like frail and delicate ladies waving fans. The sun showed them two elongated figures on gigantic steeds.

Margaret was in excellent mood. She talked of her new discoveries—Goethe, Richter, Schiller. She spoke of her longing to experience every joy and every pain. "We cannot understand what we have not experienced!" she cried. "I wish to understand all."

She talked and talked. Her voice was high. To the youth beside her it throbbed with music. He wondered what she would say if he were to tell her how much she meant to him; how much more than Goethe or Richter or a world of Schillers. He knew what she would say and how sad her eyes would look. No, he could never satisfy her ... it would take a Goethe or a Beethoven....

They rode through sunny slopes and past orchards where pink petals fell into the grass; they crossed a narrow stream and stopped to watch a waterfall. The birds sang in the trees. Young Clarke felt that he was passing through an experience which would transform the whole of his life. "This is not just a ride on a spring day; it is an epoch in my life," he thought.

And he made a vow that he would always be a friend to Margaret, no matter what other friend she would prefer to him.

They rode on in silence.

．　　．　　．　　．　　．　　．　　．

Margaret discovered Novalis; and now her desire for a life of action evaporated. The world of thought was itself an active world, for it was the motivating force of all others. Every event was now full of mystic significance for her. She saw one woman giving a passion-flower to another, who lost it. The incident brought forth a poem on the relation and the destiny of the two, whom she used as symbolic of all social relations and all destinies.

She spent hours in her oratory. Very often she left a party where she was the brilliant center of a group; and sought the solitude of her oratory.... She interested herself in horoscopes, and believed that two persons born under the same star were kindred souls. She talked to Novalis as if he were with her in her room; she recognized in him a "glowing imperfection" of mind akin to her own; found him a relief "after the immense superiority of Goethe."

But it was to Goethe that she returned, as an exhausted traveler returns to the place which gives him greatest sustenance. Goethe was her prophet; every feeling she had ever had, he could express; for every unnamable aspiration, he could find a name.

She spent a day in Boston, browsing in the Athenæum; she held imaginary conversations with the authors of old books. They were not always eulogistic conversations. Many a bookworm there would have been surprised had he heard the girl of twenty-two chiding his favorite authors, begging them, for pity's sake, to use their common sense!

The city's streets often plunged her into a mood of melancholy. The sight of an old woman returning from work, an undernourished child, a lost dog seeking his master—such things always affected her deeply. She never failed to say something cheering to the unfortunates of the streets. And she would go home and think about eternal justice and try to find the meaning of evils and tragedies and despairs.

The next year Timothy Fuller retired from the practice of law to write a history of his country. For this he must have quiet and long, uninterrupted hours. He bought a farm at Groton, a sleepy village about forty miles from Boston, and difficult to get out of once one had settled in it.

Margaret was appalled at the idea. Such isolation! How could she live without the friends of Cambridge and the books of Boston? With a heavy heart she began to pack.

The Grotonians were honest, feet-on-the-ground citizens, with no reason for bothering themselves about anything but their housework, their trades and professions, the upbringing of their children and occasional kindnesses to their neighbors. They went to church regularly, contributed to the salary of the minister, through whose sermons they quite frequently drowsed, kept their affairs to themselves and did not inquire too closely into the affairs of others. They were God-fearing, respectable, though unimaginative citizens, who knew nothing about genius or eccentricity and who doubtless would have considered themselves happy in their ignorance, had they been questioned on the subject.

Imagine Margaret in such a milieu! "I no longer lie in wait for the tragedy and comedy of life," she wrote. "The rules of its *prose* engage my attention."

She took charge of the house; she was cook, housemaid and seamstress. And she tutored the younger children. Her mother could not do much around the house, for she was not strong; the grandmother, who lived with them, was an invalid.

Eugene, the eldest boy, was now a junior in Harvard. He was a charming and attractive youth of eighteen; was merry and humorous, but without Margaret's intellectual depth, as, in fact, were all of her brothers and sisters. Margaret missed him when she went to Groton; he was her favorite brother.

She divided her days systematically, giving each hour its task. The teaching of the children took up a good deal of time. What time remained was given to the prosiest details: to mending and cooking and all the wearisome duties of the housewife.

How could she find time for her own life? How continue that development which was now as necessary to her as the summer sun and the breezes which came down from the hills?

She found the time; she stole precious moments and took them off into the woods. And soon she was lost to all the prose details, was galloping through enchanted countrysides with Heine, Carlyle, Wordsworth and Bacon. She was interested in the principles of Christianity; so she read Jahn and Eichhorn in the original.

After a while, she found a servant. This gave her more leisure, which she used in translating Goethe's *Tasso*, and sketching a number of plans for further composition. Her father prevailed upon her to learn more about her own country. She read Jefferson's letters with him. She grew closer to her mother during this time, for she had no other ties.

The times she liked best were the week-ends which brought Eugene home from Harvard. Margaret planned choice meals for him and arranged things so that she might have an hour or two with him out of doors. They roamed through browning woods and fields and talked of homely things. Eugene had a witty twist to his tongue and the facility for describing persons in a word. Margaret laughed a good deal when she was with him; and loved him because he could make her laugh.

The New England autumn lengthened, the afternoons closed in early. Margaret gave herself three evenings a week for study. Professor Farrar had sent her Herschel's Astronomy, another friend had given her a book on architecture. Both of these she read, and found both interesting. She was beginning to know her own countrymen and liked especially Jefferson and Benjamin Franklin. Her appreciation of Jefferson was pleasing to her father.

Timothy was obliged to say a good word for England that year, for England had abolished slavery in all her colonies. For years Wilberforce had been agitating about it in the House of Commons, and had Pitt and Fox to second him at times. Now the deed was done; twenty million pounds had been paid to the slave-owners. Timothy approved of this, Margaret applauded it.

Winter roared around the house, the fields and woods were choked with snow. It was well that the children did not have to go to school and that they could exhaust some of their young energy in digging paths from the house to the road. Sometimes the snow came up higher than the windows.... In the evenings Margaret sat before the fire and read Plato and Plutarch, Alfieri, Carlyle and Goethe. She felt that, one day, she must write a life of Goethe.

Sundays were not much different from what they had

always been; excepting that now they brought fewer visitors. This was a relief; visitors were tiring.

Margaret found time to write a little, but accomplished nothing that satisfied her. She heard regularly from all her Cambridge friends, who wrote her of all the happenings—the engagements, the marriages, the births and deaths.

Spring came at last and swelled the brooks that went galloping down the hillside over the stones. May came and gave Margaret her twenty-fourth birthday. She was impatient. What had she to show for her twenty-four years? It seemed to her at times that she would never do the things she longed to do: visit the places she longed to visit or meet with minds she longed to meet.

She wanted to meet Ralph Waldo Emerson. She had heard him preach, but she had not met him. For shortly after that he had gone abroad. Now he was living quietly with his mother at Concord.

Eugene graduated from Harvard that summer. This gave Margaret a day or two in Cambridge. How she loved the place! How she talked! The Farrars asked her to take a little trip with them into the mountains. She would have liked to do this, but knew she should not. And she did not suggest it to her father. Eugene's first position took him far away. He became a tutor in the family of Colonel Samuel Storrow in Virginia. There was sadness in the Fuller hearts when he left, and Margaret felt that henceforth their meetings would be few.

In October of that year Margaret first appeared in print. George Bancroft had written a paper of *Slavery in Rome*, which appeared in the *North American Review*. Margaret read it and was up in arms. What an opinion the man had of Brutus! Her anger found an outlet, and about two months afterwards, this outlet found a place in the Boston *Daily Advertiser*. She handled Mr. Bancroft very firmly, defended Brutus and altogether expressed herself very well. She did not sign her name to the article, but merely put the letter J at the end of it.

Back came an answer from a defender of Bancroft, who signed himself H. The defense was weak, the gentleman, though courteous, did not have at his disposal the knowledge displayed by "J." The honors went to Margaret.

Timothy was very proud of her. He cut out her article and he cut out the reply it had brought forth, and kept them both in a little book.

Another winter went by, another spring came. But this spring Margaret could not take long walks; her energy seemed to have gone; the least exertion tired her.

Her long period of overwork exacted its toll; she became very ill. For a time it looked as if she would not recover. Her mother took care of her, and did not leave her, day or night. Her father walked restlessly around, like one who does not know what to do with himself. His conscience gave him unpleasant pricks: He should not have allowed Margaret to assume all the responsibility of the house, when she had to spend seven or eight hours a day teaching the younger children.

One day he screwed himself up to a supreme effort, went to her bedside and gave her the first words of commendation that he had ever given her: "My dear, I have been thinking of you in the night, and I cannot remember that you have any faults."

There was a pause; then he went on: "You have defects, of course, as all mortals have, but I do not know that you have a single fault."

The unbelievable words touched Margaret to tears. She lay weeping silently; Timothy tiptoed out of the room.

His praise undoubtedly helped her back to health. Soon she was sitting out in the sun again. Timothy hovered around, more tender than he had ever been. He read to her, not what *he* wished her to hear, but what she chose to hear.

He pried a little into the secret places of her desires; and asked her finally what wish she had that he could gratify.

Her heart bounded. Did she dare to tell him that she had wanted to go to Europe for years, that this was the only thing she wanted, but that she had not mentioned it because it seemed so impossible as to be fantastic?

She told him. And he told her that she might go in the autumn.

IX

DISCIPLINE

The Farrars, learning of Margaret's illness, invited her to Cambridge for a change. She willingly accepted. Had she not great news for them at last?

What plans were made during the next few weeks! Everything was happening most auspiciously; Harriet Martineau was coming in September to spend a little time with the Farrars before returning to England. When she returned, they were going with her. "So you see, we can all go together," Mrs. Farrar said.

Margaret had never been so happy. Now she saw a rift in her clouds, a cleavage in her walls ... she was overjoyed. The future opened up to her a long vista of almost unheard-of possibilities: She would meet Wordsworth and Carlyle and Tennyson; Darwin perhaps and de Quincy....

She went home a renewed person. The atmosphere at home was different now. Margaret's illness had loosened something in Timothy, who was much more gentle and much less arrogant. Margaret thanked God that at last she was going to know an earthly father; heretofore she had called on Him for counsel and for strength.

Her relation with her mother had changed too. Now her

mother, instead of being a shadowy and rather detached person, was very dear and very loving. Margaret momentarily gave thanks for her illness, which had unlocked those two hearts and had given her some of the love that she had missed all these years.

In September Margaret went to Cambridge to meet Harriet Martineau, and to make the final arrangements for her trip abroad.

Miss Martineau received her cordially and kindly. Margaret was so moved by this long-anticipated meeting that she could not say much at first. Gradually she managed to overcome her emotion and to give her mental processes a chance to function. She saw a woman of keen insight, who found words to match her meaning; one of shrewd judgments, whose mind was master of her heart; one whose reasoning powers equaled Margaret's own. She was thirty-four years old.

They went to church together on Sunday. Margaret knelt beside the older woman and prayed for her, that her mind might be kept "firmly poised in its native truth, unsullied by prejudice or error."

The days went on. Miss Martineau spoke of Carlyle, of Hannah More, of Maria Edgeworth. Sometimes Margaret detected a certain acidity in her tone and certain little twists of judgment with which she did not agree. She was disappointed; she felt the lack of broad intellectual sympathy.

Their discussions became arguments in which Margaret found herself defending her convictions and her preconceived opinions of different persons.

"I'll see that you meet Carlyle," Miss Martineau laughed, "and soon we'll know whether you don't agree with my idea of Carlyleism."

That was what Margaret kept constantly thinking about —her meeting with Carlyle and with many others in England. They were to start very soon, as Miss Martineau's long visit to America was almost at an end. Margaret bought herself some clothes to wear on shipboard, and went home to make further preparations.

She watched the harvest moon come up out of the hills, she heard the whistle of wild geese on their way to the South. The first frosts came, the leaves dropped from the trees.

There was an epidemic of cholera in Groton. It crept from house to house. Mothers shuddered when they sent their children out to play, fathers gave words of warning when they went to work....

Suddenly Timothy Fuller was taken ill. The house was all consternation; Margaret sent one of the children for the doctor and while she waited, did what things she could....

The doctor's diagnosis was the confirmation of her fears: Timothy had Asiatic cholera.

In less than three days he was dead. He lay in the parlor and the sternness went out of his face. He had done his duty; he was a respected citizen, he had served his state. For more than thirty years he had worked hard, now he was at peace. Peace settled in a cold pallor around his mouth, unknit the frown that was between his eyes, silenced the voice which had never failed to speak against injustice. This miraculous peace transcended Timothy's limitations and laid a finger on the lips of those who had spoken sharply of him in his lifetime.

Margaret was inconsolable, but she consoled her mother. She could not bear to think what this death meant to her; she was obliged to think of it. Now she realized the value of a positive personality, now she saw why the father is the head of a household.

At night she lay looking into the darkness, wondering. Why had things happened so? Why had she, only a few weeks ago, been allowed to come close to her father for the first time? And why, now that she had achieved this closeness, this communion, was her father suddenly taken from her?

She tried to feel only thankfulness for the brief glimpse they had had of each other, but sometimes bitter thoughts edged their way into her mind. She prayed God to keep her from having bitter feelings, to help her to set herself aside and to make her obvious duty the leading motive of her life.

That duty was to take the place of her father as well as she could; to counsel her brothers and her sister, to comfort her mother. Her dearest longing she must henceforth forget —her trip to England.

On the morning of the funeral before any strangers came, Margaret gathered the children together and brought them into the parlor where their father lay. She knelt down at the head of the coffin and motioned to the others to kneel in a circle around it. Then she made a solemn vow before her God that she would care for them to the utmost of her ability. "If I have ever been unfilial in word or thought, I pledge myself, O heavenly Father, to atone for it by my fidelity to these my brothers and my sister."

The mother hovered in the doorway weeping softly. She looked at Margaret so intense in her earnestness, so dramatic in her intensity, and she thought how inexplicable the girl had always been to her, how different from all the others. Now she felt thankful for that difference; it strengthened her....

Timothy left no will and his brother Abraham, a crotchety old bachelor who combined the fighting spirit of many Fullers, undertook the settling of the estate. He did not approve of Margaret, he thought she had too much to say about everything and that she gave herself airs. It was a satisfaction to him to be made administrator of the estate; it gave him a chance to speak his mind to her officially.

He had a secret reverence for money and considered higher education for boys nonessential and for girls sheer waste. Imagine Margaret's reaction to such an opinion as this! The children's education was her greatest concern. She fought like a tigress for it. Uncle Abraham fought too. At last he had an opportunity to express himself. And express himself he did in no uncertain terms; he told her with the most brutal frankness just what he thought of her.

Margaret knew her Uncle Abraham very well. Did she not remember his nasty smile, that Sunday, almost twenty years ago, when she was sent from the room in disgrace, for having persisted in her reading of *Romeo and Juliet?* She realized that she must stand her ground, must not give him one inch. ... If she did, her brothers would all grow up in ignorance.

She stood her ground; she showed old Abraham and all the rest of them that the spirit of the fighting Fullers was by no means limited to the men.

Uncle Abraham began to acquiesce a little. But he still clung to the idea that it would be waste of money to try to educate Ellen further. She was fifteen, the best thing for her to do was look around and see if there wasn't some one who would be willing to marry her in a year or two. Here the old man had a chance to give Margaret a sly dig because of her unmarried state.

"Ellen is going to boarding-school," said Margaret.

"All waste of good money. I can't take any of her share for that." Old Abraham set his jaw.

"Then I'll take *my* share for her." Margaret's jaw was set too.

Ellen went to boarding-school. And it was finally agreed that the boys should go to college when the time came. Uncle Abraham went home declaring that Margaret was a termagant.

It was all very exhausting, all this arguing back and forth. It took the best autumn weeks, it dragged on through November. And even then Margaret did not know how much was coming to them from her father's estate.

One day toward Christmas Mrs. Fuller said, "You must

go to Cambridge and arrange about your visit to England. It must be almost time for Miss Martineau to return."

"I'll go to Cambridge, mother, but not to arrange that. I'll go to say good-by to Miss Martineau."

She went. And one of the first things Harriet Martineau did was send a note to Emerson, insisting that he call on a certain day to meet Margaret Fuller. "You must know her; she is a genius, and the most brilliant conversationalist I have ever known."

Emerson brought his younger brother Charles along when he paid the call.

But Margaret was not interested in Charles. She immediately set out to make a conquest of her "serious philosopher." She showed him frankly how much she admired him, she quoted him at length, she made many witty passes.

Emerson sat watching her in his quiet way, thinking, "I don't like that trick she has of opening and shutting her eyes; I don't like her voice. I'm a little afraid of her, she has such an overpowering personality."

He left, feeling sure that he would never get very far with Margaret. Her brilliance silenced him, her wit was a little overwhelming. "But this I can say," he thought. "She does *not* scoff about humble people, and she is not as sneering as many who do not know her imagine her to be."

And he went back to his books.

Harriet Martineau had postponed her return to England. This was welcome news to Margaret, who hoped that some way might still be found for her to go too. She remained in Cambridge throughout January. She confided many things to the older woman. She had an idea that Miss Martineau might help her to understand herself. If she could understand herself she could understand humanity. This she longed passionately to do.

She told Miss Martineau of her upbringing—her early study, the forcing process to which she had been subjected, her precocity. "I was really encouraged to be rude, for I was regarded as a prodigy by her father. This did not improve my manners. At nineteen I was the most intolerable girl who even entered a drawing-room."

Her frankness appealed to the older woman. "It is well that you recognize your own shortcomings," she told her. "When one does not see one's weaknesses, one is hampered. A recognized weakness can be overcome."

Soon Margaret was back in Groton. She looked out of her window at the stinging snow; and she thought of the peaceful English lakes, of the fences made of hedgerows and of crocuses which came in February. She was torn by indecision. She wrote to Eugene: "If I should go with Miss Martineau I would see the best literary society. If I should go, you will be with mother for a while, will you not? O dear Eugene, you know how I fear to come to a decision. My temporal all seems hanging on it, and the prospect is most alluring. A few thousand dollars would make all so easy, so safe. I pray to God ceaselessly that I may decide wisely."

The days lengthened, the birds came back, fresh spring odors gushed up from the earth, new life ran in the trees. Uncle Abraham was working away at the estate, but as yet had given no hint of its value. When Margaret was alone at night, she allowed herself the old luxury of speculation: "If we each had five thousand dollars, I would start writing at once. Then in August I'd go to England with Miss Martineau...."

One day Uncle Abraham called to tell them that the share of each of the children would be two thousand dollars.

That settled it. Margaret must not go abroad. But she must not show her disappointment.

The uncertainty of the past months, the shock, and the sorrow brought on an illness. She was not only oppressed in her body, she was benumbed in her mind. Hope left her, she was convinced that she would never amount to anything; she could not even pray.

She was twenty-six. She said over and over, attempting to draw near to her God in whom she had always trusted: "Let me now try to forget myself and act for others' sakes."

Over and over she said the words, as she made clothes for the children, as she heard them recite their lessons, as she dealt with her father's creditors. "Let me act for others' sakes."

She wondered if she would ever feel alive again. Anything would be better than this numbness, this lifelessness. . . .

She called on some neighbors. They were as lifeless as she felt. She saw poverty and she saw age which had gone beyond despair; she saw a "bloodless effigy of humanity" whose world revolved around pounds of sugar and ounces of tea. She heard the jabberings of imbecility and the dry cackle of a wandering mind. She felt sad. And thanked God that she was capable of feeling anything. . . .

She left the impoverished cottage and turned toward home. The moon was out and all the stars. She turned her eyes to the stars and asked this question: "O my Father! Thou whom we are told art all Power and all Love, how canst Thou suffer such transient specks on the transparence of Thy creation?"

She walked for a long time beneath the moon and the many stars. She thought of the rising of the sun and the coming of flowers to the fields; of the wind which came from the South and brought warmth, and from the North and brought cold. She thought of spring in the hills and of the vigor of the earth; of rich fields and warm sunsets and the timeless movement of the sea. She thought of the wondrous beauty of creation and the mystery of it.

And walking beneath the moon and the stars, she felt ashamed of her lack of faith.

Suddenly she felt all warm and glowing as if a circle of

light had closed around her. To her mind came heartening words, "The Divine Spirit of Creation cannot err, it never sleeps and will not permit evil to be permanent nor its aim of beauty, in the least particular, eventually to fail."

She turned toward home. In the quiet house set among the hills she sat thinking for a long time.

X

CONQUEST

A KIND-HEARTED NEIGHBOR, thinking that Margaret must find life dull, sent her a bundle of old magazines. Margaret looked them over and decided that first she would read a story called "The Gentle Boy," which was in a magazine called *The Token*. The name signed to this story was a man's, but from the delicacy of feeling displayed in the story and from the grace of expression, Margaret judged the author to be a woman. She thought she would like to meet her and later made inquiries. She learned that the author really was a man, and that he lived in Salem. He had graduated from Bowdoin College eleven years before and had been writing ever since. No one in his own country had paid much attention to him, but only the year before, one of the editors of the London *Athenæum* copied three of the stories which had appeared in the *Token* and frankly called their author a genius. He was considered rather a strange young man. He kept to himself, and when he went out, he went at night and took long walks along the rocky coast. He had two friends whom he had made in college—Henry Wadsworth Longfellow, who had taken George Ticknor's place at Harvard the year before, and Franklin Pierce, a young congressman from New Hampshire.

The name of this solitary scribe was Nathaniel Hawthorne.

Margaret wanted to become a writer. James Freeman Clarke told her that he thought she would find the *American Monthly* friendly. She wrote to him, "I would gladly sell some part of my mind for lucre, to get the command of time; but *I will not sell my soul;* I am not willing to have what I write mutilated to suit the public taste."

Yet she knew that in order to make a living she would have to write what the public wanted.

But she might do something else. She might teach. It would be a joy to introduce to others the poets and philosophers whom she loved.

Teaching alone would not satisfy her; she knew that only writing would do that. She had in mind especially a series of articles on German literature.

In July she went to Cambridge to say good-by to Miss Martineau and the Farrars. They thought she was very sportsmanlike in her attitude, for they knew how disappointed she was because she was not going with them. Miss Martineau admired this very much, and told the Emersons about it. "I wish you would keep a kindly eye on her," she said.

One day Margaret received an invitation from Mrs. Emerson to spend a fortnight with them in Concord. She was excited. She knew that this was the chance to make a conquest of Emerson if such a conquest was ever to be made. She was convinced that they had a multitude of common interests and that their minds would meet harmoniously if she could manage to break through his reserve. It is scarcely necessary to add that this mental conquest was the only kind in which Margaret was interested.

Emerson was in the habit of spending many hours alone. Such hours were necessary to his work and afterwards to his relaxation. He puttered about in the garden and went for long walks. Everything around him contributed to peace.

Into this serene seclusion marched Margaret. She was

electric, she threw off sparks. She was full of anecdotes, she could turn any remark into an absurdity. Her eyes danced. It was impossible not to laugh with her.

The whole rhythm of the place was changed. Now there were many syncopations. Margaret would start out with some ridiculous anecdote and suddenly would branch off into a serious dissertation on Goethe's *Elective Affinities.*

"Speaking of Goethe," said Emerson, "I've read your translation of *Tasso*. Henry Hedge showed it to me a year or so ago. It's very good."

"I tried to meet you through that. I tried all sorts of tricks, but you always eluded me. And the twice you preached in Groton, I was in Cambridge. But *n'importe!* I've met you at last."

They went for walks together through the Concord lanes and through the woods at Walden. Mrs. Emerson encouraged the companionship. It never occurred to her to be jealous. She knew Margaret's principles and she knew Waldo. Margaret called her a saint.

The serious husband was a little bothered. He thought that Margaret's lighter moods were too flippant. She made him laugh more than he liked. He did not think that so much time should be spent on the froth of conversation, witty though it was. His years of study had almost taken from him the capacity to laugh. . . .

As usual, Margaret won. It was not long before Emerson was laughing unconsciously at her and not thinking too much about it. Having achieved this much, Margaret could now afford to be serious.

They talked about her future and discussed the possibilities of authorship. Emerson did not think it was wise to make writing the means of livelihood. Teaching was quite another thing. Good teachers were needed—persons with breadth of view and depth of insight.

"There's Bronson Alcott," he said. "He is a progressive,

as you know and wants teachers who have the spiritual side of the child at heart. He is ahead of his time. This country has not gone far enough away from its Puritan traditions to accept his views on religion. He is a prophet and a seer, and the greatest genius of his time."

"I'd like to work with him," said Margaret.

One morning Emerson went to Boston and called on Alcott at his school in Tremont Street. He told him that Margaret Fuller was in Concord and that it would be a good idea if he would call on her. Alcott said he would.

He lost no time. Margaret saw a tall, tranquil man of thirty-seven with a mop of blond hair curving back from his extraordinary forehead. He talked earnestly about the dearth of spiritual nourishment in all the schools. He believed in self-analysis even among children; this was the only way to acquire self-knowledge, and self-knowledge was as necessary as forgetfulness of self. He talked the whole afternoon.

Margaret was a good listener. She now heard about the time when Abba and Bronson Alcott had visited William Lloyd Garrison in jail: many of their acquaintances refused to recognize them after that. He told her of his early struggles and was especially sentimental about his fiddle, which he had traded for a suit of clothes. He spoke of transcendentalism and a great many other abstruse things. And not till nightfall did he return to Boston.

Margaret did not agree with everything he said, but she had an idea that she would like to work with him.

When the fortnight was over she went back to Groton feeling mentally and spiritually stimulated. And she wrote to her "dear friends" and tried to tell them what the visit had meant to her.

She read prodigiously that summer: Shelley, Wordsworth, Coleridge, Southey, Harriet Martineau. Goethe she always kept before her and made notes for the *Life* she hoped eventually to write. She changed her mind several times about his religious views; now she felt him to be omniscient, now veered off a little, thought him too extreme. She had not yet formulated her own creed and had no fixed standard by which to judge his.

She kept in touch with her friends, James Freeman Clarke, Dr. Channing, Henry Hedge, the Emersons. And there was another, Samuel Ward, for whom she had different feelings. He was more cosmopolitan, more dashing, more a man of the world. He was never at a loss for a light response and he paid compliments as deftly as a Frenchman. He was a little younger than Margaret and was somewhat of a dilettante at art. He was, in short, charming. Margaret wrote him long effusions about the sun and the "tawny evergreens and oaks," called him her fellow votary and sent him flowers.

And when the autumn came she went happily to Boston to teach French and Latin in Bronson Alcott's school.

PART II
EXPERIMENTATION

I
CYCLONE

She took rooms in Avon Place and sent out prospectuses saying that she would take a certain number of pupils in French, German and Italian. She was doubtful if her work at Alcott's school would prove very remunerative.

She and Alcott had many arguments in which Margaret told him frankly wherein she differed with him: "You are too impatient of the complex ... you become lost in abstractions and cannot illustrate your principles."

He answered, "If I can unfold some of the essential conditions of man's spiritual being and turn men's minds to the culture of childhood as the primary duty, I shall be content."

He was eager that children should learn that the fundamental principle of life is Spirit. He taught them that flesh is Spirit incarnate, that Jesus attained divine Sonship by sinless living and that He is an example of what all men may become. An important part of the school curriculum was the conversations on the gospels. These were carried on between Alcott and the children; and Margaret and the other teacher, Elizabeth Peabody, reported them. As Margaret listened to these talks she wondered sometimes how long such teaching would be allowed to live in a city which had almost stoned a man to death because he proclaimed publicly that he believed all slaves should be freed.

Alcott was stimulated by Margaret who, he said, took generous views of all subjects, had the subtlest perceptions and was, undoubtedly, the most brilliant conversationalist of the day. The children loved her; her outside classes flourished. But, as usual, she had undertaken more than her health could endure and suffered constantly from headaches. Her mind was troubled too; for some reason she could not understand, she felt estranged from many of her old friends, who treated her coldly and made no effort to see her. Undoubtedly the reason for this was her association with Alcott, who was regarded by many as too radical to be tolerated. So Margaret's old loneliness came back.

Her new friends, the Emersons, never failed her; these she saw as often as she could. Abba Alcott was charming, though always harassed by the consciousness of being married to an impractical visionary. She constantly had to appeal to her father for financial help. And there was Dr. Channing, whose preaching always stimulated. "He feeds the whole spirit. After I hear him, I feel purged, as if by fire." Margaret read German with him once a week.

She was impatient, she longed for vague, ineffable things. Once she cried, "O why cannot I lay more to heart the text 'God is never in a hurry'? Let me be more patient and confident."

Harvard had its bicentennial celebration that autumn. After one of the meetings, four young Unitarian ministers got into a theological discussion about the narrowness of many of the churches. They were all very earnest young men and they wanted to find some remedy for such narrowness. They were Ralph Waldo Emerson, George Ripley, Frederick Henry Hedge and George Putnam. They called a meeting and invited James Freeman Clarke, Bronson Alcott and

Convers Francis to join them. They did not come to any final agreement, probably because Alcott started off on some of his abstractions and could not be silenced. So they called another meeting to be held at Emerson's house; and to this they invited Margaret Fuller and Elizabeth Peabody, Alcott's two assistants. And this time something definite was arrived at: They formed themselves into a club which Alcott named *The Symposium Club*. When word of this club went abroad, those on the outside smiled a little and called the group transcendentalists, a word big enough to include everything. They met once a month and talked of everything under the sun.

Between meetings they carried on their work as enthusiastically as they could. Margaret was so much impressed by Alcott's conversations with the children that she urged him to have them published. At length he agreed; and at the beginning of the year they appeared in print.

Their effect was cyclonic. Had a volcano suddenly erupted in the middle of Boston Common, the consternation could not have been greater. The Boston *Courier* started things off by declaring that Alcott should be indicted for blasphemy; a Harvard professor seconded this statement by saying that the book was one-third absurdity, one-third blasphemy and one-third obscenity. The absurdity might have passed unnoticed, but the other two counts were more than sufficient to incite the people, who became a howling mob.

One cold day in January, there was a knock on the door of Alcott's school. The mob had gathered. Alcott opened the door and saw many persons whom he knew; they called themselves the Intelligentsia; they were teachers, preachers, parents of the generation he was instructing. There were many others whom he did not know—the hangers-on, the mental riffraff who are always on the lookout for a fight.

They shouted, "Down with the Conversations!" "Retract the devilish book!" "Bring out all your copies and burn them!"

Alcott listened to them calmly, but said nothing. From the back of the group came another voice, shrill, hysterical, "Close the school, dismiss the children and hand over the key."

Alcott answered that. "No, that I cannot do."

His voice increased their anger; it was too calm to be endured. There was a growl; the man nearest to the door pushed forward and took hold of Alcott's coat. It looked as if he was to be dragged out into the street, stoned perhaps as was William Lloyd Garrison. A hard look came into his eyes, he shook off the hand that clutched his coat-sleeve, and said sternly, "You will disperse at once!"

The growl was louder this time and the crowd pushed closer.

Inside the door all the school waited. Margaret tried to go on with the lessons, but this was difficult, as the angry voices could be heard quite clearly. Little Louisa May Alcott heard them and got up from her chair. Margaret did not try to detain her. The child disappeared into the anteroom.

She saw the angry-looking crowd, and she said, bravely, "Father, the children sent me for you!"

Alcott looked down from his enormous height and picked the child up and stood there holding her in his arms. The growl died away. For a few moments nothing was heard but the cold, metallic crunching of snow under the runners of a sleigh in the street. Suddenly Louisa May called out impatiently, "Go away, bad people!"

A few faint grumbles answered her. She shivered a little, for the wind was cold. Alcott held her more closely.

Without another word, without a grumble, the crowd suddenly turned and moved off into the street. Alcott closed the door and carried Louisa May back into the schoolroom. Lessons went on as before.

Emerson was deeply grieved over the reception of Alcott's book. He wrote to the *Courier* protesting against the practice of would-be critics of picking out certain phrases and distorting them according to their own bigoted ideas, so that they appeared little short of monstrous; he pleaded for broadmindedness, for reasonableness and intelligence; he called attention to the motive of the author, which was high: "He aims to make children think ... he aims to show them something holy in their own consciousness, thereby to make them really reverent and make the New Testament a living book to them."

But the Puritan populace believed that children were conceived in sin; they could not understand the ideas of purity which Alcott was endeavoring to teach. Having eyes, they saw not, having minds, they did not apprehend.

Alcott's pupils began to drop away; the school dwindled from forty to ten. Still, Alcott would not close it. He was in debt, his family was starving. Abba wrote to her father telling him of Bronson's ill luck.

In April he was obliged to sell the furniture from the schoolroom and—what grieved him much more—to part with his library. He could not afford an assistant; in fact he had not been able to afford an assistant all winter, and his assistants knowing this, refused their salaries. Margaret gave up her outside classes and went back to Groton. She was in poor health, and looked forward to the gentle fields, the quiet woods and the bracing air from the hills. She had defended Alcott eloquently, had written to several of her "most cultivated friends," telling them frankly what she thought of them for their denunciation of him.

The thought of Groton was a soothing thought.

She would have liked to take a few months, perhaps a year, to write the life of Goethe. George Ripley was planning the publication of a series of works on Foreign Literature and had asked her to be responsible for Goethe. She was greatly tempted. But this was the situation: It would take her months to do such a work; during these months she would earn nothing. Meanwhile the expenses of the family went on. Her problem was by no means unique; many had faced it before her, many have faced it since. The creative artist obliged to earn his living will always have to face it. . . .

Margaret decided that she could not afford to take the time to write the life of Goethe.

. . . .

There was a new school in Providence, called the Green Street School. The founder, a man called Fuller, but in no way related to Margaret, offered her a thousand dollars a year to be his assistant.

She accepted this offer; and from her decision drew certain inferences: What we would like to do and what seems most important to us to do is scarcely ever related to what we ought to do. The process of spiritual discipline is ceaseless, and only when we can make our desires coincide with our duties will we attain to the highest that is in us.

The two boys, Arthur and Richard, were running the farm. Arthur was fifteen, Richard two years younger. Richard thought he would like to be a farmer all his life; he preferred the hayfields and the autumn furrows to the Iliad and the Odyssey. There were other Fuller farmers in the vicinity. One of them, a man of means with no children, was eager to adopt Richard, and Richard was equally eager to be adopted. But Margaret said no. She could not endure the idea of his education ending at such an early age. . . .

So in June, she said good-by once more and went off to Providence, in order that Arthur and Richard and Ellen and James might keep on going to school.

II

THE RADICAL

GETTING STARTED IN HER NEW WORK was an irksome business. She was to have charge of sixty girls of all ages. First she had to sort them, then she had to arrange her classes. She was to teach rhetoric, Latin, philosophy, history, poetry and moral science. She was given free rein, and so she added other things to her list—things which many would not have considered necessary: short talks on the whys and wherefores of all study. She taught the girls that study was not an end in itself, but a means to an end; what was equally important was the use to which it was put. Not material use; something much more important than that. Knowledge was the path leading to wisdom; knowledge was acquisitive, wisdom was creative. She taught that life was a long process of spiritual development, that potentially all human nature was divine, that the essential duty of every human being was to realize, as far as he was able, this divine potentiality.

The perceptions of youth are keen, and youth is quick to form judgments. If a preceptor limits his teachings to theory, youth soon knows it and becomes skeptical. Margaret applied her philosophy to her everyday life. Her pupils saw this and respected her. Their attitude toward her was reverential. They soon learned that there was nothing they could not ask of her, provided they were sincere in the asking. So they brought their youthful problems to her and she helped to solve them. She loved them, and she loved working with them, though her aspiration was toward a different kind of life.

The school building was attractive and was entered through a "wide gate, a piazza and a pretty, wide door."

The boys entered from a dressing-room on one side, the girls from a similar room on the other. The "great hall" had a thick, orange-colored carpet on the floor, its ceiling was arched. Everything was spick and span and was a joy to Margaret.

Her habit of early rising clung to her; she rose at five, sometimes even earlier, and took plenty of time to dress. She considered neatness of appearance one of the primary rules of life, and was not averse to spending as much as an hour and a half on her toilet. The result justified the expenditure; she emerged always *tres bien soignee*, in neat, well-fitting clothes. The youthful tendency to stoutness which was such a trial to her during her dancing days, had departed. She was now of more normal proportions, and, as always, she carried herself well.

She had not been very long in Providence when Uncle Abraham began to make trouble, began to harp again on his old theme—the children's education. He bullied Margaret's mother, tried to persuade her that the only thing for Richard to do was to become a farmer at once, and that Arthur should find whatever work he could do. As for Ellen ... He had used the same arguments before, but Margaret had managed to override them.

Mrs. Fuller wrote agonized letters to Margaret; she was at her wit's end, poor thing; Abraham was so positive about everything, was determined not to allow even the interest to be spent in educating Timothy's children.

Margaret had no respect for a man who awaited his opportunity to force his will on a weaker will. She wrote firmly to her mother, imploring her not to allow "that sordid man" to give her any uneasiness.

Uncle Abraham had tried to assume full guardianship of the children. Margaret bolstered up her mother's will, assured her that she was the rightful guardian and besought her not to be intimidated by the "vulgar insults" of the arrogant Abraham. "If more money is wanting... I will take a private class by which I can earn the $400 that Ellen will need. I will let her have my portion of my income with her own, or even capital, which I have a right to take. It will not even be a sacrifice for me to do this, for I am sated and weary with society and long for the opportunity for solitary concentration of thought for my book."

Again Uncle Abraham was defeated. Arthur was enrolled in Leicester Academy, Ellen went to Providence to become one of Margaret's pupils.

. . . .

Margaret met all sorts of people in Providence; she shocked her employer by attending political meetings. The Whigs were holding meetings everywhere. Tristam Burgess, the "Old Bald Eagle," came to Providence and held a fiery session. Margaret enjoyed the meetings thoroughly and considered that in attending them she had done the best thing she had ever done.

A French frigate anchored in Narragansett Bay. Margaret was entertained by the commander, and was charmed with the manners of the officers, which were "beauteous to behold and not less wondrous to one accustomed to the simple American Jack Tar." Her old desire for a life of action came back again; she saw herself in gold braid and brass buttons commanding a fleet. But women, unfortunately, did not do that kind of thing. She asked herself indignantly: Why not? Why didn't women do anything they felt like doing? She failed to see why, if they were fitted, women could not do anything under the sun. An idea for a book began to germinate; it had to-do with the limitations of preconceived ideas, with the absurdities of tradition. She knew that there had been an age which recognized not only the equality but the superiority of women. Yes, she knew that, one day, she must write a book about that.

An English Quaker came to lecture; he was said to be a great and distinguished man—John Joseph Gurney, the brother of Hannah Fry. In high anticipation, Margaret went to hear him, but was sorely disappointed. He spoke fluently enough, in the old-time, declamatory way, but he said nothing. His idea of God she found grotesque: "His Man-God seemed to be the keeper of a madhouse rather than the informing Spirit of all spirits." He was not only bigoted; he gloried in his bigotry. His smugness pained Margaret. When, at the close of the address, he asked his audience to sit for a while in silent prayer, Margaret prayed to her beneficent God to remove the scales of self-complacency from the eyes of the preacher in order that he might not go about degrading religion.

Insincerity depressed her, spiritual pride was revolting to her. She went from the meeting that night wondering why it was so difficult for people to accept God simply as the creator of good.

Richard Henry Dana was giving readings in Providence from the English dramatists. Margaret enjoyed them; and Dana's sincerity compensated for Gurney's smugness.

Writing to her family and to her friends took up a great deal of time. She took turns in writing to her family. She constantly urged Arthur to learn to express himself fluently in his letters. "I may probably be very little with you the remainder of my life and if you do not learn to write you and I, who have been such good friends, may become as strangers to one another."

She knew how precious pennies were to him, so she told him he need not pay the postage on his letters; she would pay it.

There was to be no frittering of time. To impress this on the boy, she reminded him of the years she had spent teaching them all, from the time when she was twenty-three till she was twenty-six—important years in the life of one with ambitions for a professional career. "Those three years would have enabled me to make great attainments, which now I may never do. Do you make them in my stead that I may not remember such time with sadness."

Arthur was moved by this letter; so much moved that he took great pains with his reply. It was worth the pains. Margaret wrote back encouragingly: It was the best he had ever written; at last he had given her a picture of his mind.

She encouraged her pupils in self-analysis; and all of them kept journals in which they wrote the day's happenings and their own reactions to them. Margaret was not satisfied, as were many of her acquaintances, to live in a state of negative goodness, convinced that if she did no wrong, she would be led unconsciously to do right. Hers was no such passive nature; she strove constantly to learn the why and the wherefore of the Creative Impulse in the thing created. The older she grew, the more firmly she believed in predestination.

In February of the next year, her mother went to Providence to pay her a visit. Mrs. Fuller was still at a loose end, was unable to adjust herself to the conditions which her life had so suddenly assumed. She, who had grown up believing in man's supremacy and had made herself utterly subservient to her husband, was now like an orchid which had no trunk to cling to. She respected Margaret's judgment more than that of any other woman, but it was sometimes hard for her to accept it as superior to that of Uncle Abraham. For Uncle Abraham was her dear husband's brother, whom her dear husband had undoubtedly loved. . . .

Things were very difficult for her.

She enjoyed her visit as much as she ever expected to enjoy anything in life again. She even thought of letting the farm at Groton and settling in Providence. Arthur might enter Brown University, Ellen was with Margaret. She would have three of her family with her.

She was more dependent on Margaret than she realized,

and her admission that she had enjoyed her visit more than she ever expected to enjoy anything in life again, was evidence enough that she was not inconsolable.

Toward spring an emergency arose which caused Margaret great anxiety. No specific mention is made in any of her letters as to what it was, but there is no doubt that it concerned one of her brothers. She was faced with the necessity of applying to Uncle Abraham for funds. This was not easy for her to do, but she put herself completely out of the picture and wrote to him.

Evidently Uncle Abraham rose to the situation, though the temptation must have been great to humiliate them. For, as Margaret frankly remarked to him, she knew very well that he was not partial to any of her father's children.

She wrote bright accounts of all her doings to Emerson, to James Freeman Clarke, to Dr. Channing and to that other "fellow votary," Samuel Ward. Now and then she went up to Boston, to the theater and to concerts. Once she went to a fancy dress party given by Mrs. Thorndike. It was the largest affair she had ever attended. When she arrived, everything was at its gayest. Débutantes were there from all lands and from all times. Solemn pilgrims talked with courtesans; Spanish dancing-girls coquetted with red-robed cardinals; Creole belles dropped dainty handkerchiefs in the paths of pirates.

Margaret was enchanted. But she did not have much opportunity for looking on, for, the first thing she knew was that some one was before her introducing a pale young man as serious as the solemn pilgrims. This was Theodore Parker. Margaret willingly forgot the pageant. She had heard admirable things about this young man: How he had worked to secure a college education; how remarkable was his knowledge of languages, how advanced his nonconformist views.

They were soon deep in talk, and were about to begin a discussion of Spinoza, when some one came up and claimed

Margaret for supper. During this part of the proceeding, she had a close-up of Daniel Webster eating oysters!

Afterwards she danced.... And left the party very late, feeling stimulated and greatly fortified for her work.

Another spring came, the lilacs blossomed again, japonica flamed in all the gardens, the frogs were clamorous in the ponds. Margaret was twenty-eight. She thought of all she wished to do: the life of Goethe, which was still unwritten, the countless essays. She thought of Harriet Martineau, whose book on America she had read and frankly criticized: "Such a crude, intemperate tirade as you have been guilty of about Mr. Alcott, a true and noble man, a philanthropist whom a true and noble woman also a philanthropist should have delighted to honor; a man whom Carlyle would delight to honor; a man whom the worldlings of Boston hold in as much honor as the worldlings of ancient Athens did Socrates. They smile to hear their verdict confirmed from the other side of the Atlantic by their censor, Harriet Martineau."

She lost no time in sending this letter off to Miss Martineau.

And she thought of more tender things, such as the spring is likely to bring to one's thoughts. Her "fellow votary" had seemed of late not quite so ardent; was he, perhaps, growing tired of her? His letters were filled with superficial observations, like the letters of a lover whose conscience urges him to write but whose interest has gone. In her thoughts she clung to him; he dwelt in a chivalrous and enchanted land, like a god almost, remote from all prosaic worries, from all burdensome cares. He spoke a language that no other spoke. ... What happiness to dwell with him in his chivalrous and enchanted land and to speak the language that no other spoke! She re-read his last letter and deep melancholy seized her....

Fanny Kemble was touring the country. Margaret went to see her in *Much Ado About Nothing*. She was as excited as a child, could scarcely wait for the curtain to go up.

At last Beatrice appeared. But what a Beatrice! You would have thought the stage was chalk-marked for her, so studied were her movements; she was conscious of every intonation of her voice, as if she were listening to herself playing the part. Instead of an exuberance of wit she displayed studied coquetry, instead of high intellect a certain crafty intelligence. . . .

Margaret was bored. She went home tired and irked because her brain was not on fire nor was her heart moved. She had her glass of milk, she went wearily to the mirror and let down her beautiful hair. The face which looked back at her had lines around the eyes and a somber droop to the corners of the mouth. . . . She turned away and prepared for bed.

The next night was much better. The play was *The Stranger;* and it was only by the exercise of great will that Margaret kept herself from rushing up to the stage at the fall of the curtain.

And that night when she looked in her mirror she saw a woman with mysterious lights in her eyes; and she thanked God that she was able to experience exalted moments.

The interesting thing was that the older she grew the more intense became these moments. She never knew when they would come, for they came suddenly, with no warning, caused by simple things like a sunset or low mist hanging over a garden; by water lilies lying motionless between broad leaves. Less simple things caused them too: the grandeur of a stretch of sand-dunes, Beethoven's Fifth Symphony, Raphael and Michael Angelo.

Her melancholy was as deep as her exaltation was high. Often when she went home after a trying day at school, she found unpleasant letters waiting for her. Uncle Abraham was on the war-path again and her mother was distressed.

She lost no time in dealing with Uncle Abraham, she never failed to send her mother a heartening word.

One Saturday she went up to Boston to see an exhibition of pictures at the Athenæum. She had been rather low in her spirits of late and felt the need of stimulus.

She received it. "I seemed to breathe my native atmosphere and smoothed my ruffled pinions."

Looking at a Christ of Raphael, she was lost in spiritual ecstasy; she thought of St. Theresa and longed to sacrifice herself for some great cause. She thought of the visions of St. Catherine of Siena, and she bowed her head and prayed that she might overcome her haughty manner and the proud arrogance which was the heritage of many Fullers.

She sat for a long time among the books she loved and listened for whatever thoughts would come to her. She heard: "There is a gloom in deep love as in deep water; even the Muses approach it with a timid step and with a tremulous and melancholy song." And the recurring questions came to her again: "Why have I not yet experienced the heights and depths of love? Is it because I have lived thoughtfully, seeking to be wise? Why am I destined to be loved by those I cannot love and why do I love some one who seems to have grown cold to me?"

Her thoughts wandered here and there. She thought of George Sand and her many loves: of her tenderness with Chopin and her passion with Jules Sandeau and Alfred de Musset....

And while she sat there alone and lonely, George Sand was making plans to take Chopin to a warmer climate where he might go on writing music; old statesmen were marrying young wives, in order that their names might live; a young queen was on the throne of England....

Life went on and on; active life on one side, thought-life on the other. Margaret thought of her long association with books. Was it possible that a life with books unfitted one for a life with persons? There were times when books did not satisfy, when she longed to take life to her with all its gifts—its good and evil, its joy and pain, its ecstasies and despairs. And her soul cried "Must I always remain lost in a maze of trivial tasks and homely, sordid problems?"

She got up, went again and stood before Raphael's Christ and prayed that she might become more like him. Then she went out into the sun.

She saw Emerson as often as was possible. To him she could speak freely. She told him that it was he who had first opened her mind to the meaning of the inward life, that every time she heard him speak, her torch was kindled again. "Several of your sermons stand apart in my memory, like landmarks in my spiritual history."

She usually did most of the talking. Sometimes the frankness of her self-analysis shocked Emerson, who was much more reserved than she, who kept his best thoughts for his lectures. Margaret, on the other hand, gave freely of hers, and could not have repeated them. She had an insatiable habit of getting at the bottom of people's minds.

Once she went for a walk with Oliver Wendell Holmes and drew him into a discussion of this question: "What view should a man of science take of his relation to eternal interests and his temporal pursuits?" Her constant query; how reconcile immediate activities with eternal principles. Holmes answered her indifferently; he saw no reason for bothering himself about such things; the main thing was to keep on with one's job. Margaret was disappointed. Afterwards she made this note: "I realized that after our talk, that my mind was as superior to his as it is inferior to many others."

Her frankness went both ways; when she saw herself superior, she admitted it. When she chanced to meet minds she thought superior to hers, she paid homage to them generously. This frankness led many persons to misjudge her—

to say that she was egotistical, conceited, a "mountainous me."

It is ridiculous to think that a person of superior mentality does not know that he is superior. Margaret's mistake lay in her too free expression of this knowledge. When she made the statement that of all those she had met she found no intellect comparable with her own, she was absolutely truthful. She had made a penetrating study of herself and she knew, better than any one else, what her mind contained. She had set out at an early age to make herself superior in intellectual attainments; that she should become so was only natural. But that she should be proud of her superiority is inexcusable.

Her *spirit* was not proud; and her great task was expressing humility of spirit through a personality which was anything but humble. She prayed constantly that she might learn to do this; she prayed that her intolerance of stupidity and of vulgarity might be transmuted into kindliness. And in time it was.

That was the summer in which Emerson gave his historic address before the graduating class of Harvard Divinity School. It was an impassioned plea for self-reliance and for clearness of thought. "Cast conformity behind you and acquaint men at first hand with Deity."

It caused a howling tempest; the fundamentalists attacked him, said that he was destroying the foundations of their faith; the modernists defended him. Margaret wrote him a congratulatory letter. Emerson, digging in his garden, heard the protests and the defenses in silence. The summer went on.

III

DYNAMICS

MARGARET DECIDED TO LEAVE PROVIDENCE. She was working on her life of Goethe, had already translated Eckerman's *Conversations;* the creative impulse was clamorous within her. But she must have solitude. She wrote to Dr. Channing: "I am weary and want rest ... my mind has so long been turned outward and longs for concentration and leisure for tranquil thought ... my energies have been much repressed. ... I do not wish to teach again at all."

Her mother had managed to sell the farm at Groton, but the family was to spend the winter there. Richard was general manager of the place, Arthur was away at school. Richard was beginning to weary of farming and wrote telling Margaret that he, too, would like to go away to school. She answered that there was no immediate hurry; that since this was the last year that they would spend at Groton, she thought it best for him to remain till spring. She said that she would tutor him in Latin and composition and that Ellen would look after his French. For this she asked that he compensate her by willingness to take her advice and by neatness in his dress, politeness in his manners and devotion to the wishes of their mother.

The last day at school was very trying. After all the lessons were heard, Margaret thanked the pupils for their coöperation, their loyalty to her wishes and their aspiration to become what she had outlined to them. She assured them of her friendliness and told them that they might always call on her if they felt so inclined. Then she dismissed them.

But they would not be dismissed. For many minutes they sat there quietly weeping. This affected Margaret deeply.

Finally she went among them, said good-by to each one, then slipped out of the room.

At Christmas she was in Groton and the fields were white. She looked out at them and wondered where would be the next place that she could call home. The future was precarious, she had no work in view, the boys must go to school, Ellen and her mother must not be allowed to worry. If she could possibly avoid it, Margaret wished not to teach again, but if it became necessary, she would. In the meantime, she hoped for peace and rest and the leisure to do what she wished, more than anything else, to do.

She had not much peace; she was ill all winter. She had not much rest; she was busy tutoring Richard and Ellen. The winds whirled around the corners of the house and made mournful sounds in the eaves; the cows huddled together when Richard let them out for water; the cold glittered on the snow and made figures on the window-panes.

When she was well enough, Margaret went to Boston for a few days. She called on Bronson Alcott and found him greatly changed; he was paler, his eyes had gone further into his head, there was a deep line on each side of his mouth. He had been through great difficulties; and now his school was closed and he was up to his ears in debt. His family looked half-starved. He had steadily backed William Lloyd Garrison in his abolitionist movement, and one day, went a step too far by admitting a little negro girl to his school.

That was too much for Boston. The parents came storming to the school again, this time to take their children home. They saw a little group sitting in a pool of sunlight around their great, gaunt teacher. One woman, who had always been friendly toward the Alcotts, went up and jerked her child out of his chair. "Come, Charles," she said, "I didn't know that you were associating with black scum." Venom in her voice.

It released other venom. In a moment, the whole twenty of them were all talking—high and shrill and bitter. What a picture they made to the quiet, serious, gaunt-looking man with the peace of God showing in his eyes! They hurt him more than he could bear. Suddenly he called "Silence!"

Taken so unawares, hypnotized by the force of Alcott's personality, the crowd stood staring, their words abruptly checked.

Alcott questioned each of the children about leaving. There was not one who did not ask to remain. Last of all he questioned the little colored girl, a pretty mulatto child. She said, "My father said you would teach me how to save my race."

Save the race! Save the race of black men who were no better than animals! Some of the foremost of the crowd went a step or two toward the door. This was the signal for the next move. In strode a blustering man with a bull-dog face. The crowd fell back a little to make room for him. He stood in the pool of sunlight in front of Alcott. "Sorry, Mr. Alcott, but I've got to close you out of here. Your creditors have turned to the law. I'm the Sheriff."

It was a dramatic gesture. The crowd showed its appreciation by grunts of approval. Alcott's two children Anna and Louisa May got up and went to him. As on that other day in midwinter, Louisa May was spokesman: "Go away! You are making my father unhappy."

Charles' mother answered the child. "Yes, we'll go, Miss Impertinence, and not a living soul of us will come back."

Alcott saw that there was nothing to do but leave. He waited till the triumphant crowd had departed and the children had gathered up their books. Then he helped Anna and Louisa May into their coats, took his old hat down from its peg and with a child on each side of him, went out into the street, crossed the Common where the winter sun lay on the snow, and walked slowly home.

Margaret was deeply touched by this story, and asked Alcott what he intended to do next. He did not know. Emerson had tried to find work for him but could not. There was no school committee which would consider him for a moment. "All right," Emerson had said, "then devote your time to writing."

That was all very well in theory, Alcott said, but what about his family? The returns for writing were slow....

As a matter of fact, Alcott had never supported his family; and if it had not been for his wife's father, they would have been obliged to seek help from charitable institutions.

Margaret left him, feeling that her problems were simple compared with his.

She had another memorable meeting at that time; she met Allston the painter, and was so fascinated that she forgot to make herself interesting! Usually it was she who did the talking; this time it was Allston. "He flamed up into a galaxy of Platonism," she wrote in her journal.

Into this journal went all her secret thoughts, all her questionings, all her self-analyses. She thought that writing her ideas clarified them....

While she was in Boston she looked around for a house. She found one at Jamaica Plain, which appealed to her. It stood back from a winding stream called Willow Brook, in a good-sized plot where there were trees and where rocks jutted up out of the earth. In the summer the rocks were covered with cardinal flowers. There were open spaces at Jamaica Plain, and there were beautiful vistas. Narrow paths wound around Jamaica Pond and in the spring the fronds of weeping willow bent down into the water....

Margaret took the house.

She went back to Groton and gave the family an enthusiastic description of the place; and while the sharp winds drove the snow along in swirls and Richard's cattle huddled in their stalls, she laid out plots for candytuft and columbines and old-fashioned gillyflowers.

In March she visited the Emersons. Elizabeth Hoar was staying in the house too. She was to have married Emerson's younger brother Charles, but Charles had died. Elizabeth remained faithful to him and frequently visited at Waldo's house, where she was to have lived. Emerson called the beautiful Miss Hoar, Elizabeth the Wise. Wise she was in a quiet, tender way.

She and Margaret shared the same room. They got on very well together and talked away into the night. Margaret wrote to Eugene saying that they talked too much for her strength.

There were other guests in the house, Emerson's brother William and his wife, from New York. Margaret did not find much similarity in the two brothers: "Mr. William is as unlike his brother as possible. He is very gentlemanly, very amenable, very clear-headed, but a mere business man. He strikingly resembles Governor Everett in his way of speaking."

She did not see much of Waldo till afternoon. All morning he was shut up in his study and she was busy writing or reading. They met after twelve, when Emerson read aloud to her. Afterwards they talked. Now that friendly relations had been established, Margaret did not have to make any special effort to please him; there were fewer fireworks about their conversations now. Emerson asked Margaret's opinion of his writing; sometimes she disagreed with his ideas. He always listened eagerly to her reasons for disagreeing and not infrequently was won over to her opinion.

She told him that she expected to move her family to Jamaica Plain about the end of April. Already there was a band of workmen in the house, repairing and decorating. She gave spirited accounts of the Bedlam that was going on there. She had decided to start a kind of symposium in Boston, for women. She had not made a complete outline, but she suspected that her subjects would be Nature, Literature, Characters of Great Men, and the like. "My idea is to systematize thought, to give precision and clearness of expression (shades of Timothy!), to learn what pursuits are best suited to us and how we may make the best possible use of our talents. The idea might be said to revolve around the question, 'What were we born to do and how shall we do it?' I know it is an ambitious plan, but it should work itself out. And I know also that if it does not succeed in Boston, it never could in any other city in the United States."

Terribly earnest she was in her desire to make individuals out of women. Her earnestness sometimes ran away with her sense of humor, which had never equaled her wit. Indeed, it is a question whether very successful persons ever have a sense of humor. If they had, it is doubtful if they would be so successful, for they could not then take themselves so seriously.

Emerson was interested in her project and thought she would make a success of it. Margaret talked it over with George Ripley's wife Sophia, who had a long head. They considered who they thought would be interested and found more than twenty. This was encouraging.

But Margaret was not happy. She was more and more convinced that her fellow votary's interest was on the wane. She had hoped that he would look her up while she was in Concord, had visualized a walk under the March moon, a talk in some secluded place, at least a concert. She had so many things to say to him! She never forgot the charming way he listened to her and the deferential way he replied. She did not say them, but went back to Groton to superintend the packing.

The place was in an uproar, "all dust and Babel." Arthur came home to be with the family during the last few days. He wandered around among the packing cases, not knowing what to do with himself. He was a little intolerant of Richard the farmer, whose clothes smelled of the stable. Margaret hoped he was not going to allow himself to become vain.

One day after crocus time, three wagons moved over the road from Groton to Concord, from Concord to Boston, carrying the Fuller furniture and effects. And before the leaves were thick along the Jamaica way, the Fuller family was settled in the house which listened to the low chortles of Willow Brook.

It was a busy summer. Margaret outlined her plans for the autumn, kept the household accounts, helped Richard with his lessons. Mrs. Fuller pottered about in the garden behind the house, the cardinal flowers dripped over the rocks.

The Transcendentalists were very active that summer. Thoroughly impatient with the narrowness of Puritan orthodoxy and somewhat alarmed at the spreading materialism, this group decided to start a counteracting influence. With such a force as Plato in the world and Plutarch, Socrates and Seneca, and with such later comers as Kant, Jacobi, Hegel, it seemed worse than stupid for the country to shuffle along in the wake of the tattered banners of Puritanism. The gloom of Puritanism was repellent to these courageous men and women who went delving into the motives of human action; its bigotry they considered a refutation of individual intelligence. They looked past creeds to a brighter Source for their spiritual guidance and visualized the day when the whole country would be moved to seek a similar Source. "All mine is thine" sounded forth to them in ceaseless benediction—from flowers and from stars, through the poetry, the art and the heroism of the ages, through their own aspirations. Their maxim was "Trust, dare and be; infinite good is ready for your asking; seek and find."

They were honest critics of their time, they were smashers of shams and destroyers of hypocrisy. They dared to be individuals in a world they saw fast becoming standardized. Perhaps they were inclined to take themselves and their mission in life too seriously. Was this a fault? The records of their achievements, more alive to-day than in their time, are answer enough to this.

Margaret went to the meetings when she had time. She always entered the room with a sweep and a flourish. One would not have been surprised had a herald blown a trumpet as she was about to cross the threshold. Seated in the room, she raised her lorgnette—symbol of a duchess—and scrutinized every face. She listened well; and while the other speeches went on, she gathered together that remarkable energy, which, when her turn came, always made her the most powerful and the most eloquent of all. Dr. Channing said that she seemed to be the medium for all the circulating life of the place. "Her opening was deliberate, like the progress of some massive force gaining momentum; but as she felt her way, the sweep of her speech became grand. The style of her eloquence was sententious, free from pettiness, direct, vigorous, charged with vitality."

Thanks to her years of study, she had a world of information at her disposal. She picked her steps carefully through that world, stopping to gather only such items as were relevant to her subject. She could go swiftly to the kernel of truths. While she spoke, the others listened in a kind of rapt ecstasy. They always found something new in her interpretations of old truths. "There were seasons when she seemed borne irresistibly on to the verge of prophecy and fully embodied one's notion of a sibyl."

Afterwards, when she had left them, they asked themselves what was the secret of her remarkable power. All agreed that it was genius, but what was genius? Dr. Channing arrived at a conclusion about Margaret's particular genius: "She blended feminine receptiveness and masculine energy. By the vivid intensity of her conceptions, she brought out in those around her, *their own consciousness.*" That was probably as correct an analysis as anything; she undoubtedly combined both masculine and feminine characteristics to a marked degree. She realized, long before the psychoanalysts came along, that each individual is by nature both masculine and feminine; she recognized the masculine and feminine principles in all life—the eternal opposites, which, for fulfillment, are united. She was forming her profession of faith which, in a short time, she was to issue as her Credo: "Man is himself one tree in the garden of the Spirit. Wherever man remains embedded in nature, whether from sensuality or because he is not yet awakened to consciousness, the purpose of the whole remains unfulfilled." With such convictions, how appalled she must have been at the advancing materialism!

After the highly charged meetings of the Transcendentalists, Margaret was a nervous wreck. The headaches which were the result of her early "forcing process," came back with increased intensity, and sleeplessness accompanied her long nights.

IV

THE SIBYL

THE SUMMER was a disappointment. Nothing happened as she had hoped; there were no confidences with the one she loved, no quiet walks around Jamaica Pond, no happy evenings under the stars.

She waited till the end of August, when she wrote: "You do not wish to be with me. Why try to hide it from me, from yourself? You are not interested in any of my interests; my friends, my pursuits are not yours.... The sympathizing contemplation of the beautiful in Nature, in Art, is over for us—that for which I loved you first and which made that love a shrine at which I could rest upon my weary pilgrimage.

"You come home, to go away again, and make a call upon me in the parlor . . . you write me to say you could not write before. My heart deceives me widely if this be love."

She heard from him. From her answer, it is evident that she can build no more aërial castles in which to house her dreams:

"My Dearest Samuel:
"Although I do not feel able at present to return a full answer to your letter, I will not do myself the injustice of preserving entire silence.

"Its sincerity of tone is all I asked. As I told you, I never should make any claim upon the heart of any person on the score of past intercourse . . . but on the minds of those who have known me, I have always a claim. My own entire sincerity in every passage of life gives me a right to expect that I shall never be met by unmeaning phrases or attentions.

"For the rest, believe me, I understand all perfectly; and though I might grieve that you should shut me from you in your highest hour and find yourself unable to meet me on the very ground where you had taught me to expect it, I would not complain or feel that the past had bound either of us as to the present. . . . I had thought that in ceasing to be intimates, we might cease to be friends. I think so no longer. My attachment was never so deep as now; it is quite unstained by pride or passion; it is sufficiently disinterested for me to be sure of it. Time, distance, different pursuits, may hide you from me, yet will I never forget to be your friend, or to visit your life with a daily benediction. . . .

"Do not bid yourself remember me, but should an hour come, by and by, when you have any need of me, you will find me in my place and find me faithful to you."

Samuel Ward was a close friend of Ellery Channing's. He was obviously a man of moods. Channing took him to task for frigidity in friendship. Ward justified himself by saying that Ellery expected too much, and was not willing to reciprocate. "Until he met Emerson, I never heard of his having any friend but me, and no one ever appreciated his genius more fully than I did then. Naturally he idealized me. When he went West (1839) he used to write me the wildest letters of devotion and gratitude, to which I never attempted to respond on the same plane," Ward wrote to F. B. Sanborn some years later.

And now Margaret found him faithless.

One day in November she went into Boston to begin her famous Conversations. She carried some books for reference and a large bunch of chrysanthemums. She was not entirely easy in her mind and kept wondering what she would do if she detected a feeling of criticism in the class—if, for example, the class regarded her as a self-exploiting Corinne, displaying her superior talents. She knew that the majority would have no such thoughts, but there were others whom she did not know personally.... Might they not think her a little ridiculous?

A chill wind answered her, and a rapid scuttling of leaves.

She had arranged with Elizabeth Peabody to use her rooms in West Street for the classes. She was heartened by Elizabeth's greeting; she at least did not regard the venture as ridiculous. Margaret arranged her chrysanthemums very tastefully around the room and glanced at her watch. Almost time for the first arrivals. Then she disappeared, so that she would not have to face the first arrivals.

She made her entrance like a prima donna, looking very stately. Her heart was racing and her mind was saying, "Courage! You know that you have friends among the group."

There were twenty-five women in the class, and an attractive group it was, with not the slightest undercurrent of criticism detectable. What a relief! Besides Elizabeth Peabody, there were these: The other Elizabeth from Concord, whom Emerson called the Wise; Emerson's wife, Lidian, and the fragile Sophia Peabody, who was to marry Hawthorne when the roses were out; Lydia Maria Child, of course, who remembered the days when she and Margaret studied metaphysics together—the days of the magnificent cloak; Theodore Parker's wife and the wife of Horace Mann, who had to override her husband's prejudice against Margaret (*there* was a person who thought her ridiculous); and the charming Maria White, who was going to marry one of Margaret's bitterest lampoonists, James Russell Lowell. A very eclectic group!

Margaret told them that she wanted them to talk; the purpose of the classes was to explore hidden depths, to bring latent ideas out of hiding, to burrow far below the surface of their minds....

It sounded so much like bluestockingism that the whole room became as silent as a tomb. Margaret persevered, however; began talking about Apollo and Minerva and calm, cow-eyed Juno. She plunged at once into the meaning of these deities. It was such a revelation to the majority of the eclectics that some one said something.

That started the discussion. Before long, half a dozen were talking, and when the two hours were up, every one felt much stimulated. Not all the twenty-five had joined in the discussion, but ten or twelve had. This was encouraging.

Margaret was satisfied with the first meeting; there had been not the slightest evidence of criticism. On the contrary, she felt herself more than ever a high priestess; realized that all those women regarded her as something a little more than human. And she knew that she would always have to play the part of sibyl with them, if she was to make the conversations a success.

The Transcendentalists were planning a magazine. It was

to be called the *Dial,* and Margaret was to edit it, with Emerson and Ripley for her assistants. She was very busy; she taught classes of girls at her home, the Conversations were held every Saturday.

Her translation of Eckerman's *Conversations* was published. This was encouraging; and it made her more eager than ever to go on with the Life of Goethe. But, as always, there seemed to be no time for it. She thought of the constant struggle that went on because of lack of time or lack of opportunity or lack of funds. A young German, Richard Wagner, had dashed off to Paris with an unfinished opera in his pocket. He had high hopes for its acceptance. Acceptance meant a guarantee, an advancement of money, and the leisure to go on with the work. The opera was based on Bulwer Lytton's book, *Rienzi.* Wagner was confident that it would sell....

It was rejected.

The sensitive and tubercular Chopin was at Vallombrosa with George Sand, trying to get back health enough to enable him to go on with his compositions.

In England a new humor had appeared, and one spoke names like Sam Weller, Nicholas Nickleby and Sairy Gamp as if they belonged to one's cronies. There were many stories about the creator of these characters—how he had once lived in jail with his family because his father could not pay his debts; how he had always been hungry; how he never lost sight of a vision he had, that one day he would occupy an honorable position in the world.

Margaret thought of this man Charles Dickens and of the obstacles he had to face. She plunged into the new work she had agreed to undertake—the editing of the *Dial.* What a departure it would be! "A perfectly free organ for the expression of individual thought and character ... this journal will aim not at leading public opinion but at stimulating each man to judge for himself and to think more deeply and more nobly...."

Anything to prevent the country from forming itself into a flock of sheep who never veered an inch from the beaten track!

She wrote to her friends for contributions: To William Henry Channing, who was preaching at Cincinnati; to Henry Hedge, who, as a Harvard student, had prophesied great things for Margaret. How many years ago that was! He, too, was a minister, with a church in Bangor. Margaret wrote to him: "My friend, I hope you will make this the occasion for assailing the public ear with such a succession of melodies that all the stones will advance to form a city of refuge for the just. Let me hear from you directly."

She did not hear from him. She waited for over two months, then she sent a more urgent note: "Henry, I adjure you in the name of all the Genii, Muses, Pegasus, Apollo, Apollyon—to send me something good for this journal before the first of May."

Meanwhile there were other letters going about. Emerson wrote to Carlyle, who sat in his cozy, thirty-five-pound-a-year house in Chelsea, sipping strong tea and brooding over the frivolity of the world. And this is what he read when Emerson's letter came: "My vivacious friend Margaret Fuller is to edit a journal, which I think will be written with a good will, if written at all." A few weeks later Carlyle read this: "I have very good hope that my friend Margaret Fuller's journal will give you a better knowledge of our young people than anything you have had."

The young people were in revolt. They were weary of the moth-eaten standards and of the professions of faith which never became works. And they were piqued that all their intellectual fare should still come from abroad, though their own country was over two hundred years old. It was time, they thought, that some one produced something indigenous to the soil. True, there was Longfellow, who had brought out a couple of volumes of poems, but there was nothing startlingly original about them in thought or in form.

A pride of country was in those ardent young souls and not one of them was more ardent or more proud than the editor, Margaret Fuller.

The contributions were slow in coming. The ardent souls required a great deal of kindling, it appeared. Margaret exerted all her powers of persuasion, cajolery and expostulation to pry the contributions out of the contributors. Even Emerson had to be hounded.

At last, when the sun scorched the grass on the Common and urchins splashed half-naked in the Frog Pond, the first number of the *Dial* appeared. It was three months late, but what of that? A start had been made.

Margaret was exhausted but jubilant. "I'm living like an angel and don't know how to get down," she wrote to Emerson.

Those were cyclonic days in Boston. That first number of the *Dial* brought a howling storm up from New York and Philadelphia. In New York there was a magazine called the *Knickerbocker,* which rather fancied itself. It doubtless saw that the *Dial* had stuff in it such as it had never been able to produce; it showed its pique by laughing at Emerson's contribution and by parodying Alcott's. The Philadelphia *Gazette* was the other particular storm-brewer. It called the editors of the new journal by a variety of names, none of which was complimentary, and declared that they were madder than the Mormons.

There was criticism from the Transcendentalists themselves. There was Parker, unimaginative, scientific, feet planted firmly on the ground; he had all the traditional prejudice against women in men's places; he thought that editors' chairs were seats for men only; he said the *Dial* was too feminine, was lacking in full-blooded masculinity.

On the opposite side stood Alcott, then at the pinnacle of his idealistic theories. Like a prophet of old he stood, exhorting fire and brimstone to come and destroy all existing institutions. He would have the *Dial* the torch which must start the conflagration.

Between the two extremes stood Margaret....

There was much unholy laughter in the air. The Boston *Post* made daily caricatures of Alcott and his iconoclasms, of Emerson and his optimisms. Across the river, Oliver Wendell Holmes amused himself and a few others by aiming his sling-shot at William Lloyd Garrison, Wendell Phillips and any other abolitionist whose name he happened to know.

Two years previously, the chosen poet of the graduating class, James Russell Lowell, had shot his dart at Emerson for his antislavery ideas. But he had changed since then; for he had fallen in love with Maria White, a young woman of character and a professed sympathizer with the abolitionists.

It was a time of prolific granting of honorary degrees. Every governor of Massachusetts was eligible for a degree of some sort, no matter what his politics or what his principles may have been. And that summer Theodore Parker received the Master of Arts. But Emerson remained unnoticed, and was to remain unnoticed, as far as Harvard was concerned, for many years.

Margaret was in great demand. She had many friends, and she had a few enemies. The strange young hermit of Salem, whom Margaret had discovered, one winter evening at Groton, when she went through the pages of a bunch of old magazines, could not overcome an insidious intolerance of her. And while he went off by himself, dodging down side streets to avoid meeting any one, wandering through the woods and listening to the ceaseless moan of the sea, she wrestled with printers and typesetters, wrote letter after letter to her contributors, settled the accounts of her household, helped her brothers materially, mentally and spiritually, met every Saturday for her Conversation classes, had classes in her home, wrote articles, edited articles, attended dinner-parties and tea-parties and saw every one who sought her counsel.

For some mysterious reason, all these activities grated on Nathaniel Hawthorne. He had met Margaret some time before and he had at last made up his mind to marry Sophia Peabody. Sophia adored Margaret. Was that it? Was he jealous? Perhaps he was jealous of Margaret's social success. Hermit though he was, he may have had a lurking, subconscious desire to be the center of an admiring group. It would seem, from the form his antipathy took, that there was some deep repression back of it. He may possibly have been more attracted to Margaret than he knew....

Margaret had no prejudices. She knew that Theodore Parker did not like her, but that did not alter her opinion of him. She never forgot an early maxim she had made for herself: "Make the emotions the servant, not the master of the soul."

She had recovered from her disappointment in Samuel Ward, for now she understood what had happened to him all of a sudden. He had met the charming Anna Barker, who had been Margaret's model when Mrs. Farrar took her in hand. Naturally, he had fallen in love. Now he was married to Anna Barker, and Anna Barker was one of the Saturday morning group who regarded Margaret as something more than human.

Her old friends were scattering. James Freeman Clarke was in Cincinnati, editing the *Western Messenger* with William Henry Channing. The most interesting thing about the *Western Messenger* was that it was the periodical in which Emerson's first poems were published. Margaret's brother William Henry was in Cincinnati in business; and Ellery

Channing was there, supposed to be studying law. But he wrote poetry more than he read law. Henry Hedge was still in Bangor preaching.

Some of Margaret's days were weighted with the tedium of domestic duties. These she called laughingly her rye-bread days. Once she wrote to Arthur, who was in Westfield teaching school, "We banquet on pork rather more constantly than is agreeable to a 'true believer' like myself!" Her letters were by no means mere recitations of events; nearly all of them held such advisory messages as, "In all relations with our fellow-creatures, never forget that if they are imperfect persons, they are immortal souls, and treat them as you would wish to be treated in the light of that thought."

She often became conscious that she sounded rather solemn in her letters, and added, "I will not play minister much, lest I make you averse to writing to your affectionate sister Margaret."

Richard was in Concord preparing himself for Harvard. Margaret had sent him off with a letter to Emerson and hopes for studious days. He was now keen to advance himself, though there were times when he longed for new-mown hay and the warm, pungent smell of freshly plowed fields. Emerson said that he would keep an eye on him, and Richard began five months of grinding study with only himself for tutor. He took one room in a vacant house, and entered on a monk's life in his quiet, sparsely furnished cell. Every morning a pint of milk was left at his door and on Saturdays he had the luxury of a loaf of brown bread, though necessity made him forgo the beans. "My breakfast was made on a thick piece cut out of the brown bread loaf, with a dipper of water. I then put some potatoes in the ashes of my peat fire, which were only baked at noon. These with milk made me a wholesome and agreeable dinner. My supper was brown bread with water. I purchased no meat, butter, coffee or tea.

...I studied fourteen hours a day and only occasionally exercised when invited to walk by Henry Thoreau or Mr. Frost."

Sometimes he was invited to have tea at a neighbor's house —at the Hoars, the Emersons, the Frosts. Mrs. Emerson was a kind soul and, every week, sent gifts of pies around to those in need of such help. She always included Richard. Mrs. Samuel Hoar also kept a motherly eye on him and frequently sent him a substantial meat-pie. Elizabeth heard him recite his lessons, once or twice a week.

Margaret had written to him advising him not to remain too much by himself. "The mind works better when quickened by really good society and easily makes up for the loss of an hour or two. You might not again have the opportunity of cultivating such persons as Miss Hoar and Mr. Thoreau."

And that was why he asked Elizabeth to hear him recite his lessons.

Margaret had discovered Thoreau some little time before. She was visiting the Emersons and Thoreau was living there as Emerson's "working man." Margaret wrote at the time to Richard: "He (Thoreau) is three and twenty, has been through college and kept a school, is very fond of the classics and an earnest thinker, yet intends being a farmer. He has a great deal of practical sense, and as he has bodily sense to boot, he may look to be a successful and happy man. He has a boat which he made himself, and rows me out on the pond. Last night I went out quite late and stayed till the moon was almost gone.... There was a sweet breeze full of apple blossom fragrance...."

That was the year before; now Margaret went again to stay with the Emersons. She and Waldo walked for hours through the woods, through the meadows, along the shadowy slope by Walden Pond. Margaret thought what a splendid figure Emerson was in his long, blue cloak.

She opened all her doors to him and he listened quietly.

She told him fancies that she had, about days and talismans and precious stones. It was pleasing to her, she said, that those whom she especially admired should have names of archangels—Raphael and Michael Angelo, and that Kant and Swedenborg should bear the name Emanuel. William was another name she liked; it meant the Conqueror to her. "Of course it was Shakespeare's name," she said with feeling.

She believed that ill luck attended some precious stones and good luck others. She spoke of sapphires stolen from the eyes of old gods and of the tragedy which always befell the owners of them. She talked of idols made of jade and resting in Chinese temples, and of ancient musical instruments. The sistrum used by the Egyptians in the worship of Isis had strange attractions for her. The fact that it was kept always in motion attracted her; she agreed with Plutarch's interpretation of its symbol—that mankind needed constant agitation to keep his soul from stagnating.

She never tired of talking of the influences of the sun, the moon, the sea, the air—"all mysteries which flutter, blow, skim, lave." She was a sun-worshiper, a star-worshiper, a worshiper of all splendid evidences of divine creative power. ... She liked to think of the mystic significance of old rings and the curiously wrought gems found in Egyptian temples. She spoke of the moon-shaped talismans made of chased silver and worn as a charm against disease; and she spoke of the jewels which were buried in the tomb of Queen Aahhotep, the mother of Ahmes, first king of the eighteenth dynasty; of the bracelets of lapis-lazuli, cornelian and gold, curiously strung together to form a checker pattern; of carved sapphires set in the bodies of golden serpents; of chased gold lotus-flowers set in the handles of bronze mirrors; of jeweled anklets and rings with magical powers.

Of the veiled women of Turkey she spoke, and of the fire-worshipers of the Monsul Mountains and their sacred dance. She mentioned the dancing virgins of Thibet, who swear eternal chastity. She talked of Sita, the beautiful wife of Rama, a descendant of the sun. A demon desired to possess Sita and devised means whereby he might gain access to her apartment. He dressed himself in priest's robes, persuaded her to accompany him on a pilgrimage of worship, took her in his chariot to a fair city built upon an island of the sea.... She recalled the story of Sakuntala and the signet ring which had power to restore lost love; and of the insolent versemaker of Samarkand, who offered a city for the mole on a lady's cheek. Of pillared temples and almond-groves and sacred lotus-flowers she spoke; and of the songs of Sappho and the destiny which shapes each human life.

Growing confidential, she mentioned her own fight and the particular demon who worked his will with her, clogging the stream of her thought, giving her headaches, taking from her the will to do what must be done. "It refuses to be analyzed ... but it is there and always has been.... It is most obvious in the eye of the person possessing it. As we look on such eyes we think of the tiger, the serpent, beings who lurk, glide, fascinate, mysteriously control."

Emerson did not accept her theory about demons.... And yet, when she spoke of them and of all the pagan subjects which were so fascinating to her, there was a strange expression in her eyes; and he recalled that some one had likened her eyes to those of a snake.

He listened quietly to her, but he did not give her confidence for confidence. This reserve was disappointing to her. Many times she tried to break it, tried to enter those inner rooms which were so firmly locked. But she could not. And she felt lonely and forlorn.

Once at such a time of loneliness, she wrote an impassioned letter to the only person who she felt could have understood her great heart hunger—Beethoven.

Always, for her supreme satisfaction, Margaret had to return to her world of fantasy....

V

BROOK FARM

THE MONTHS flew on and season followed season. Her busy life was taking from Margaret the ability to idle. After visiting her friend Caroline Sturgis at Newbury for ten days, she wrote to Richard: "I should not like such a life constantly. There are few characters so vigorous and of such sustained self-impulse that they do not need frequent and unexpected difficulties to awaken and keep in exercise their powers."

One would have thought those ten days made a welcome hiatus in Margaret's life; they sound idyllic enough. Miss Sturgis had a little green boat with an orange rim in which she rowed Margaret to a quiet cove on the river, where trees bent down and where dragon-flies balanced on the tips of reeds. There they drew the boat up and there they sat reading aloud or silently, or dreaming and dawdling while the birds sang in the trees and the cicadas made a quiet hum.

Margaret rather proudly told Caroline about Richard. One gray morning he started off from his Concord cell and took the road to Cambridge. He had a bundle under his arm in which were clothes and sandwiches, and in his pocket he had a letter from Emerson to Josiah Quincy, the president of Harvard. He was starting out to face the hardest ordeal of his life so far—the entrance examinations for college. More than the entrance examinations really. What he wanted to do was write off the freshman year and half of the sophomore.

He presented himself at the president's office, drenched and disheveled, for he had met with a shower as he trudged along. He apologized for his appearance, but Quincy said he didn't mind his looks in the least, as he had been a farmer and knew all about summer showers. His tone was kind, and Richard felt heartened.

Soon the ordeal began, soon he was lost in a maze of Latin verbs—of gerunds and gerundives and vague subjunctives; of tricky nouns belonging to he couldn't think which declension; of vocatives and ablatives and irregular accusatives. He took a little time and gradually the maze cleared up....

Some time later he went to the president's office to learn his fate. His knees were a bit shaky, his hat-band was quite wet....

To his astonishment he learned that he was eligible to enter the second half of the sophomore year! As well as he could, he got himself out of the office and ran almost all the way to Jamaica Plain to tell Margaret the news. She was delighted. "Now that you are going to college, I must look around for a house in Cambridge."

But not just yet. First must come a few weeks of absolute rest from the usual routine.... She started off with a visit to Caroline Sturgis; and while they dawdled in the green boat with the orange rim, Margaret outlined in her mind the next book she would write.

. . . .

Her friends the Ripleys had been adventuring during the past year. George had finally become so weary of the narrow attitude of the church that he resigned his pulpit in Purchase Street and took Sophia to board at a dairy farm in West Roxbury. It was a cheerful and picturesque place with the scent of pine woods in the air and the Charles River not so far away. Meadows sloped back from the house and in the mornings the dewy fragrance of clover blossoms came in through the open windows. The Ripleys were delighted with the place.

George was not satisfied with the Transcendentalists. They

met regularly, talked of this and that—the relative values of Kant, Hegel and Schleiermacher; Alcott held forth at length, read reams of Plato; but to what did the readings and the discussions lead? To more readings and discussions. It was all very interesting to meet and talk of the supremacy of man, but talking of it did not demonstrate its truth. George wanted to *realize* some of their ideals, to make them take concrete form. How he and Sophia talked, trying to arrive at some plan by which this might be done!

First of all, they must find a place, preferably a farm which would "insure a more natural union between intellectual and manual labor." That is, they wanted to start a community where the thinker would use his hands and the laborer his brain. It would be made up of "liberal, intelligent and cultivated persons, whose relations with each other would permit a more wholesome and simple life than could be led amidst the pressure of competitive institutions!" It was to be self-supporting, and naturally it was to be harmonious in all its parts.

George and Sophia looked around and found a farm of a hundred and seventy acres which seemed to be exactly what they wanted. It was owned by a man called Ellis, and was a beautiful farm through whose meadows ran a twisting brook.

But how could one buy without money? All the assets that the Ripleys had was their library. George wrote a long letter to Emerson, telling him about the farm and what he wanted to do with it. He wanted buildings enough to house ten families; he wanted a school building. He wrote about a plan he had, of forming a joint-stock company....

One day when the snow was melting and the sun lay about in the puddles, he and Sophia went over to the Ellises and closed the deal for Brook Farm. A little later, when the daffodils were up and the frogs were shouting in all the ponds, the first families moved in. There were fifteen besides the Ripleys, who had pledged their libraries to pay their share. Among the fifteen was Nathaniel Hawthorne.

It took six months to get things started. Ripley's sister Marianne took charge of the school, Hawthorne chose to be chief plowman. He liked the dim woods with their shifting shadows; he liked the slopes of meadowland and the groves of evergreens and the quiet valleys where marsh-marigolds stood beside the brook.

The farmhouse was called the Hive. Around it clustered mulberry trees and a scattering of spruce; a spreading sycamore gave it a stateliness in keeping with its new function. The Hive looked toward the rising sun.

It was not long till another house had to be built. It rose on a sunny upland, the highest point of the farm, and was reached by a flight of steps. This was the Eyrie, and here the Ripleys lived. In the parlor to the left of the hall was a piano which was used by John Dwight to teach music.... The Eyrie had four small dormitories for the pupils of the school.

The next building to go up was simply The Cottage. It was in the form of a maltese cross and it had four gables. It was a picturesque place and was the most tastefully furnished of all the houses. Later on, it became known as the Margaret Fuller Cottage. Why it was called this no one seems to know. Lindsay Swift says it is probably the only house in which Margaret never stayed when she visited the community.

Margaret was not a member of the association. The scheme did not appeal to her; neither did it appeal to Emerson, Alcott, Channing or Elizabeth Peabody. But all of them went occasionally to visit the colony.

Margaret went for solitude and relaxation. Since her purpose was understood, she was allowed to be by herself as much as she chose. But her reception was majestic. One of her most devoted admirers was Georgiana Bruce, a young woman of twenty-four, who taught in the school. She was an English girl with her living to earn. Since teaching did not take up all her time, she did other things—ironing, washing dishes, preparing vegetables for meals. She was a vivacious girl with a quick tongue and a quicker temper, was very susceptible to personality and of a romantic temperament. She adored Margaret, and always gave up her room to her at the Eyrie.

And what preparations she made when word came that Margaret was on her way! Flowers were gathered and favorite foods were cooked; there was a hurrying and a scurrying. The only decorated china cup in the place was taken down from its shelf, the best doily was set aside for Margaret's breakfast tray. Georgiana always gave herself the thrill of taking Margaret's coffee to her room in the morning.

Just before Margaret arrived, Georgiana slipped up to her room which was polished and sweet-smelling and flower-laden, and lighted incense which she had walked several miles to procure. When Margaret arrived—the high priestess indeed!—the fragrant smoke was rising from its little urn; and Georgiana, with blushes and stammerings, received her deity's word of praise. Then down she went to make a pot of tea for her in the good, old English way.

George Ripley paid tribute to Margaret too; he named one of his cows for her!

Margaret smiled happily at all of this. But she could never take Brook Farm seriously. It all seemed such a game to her! Oh, enthusiastic enough, sincere enough and idealistic after a fashion. But sometimes the desire to be absolutely natural ran away with good taste; sometimes the passion for spontaneity introduced a certain crudeness into the life. It seemed indeed as if some of the members wished to dispense entirely with good manners, as if there lurked somewhere within their consciousness the idea that to be crude meant to be manly.

In the evenings when the work was done, when the cows

were milked and the hens securely locked within their houses, when the carpenters' hammers were silent and the printers' dummies were placed in an orderly row, all the company gathered in the large room where the fire crackled, or in the barn where corn awaited husking and there they proceeded to make merry. She liked the freedom of the place, which allowed one to come and go without question.

In the large room where the fire burned, the company danced and sang, put on romantic costumes and declaimed immortal lines. Margaret, sitting in the chair of honor, thought of the sad, tempestuous, triumphant days at the Misses Prescott's School, when she painted her face and aped the ways of women whom history, mythology and polite gossip have eulogized or damned. And she thought how interesting and strange it was that there seemed so few pastimes for grownups with mature intelligences; that a pastime must always be something which set the mind in abeyance. She wondered if it would always be so; if great historical events and great moral events would be commemorated in such childish pageant, such naïve parade; if the great nation composed of all the United States would find its chief amusement in strutting about in fancy costumes imagining itself to be other than what it was.

These experiments in community living—there was something very youthful about them, she thought. The idea of doing things in crowds was essentially a youthful idea. To the mature mind alone belonged self-sufficiency, to the mature mind belonged the ability to find happiness in solitude. Margaret visualized her country in the future as deficient in the accomplishments achieved in solitude, but supreme in mass production. "The essential motive of life—soul-expansion—will be slow. Superficial benefits will be many, for our country in its childishness, judges from appearances. Luxury, prosperity, will choke the spirit."

She looked around the circle. Her eyes found Emerson,

who, like herself, did not belong to the community but came occasionally as a guest. She breathed a prayer of thanksgiving for such men as Emerson: "Thank heaven for the *individual* man. If the nation goes astray, if the national point of view is muddled, there always remains the exceptional individual, who can show that we are not really independent despite brave acts and heroic encounters, despite treaties and declarations, unless our independence leads to freedom—freedom from fraud and meanness, from selfishness, from public opinion so far as it does not agree with the still, small voice of one's better self."

Her thoughts particularized regarding Emerson: "History will inscribe his name as a father of his country, for he is one who pleads her cause against herself." She meditated on the different kinds of great; on the great whom the world at large could laud because their deeds were showy, were sensational. History was full of them; they were the geographical conquerors, the aggressive leaders of one nation against another; their kingdom lay across the two dimensions of land and sea; their conquests were easily reported, hence were easily understood. But there were others, those whose struggles were waged in less easily definable realms. They it was who sought to assimilate the spiritual laws by which man lives. They were not so readily acclaimed. Their kingdom lying in a realm which the majority do not easily apprehend, they were not so vociferously followed. But their adherents, though few in number, were more highly developed; and their eyes saw further than the others.

She looked at another figure who had come into the room when the festivities were at their height—a beautiful young man with a high forehead and brooding, introspective eyes. His hair was long and looked as if it was rather hard to manage. He kept rubbing the palm of his right hand with the fingers of his left. This was because he had been plowing all day and his hand was blistered. This young man was Nathaniel Hawthorne. He felt ill at ease. The social gatherings in the evenings were not as agreeable to him as the more active life of the community. He was a solitary individual, had never practiced the art of the social life. He felt particularly self-conscious when Margaret Fuller was in the room. Her personality dominated all others; he was afraid of her frank and rather caustic tongue. He need not have been. In the group Margaret, the revolutionary, felt conventional. She did not speak to him. She sat there, trying to adjust the first impression she received of the author of the *Gentle Boy* with the beautiful and somewhat retiring young plowman of Brook Farm. He was not unlike what she expected him to be; he was sensitive, was more feminine than masculine, more negative than positive, seemed almost to be afraid of life, to shrink from life's deepest experiences. He seemed like a man who had not found himself.

On Sunday evenings there were lectures in the large room. Margaret, Emerson, Channing and Alcott were the most noteworthy speakers who came in from the outside. George Ripley frequently spoke. The audience was not always as attentive as Margaret would have liked. "They showed a good deal of the *sans-culotte* tendency in their manners—throwing themselves on the floor, yawning and going out when they had heard enough. Yet, as the majority differ from me, to begin with, they showed, on the whole, more respect and interest than I had expected. As I am accustomed to deference, however, and need it for the boldness and animation which my part requires, I did not speak with as much force as usual. Still, I should like to have to face all this; it would have the same good effects that the Athenian assemblies had on the minds obliged to encounter them."

She usually started off hopefully; she launched the bark of her eloquence far from the shoals of triviality; she sailed through metaphor, through analogy into a sea of legend, of myth, of mystic fable. A few of her hearers followed her;

the majority wearied early and with loud yawns got up and left the room.

At the end of her sojourn she summed up her impressions: "I have found myself here in the amusing position of a conservative. Even so it is with Mr. Ripley. There are too many young people in proportion to the others. I heard myself saying, with a grave air, 'Play out the play, gentles.'"

After another visit, a year later, she wrote: "The tone of the society is much sweeter than when I was here a year ago. There is a pervading spirit of mutual tolerance and gentleness, with great sincerity. There is no longer a passion for grotesque freaks of liberty, but a disposition, rather, to study and enjoy the liberty of law. The great development of mind and character observable in several instances, persuades me that this state of things affords a fine studio for the soul-sculptor."

VI

CONTROVERSY

WHEN ELLEN FULLER was twenty-one she went to visit her brother William Henry in Cincinnati. While there she met Ellery Channing who was supposed to be studying law. The meeting was epochal; they fell in love.

Ellery was a hot-headed young man of twenty-seven, who wrote poetry and spent long hours idling in the sun. He wanted to marry Ellen at once. When she mentioned a wedding-gown and bridesmaids and the other accessories which mean so much to a young bride, Ellery pooh-poohed the idea. What did those things matter after all? Ellen agreed to be married in Cincinnati, provided her mother approved.

He followed this up with a letter to Margaret in which he tried to explain in what manner he loved Ellen.

Against her will, Mrs. Fuller gave her consent to the immediate marriage. She did not entirely trust such sudden flares of passion, she would have liked them to wait a little while, to test the quality of their love....

Ten days after receiving Mrs. Fuller's consent, Ellen and Ellery were married. They remained in Cincinnati and to them came many packages from the East. We are to imagine those first idyllic days, and the outpourings of Ellery's impassioned feelings....

There seemed to be a dearth of reading matter in Cincinnati. Ellen wrote to Margaret asking her to send some books. After a few months, only the lightest of literature was required. To Ellery Margaret sent better books, some of which he acknowledged in this fashion: "I have to-day received the Shakespeare sonnets. Whether I read them or not depends on my fancy. I do not read now, I am chiefly engaged in doing nothing. I own to a large penchant for this species of occupation. It is a pleasant thing to do nothing....

"Affairs... I have none of them! I may wake up some day and find I have been doing something, but no one will ever tell me of it...."

Ordinarily, such a letter would have amused Margaret. A gossamer touch she enjoyed as much as any one, the amusing nonsense which came from an irresponsible nature usually brought a smile to her face.

But this was different; this man had married Ellen. He had next to nothing to live on, Ellen had next to nothing. How were they to live? How were they to bring up a family? What did Ellery know of responsibilities? He was in his habits of thought a dilettante; so he must be in his mode of living. His response to life was a gossamer response; he went from experience to experience, touching each lightly, exuberant mostly from his lips. Life appealed to him mainly through his senses. "The senses," thought Margaret, "have their own function, but it is not the only function. It is to provide the bridge which reaches from the mind to the soul." But if one refused to cross the bridge? What then? The irk which comes from too long sojourn in one place; the irritability caused by dwelling in a space too much confined; resultant lack of harmony, eventual inability to find peace.

Thus Margaret reasoned. With her genius for looking deep into the natures of human beings, she could see clearly down the path of years; and she feared that Ellen was destined for much unhappiness. For Ellen was a hot-headed little thing, was petulant, was of a youthful temperament. How was she going to accept the timeless problem of meeting each day's necessities? How was she going to readjust herself to pinch and save? How face the natural outcome of marriage—the bearing of children—under conditions far from ideal?

Might Margaret not have to assume the responsibility of Ellery and Ellen? Assuming responsibility was as natural to her as reading. Deep within her was a characteristic which was as essentially a part of her as were her hands, her eyes, her lovely hair. It was her duty toward those she loved. Duty to her was not a stern-faced old hag with a whip in her hand; it was a gentle creature compounded of love and tenderness who recognized the kinship of one human being with another, who recognized as of more immediate kinship the different members of one family. This closer kinship being arranged by some power for reasons beyond the reach of ordinary understanding, imposed upon its members certain obligations. Loyalty and love and devotion were some of them. It should be as natural for one member to work for the well-being of another member as for himself. This Margaret believed, and this she endeavored to live as fully as she could.

For Ellery and Ellen she would do anything within her power. But at present there was little reserve power for her to use. The *Dial* was a vampire that sapped all her energy and left her spent and listless at the end of each day. She wondered if it was worth all the energy she spent on it. Certainly there were many diverse opinions about it. Theodore Parker kept insisting that it lacked masculine virility. His opinion did not give Margaret much cause for worry; she realized that there was a vast realm into which the Reverend Theodore would never penetrate; that he was one of those worthy but unimaginative individuals who divide their minds into pigeonholes and who spend most of their time fitting each experience into its particular niche. Should such persons ever encounter anything for which they had failed to provide a suitable haven, the encountered thing was regarded as too trifling to merit much attention. Never by any chance did it occur to them that additions should be made to their mental pigeonholes. They might be called the limited editions of humanity for they were infinitely precious in the eyes of many and they usually arrayed themselves in imposing garments.

In a letter to Emerson Carlyle commented on the *Dial:* "It is all spirit-like, aëriform, aurora-borealis-like; no stalwart Yankee man with color in his cheeks and a coat on his back."

This comment made Margaret think: If any created thing was to live, it must have form; it must have a healthy body and plenty of red corpuscles. She had thought that her *Dial* was steadily gaining in vitality; Carlyle's words were disheartening. Then suddenly she remembered what a crank Carlyle was; how he had said that he could see no virtue in any of the poets and that he considered it a waste that Shakespeare had not chosen to write in prose. This heartened her a little.

But she was confused, was dissatisfied, was mentally ill at ease. She could not depend on her contributors and had to keep cajoling them, imploring them, beseeching them to send their copy in on time. They were as irresponsible as school children; Margaret was weary of them and of the whole business of editing. She wrote to her mother who was visiting her relations at Canton: "I am in a state of extreme fatigue; this is the last week of the *Dial* and as often happens, the copy did not hold out and I have to write in every gap of time.... I am now quite unfit to hold a pen."

She realized that she could not go on. This decision had been germinating for some time; it almost came to fruition after Ellen's marriage; it came to full fruition when Margaret received a letter from her brother Eugene, who said that he must have three hundred dollars immediately.

Margaret's share of her father's estate had dwindled to five hundred dollars; she was not earning as much as usual, for her work on the *Dial* took so much time that she was obliged to curtail the number of her pupils. Her salary as editor of the *Dial* was to have been two hundred dollars a year. But at the end of the first year no money whatever was forthcoming. Willingly she gave her services and continued to give them, trusting that her reward would be in such coinage as is not reckoned in dollars and cents.

At times like this, with Eugene writing frenziedly from New Orleans and Ellen embarking on a questionable marriage, Margaret realized rather poignantly that the more ordinary coinage has many uses for which no idealistic substitute is ever adequate. She wrote to Eugene telling him that he would have his three hundred dollars and she decided definitely that she must give no more time or energy to the *Dial*. She wrote to Emerson, telling him of her decision: "I grieve to disappoint you. I am also sorry myself, for if I could have received a maintenance from the *Dial*, I could have done my duties to it well and my time might have been given to my pen, while now, for more than three months, I have been able to write no line except letters.... If you carry it on, I should like to do anything I can to aid you."

While she waited for Emerson's letters of acceptance, she reviewed her work of the last two years. She had opened people's minds to Goethe and to Schiller; had tried to show them the supremacy of the human spirit in the face of apparently insurmountable obstacles. To illustrate this theme, she had taken Beethoven as her example—Beethoven the master; Beethoven the man of affliction and of nameless grief. She had tried to tell her smug, provincial, bigoted New England that man was not made for society, but society for man; that the present was compounded of the past and of the future and that time was timeless; that the only hope for man was grounded on his destiny as an immortal spirit and not as a comfort-loving inhabitant of the earth or a subscriber to the social contract. She had tried to teach that a widespread diffusion of knowledge unless accompanied by a correspondent deepening of the sources was likely to vulgarize rather than to raise the thought of a nation; in short, that real culture could not be acquired from external sources but must come from within the spirit of mankind.

To her ambitious countrymen she had lent an ear and opened a door, so that now the readers of her *Dial* had a bowing acquaintance with the names of Dwight, Cranch, Thoreau, Channing and Lowell. She was the first to do full justice to Nathaniel Hawthorne.

Her sage, her prophet, her noble Emerson she had introduced as often as he would allow himself to be introduced. She regretted that his influence did not as yet extend over a wide space; but she understood the reason why it did not: "He is too far beyond his place and his time to be felt at once or in full, but his influence searches deep and yearly widens its circles."

She mourned with Emerson, who was in great sorrow. His little son Waldo had died. Margaret's sorrow found outlet in these words to the parents: "He was the only child I ever saw that I sometimes wished I could have called mine."

She wondered if she would ever have a child of her own. She was inclined to sentimentalize a little over the mystery of birth, chiefly because she saw in children the symbol of second birth, of that state of receptivity each individual must acquire before he enters into a conviction of eternal life.

Emerson gladly assumed the responsibilities of the *Dial*. The additional work would keep him from brooding over his sorrow, would take him out of himself. He sometimes thought that his self-imposed solitude was none too salutary for him; there were times when he needed the impetus of a new interest. He hoped that the *Dial* would provide it.

Thoreau, who still worked for him, at once started out canvassing for subscribers, and down in New York, the bluff, good-natured Greeley gave gratuitous publicity to the periodical in the pages of his *Tribune*. Freed from the burden of editing, Margaret went to Canton for a rest, and there, with the spring winds to soothe and the spring birds to hearten, she took up her work of writing. She was busy on a translation of the letters between Bettina von Arnim and her friend Caroline von Günderode. A few years before, there had appeared the correspondence between Goethe and this Bettina, a charming child bubbling over with merriment. The letters interested Margaret so much that she began searching to see what more she could learn about the exuberant Bettina. She found an even earlier correspondence, between Bettina and an older woman, a canoness, who mixed with the outside world. This woman was Caroline von Günderode.

She was charmed with these letters. Bettina was sixteen when they were written; she went "bounding over the fences of society as easily as over the fences of the field . . . never hushed into silence . . . flying and singing like a bird, sobbing with the hopelessness of an infant." To Margaret she typified the "pervasive, vital force, cause of the effect which we call nature." Günderode was her opposite, her ideal: "A soul so delicately appareled, a woman so tenderly transfigured. . . ."

Günderode later drowned herself because of the narrowness of the world. Bettina lived and followed every freakish fancy "till the enchanting child degenerated into an eccentric and undignified old woman."

Margaret understood the reverence which a younger woman

feels for an older, who represents all that youth hopes to achieve.

She was thirty-two. She looked at herself in the mirror and she saw that her hours of concentration, her concern for her family, her constant adjustments to circumstances were leaving their marks on her face—a line on each side of her mouth, many lines under her eyes. . . .

Ellen had a child, a little girl whose name was Margaret Fuller Channing. Mrs. Fuller was with her and Ellery was beginning to think of practical things, had visions of a small farm in New England—a simple cottage with trees before the door and a patch of land where he could dig and plow and breathe familiar air. He wanted to collect all his poems; they were the only evidence he had that he was not only a poet but a person of industry as well. . . .

Margaret, too, wished that he and Ellen would come East. And she spoke to Emerson about the possibility of finding them a place in Concord. Emerson suggested that Ellery build a cottage himself. Stearns Wheeler had put up a shanty near Flint's Pond, Thoreau was thinking of building one, so that he could live among the birds. Margaret said she could not visualize her brother-in-law at work with hammer and nails.

She wanted to live in Cambridge. She looked around and found a house in Ellery Street, and decided to move the family there as soon as the Jamaica Plain year was up. She was reading Tennyson's new volume of poems. "One of his themes has long been my favorite—the last expedition of Ulysses. In Dora, Locksley Hall, the Two Voices, Morte d'Arthur, I find my own life, much of it, written truly out."

She was daily writing her life; to many she was a prophet, a sibyl, a seer. Emerson called her simply *The Friend*. At Emerson's house she always found peace. She went to stay there that summer; she had reconciled herself to his reserves and no longer tried to force an entrance to those secret rooms whose doors were closed to her, as they were to everybody else.

Margaret clung to her idea of the threefold life: "You cannot solve a problem by denying it, you cannot find spiritual life by denying physical life. Everything is comprehensive and unity comes only by the establishment of harmony in threefold life."

Emerson disagreed with her. He steadfastly denied the *fact* of human nature, was an uncompromising idealist. Margaret sought the ideal through the real. Denying the existence of the real was evading the fact, like denying that night was dark or that ice was cold. . . .

It was a serious age; the air was full of the voices of the reformers. Here came a fiery Gabriel who would drive all lawmakers out of the state; here was a newspaper which threw a bold slogan across its front-page colunms, "The World Is Governed too Much." A church threatened to throw out one of its leading members because he tossed his cap into the anti-slavery ring. He retaliated by formally excommunicating the church. The spirit of the antinomians who used to hold meetings in Anne Hutchinson's house in School Street, came back again. And there came phrenologists, mesmerists, fortune-tellers. The élite of the town went to private séances where their characters were revealed to them through their writing; the educated listened to Parker and Brownson and Ripley expounding the philosophy of Kant and Hegel; the less enlightened met periodically and washed each other's feet in preparation for the second coming of Christ. The sacred institution of marriage was attacked as being the "fountain of all ills"; there was bold mention of the burden of child-bearing and its ill effects on women. Money was denounced; there were cries of "Back to the Land" and "Away from the Vice of Cities!" Politicians went about advocating free trade; there was a clash between capital and labor. Alcott preached what Carlyle from Chelsea called a potato gospel; Charles

Burleigh was blasphemous because he wore a beard which resembled that pictured on the Christ. Lowell was now an out and out abolitionist, hence a radical, a barbarian. When he gave up trimming his beard he was even more decried. . . .

In one of the first issues of the *Dial* under Emerson's editorship, the editor described a Convention of Friends of Universal Reform: "Madmen, madwomen, men with beards, Dunkers, Muggletonians, Come-outers, Groaners, Agrarians, Seventh-Day Baptists, Quakers, Abolitionists, Calvinists, Unitarians and Philosophers—all came successively to the top."

Among them moved Margaret, with no ax to grind, no scimitar to sharpen—unless it was the scimitar of her wit, and there were but few stones strong enough to bear the edge of that.

VII

PASTORAL

SHE HAD HER WEEKS of solitude, she finished the Günderode-von Arnim letters. Her translation was excellent. Understanding so well the mystical, fanciful, fantastical German girls and their consequent floweriness of phrase, she felt all the meaning of the letters; having at her disposal a generous vocabulary, she transmuted the feeling into an almost perfect mold of words.

Unfortunately, only about a quarter of the letters were published. They appeared in a thin pamphlet and they were unsigned. Elizabeth Peabody, who kept a bookshop of foreign literature, was responsible for their publication.

In the early autumn Margaret moved her family back to Cambridge. Her classes went on, the Conversations continued. There were those—on the outside—who smiled at the solemnity and sumptuousness of the Saturday morning meetings; and there was that acid-tongued woman across the sea, Harriet Martineau, who quite failed to understand Margaret's motive and called it little short of destructive. Destructive of genius, feeling and sound activity she went on to say, and deplored the fact that Margaret did not fall in love and marry a strong American man with plenty of brawn and not too much idealism. Margaret would have liked nothing better than to have married during her formative years; her frequent outbursts of loneliness, her frank longing for a great love, are proof of this. But she could not marry where she did not greatly respect, neither could she revert to Amazonism and club an unwilling victim to the altar. . . .

Some one suggested that she hold extra meetings for the Conversations in the evenings, in order that men might attend. Margaret thought that this was a good idea; the men, most of whom were classical scholars, would carry forward the ideas which her lack of knowledge prevented her from developing as much as she wished.

They assembled. The Ripleys came in from Brook Farm, bringing a breath of the stables with them; Alcott was there in all his solemnity; Henry Hedge was in town from Bangor; Emerson pried himself out of his study and brought Stearns Wheeler, from whom he expected much; James Freeman Clarke, now the rector of the Church of the Disciples in Boston, forgot his parish duties for a night; Jones Very came in from Salem; William Story, the sculptor, was there too, and all the usual women, looking more "sumptuous" than ever.

Margaret spent a great deal of time dressing that night, and made her usual prima donna entrance, head high, eyes half-closed, lips smiling a little. She felt charged with some powerful force and she had great hopes for the success of the evening. It would have been perfectly natural for her to feel proud that night. Were not several of the greatest thinkers of the day assembled to hear her?

Her subject was the humanizing of the old Earth-Worship by the Greeks. Something for Stearns Wheeler to enlarge upon, surely! She started off, "What was a seed in the Egyptian mind became a flower in Greece." A very neat beginning. Then she paused, looked around, raised her lorgnette.... Not a sound. All the men shifted a little in their chairs, as if settling themselves more comfortably to enjoy the show. Margaret wondered what she could do to make them talk.

She called on Emerson. He said that he was no conversationalist, as she knew very well, and referred her to Stearns Wheeler. Wheeler finally opened his lips and told a few mild fables. Margaret felt like saying, "Yes, I know; fables are all right for demonstration, but what I want is *ideas!*"

She appeared to be the only person who had ideas. And the meeting resolved itself into a lecture by her. At the end every one clustered around her and told her how entertaining she had been.

Yes, but that was not the idea, she said. She wanted some one else to do some of the entertaining.... All these men ... and not one of them would say a thing. Not even Alcott.... "Next time, I hope the talk will be more general," she said.

It was. It was so general that Margaret kept turning her head this way and that, to see the different persons who were making it so. Clarke started the ball rolling by asking Margaret to compare Venus with the Madonna. In a moment Alcott's boom was heard, then Emerson's quiet tones, then Stearns Wheeler's.... The evening was a great success....

Emerson soon gave up attending the meetings; the journey from Concord to Boston was too tiring, he said.

Visitors often came; for now the whole country knew about the Conversations and about Margaret, and many who came to Boston were eager to have a look at the woman who was called prophet, sibyl, seer. Mrs. Horace Greeley frequently came up from New York, and always timed her visits so that they included a day on which a Conversation was held.

When she went home, she talked about Margaret till Horace began to say sly things to her about all the ridiculous woman-worship there was in Boston.

Margaret was happy in her home life now. She took long walks with the boys who were both in Harvard; they walked along by the river's edge and went among the graves in Mount Auburn cemetery. Ellen and Ellery were in Concord after having spent the winter in Cambridge. They had a red cottage on the turnpike near Emerson's place, which Thoreau had put in order for them and for which they paid fifty-six dollars a year. Ellery was as moody as ever and was so disagreeable at times that Alcott once exclaimed that he could put up with him all right as long as he did not have to live in the same house with him. Ellen was gentle and soft, and self-effacing as her mother had been when Timothy was alive.

Hawthorne was married to Sophia Peabody. They lived in the Old Manse in Concord and seldom saw any one but themselves. Sophia wrote sonnets to Margaret, addressing them to "A Priestess of the Temple Not Made with Hands." And she wrote many letters to her addressing her "Dear, Most Noble Margaret!"

Since his marriage, Hawthorne dared to make friendly overtures to Margaret. One day he received a letter from her, asking him if it would be possible for him to take Charles Newcomb into his home to board for a time. Newcomb was a sentimental youth who wrote a little and thought a good deal about his soul. He was one of the first boarders at Brook Farm and he decorated his walls with pictures of the saints. Sometimes in the night those who had rooms near him heard him chanting the litany and saw a light under the crack of his door; and they imagined Charles making genuflexions before his pictures and his images. He was a student of all the literature of mysticism and he considered the amusements of the community frivolous and unnecessary. He allowed himself the luxury of skating when the ponds were frozen over. Sometimes he skated on Sunday. If the day were bright and his eye happened to catch sight of a church-spire glinting in the sun, he would remove his skates, follow the shining spire, enter the church, skates in hand, walk up to the altar and kneel down for a few moments of meditation. Then out he would go again, back to his pond and his skating. His chief occupation was communion with nature and with himself. Nature, he never, by any chance spelled without a capital. He was as sensitive to "atmosphere" as an impresario and on more than one occasion, changed his seat at table because he imagined the woman sitting opposite to him was trying to attract his attention in an indelicate way. He had long, unruly hair and his eyes suggested secret knowledge; there was about him an air of mystery which some women found extremely attractive. He was pale, and slight and languorous—an ascetic youth, who hated intellect with the ferocity of a Swedenborg! The only work he ever had published was an essay called *Dolon* which appeared in the *Dial*. He and Margaret walked together through the pine grove and exchanged confidences about their souls. When she did not see him, during her visits to Brook Farm, Margaret wrote him neat, little notes, folded threecornerwise. And she approached Hawthorne about taking the youth to board.

Hawthorne wrote in reply: "... as to our friend Charles Newcomb, I heartily wish I would have the privilege of his society next summer. But it is *not* possible, for a reason at present undeveloped, but which I trust time will bring to light.

"How strange, when I should be so glad to do everything that you had the slightest wish for me to do and when you are so incapable of wishing anything that ought not to be! Whether or no you bear a negative more easily than other people, I certainly find it easier to give you one, because you do not peep at matters through a narrow chink, but can take my view as perfectly as your own....

"I have skated like a very schoolboy this winter. Indeed, since my marriage, the circle of my life seems to have come round and brought back many of my school-day enjoyments and I find a deeper pleasure in them now than when I first went over them.... As for Sophia, I keep her as tranquil as a summer sunset.... I sometimes wonder how she is able to dispense with all society but mine. In my own case there is no wonder....

"She sends her love. Of course you will be in Concord when the pleasant weather comes, for a month, or a week, or a day. And you must spend a proportionable part of the time at our house."

Margaret went to Concord as often as she had the leisure for visiting. Emerson was in New York that winter giving a course of lectures. Thoreau wrote telling him the most important gossip. There were four in the Emerson family besides Thoreau—Madam Emerson, Waldo's mother; Lidian, his wife; and his two small daughters Edith and Ellen. Elizabeth Hoar was still flitting from house to house; Alcott was living in the Hosmer Cottage for a while with his English friends Charles Lane and Henry Wright. When the weather grew warmer, they were going to try an experiment at community living at a farm called Fruitlands not far from the village of Harvard. Occasionally in the evenings, this group met at Emerson's house when Alcott held forth on Platonism or Christian mysticism; or on Milton, Bacon and the Origin of the Mind.

The wind circled around and whined in the chimneys; snow stung the window-panes. Indoors, the group sat comfortably before the open fire. When it grew late and they got up to leave, they found the front door banked with snowdrifts; and Thoreau had to put on his high boots and make an attack with the shovel.

Ellery Channing was still engaged in doing nothing beautifully. Hawthorne declared that Ellery could idle with greater grace than any one he knew. Ellen was not well, had not been well since her marriage. She always felt tired, and her back ached. Sometimes Ellery helped her with the work; but he did not find dish-washing to his liking, and wished that they could afford a maid.

The snows melted and the winds grew soft. Margaret walked past Walden Pond and found a spreading tree with a friendly trunk. She lay back against it and closed her eyes; spring sounds came to her—the call of a linnet, the trill of a thrush. The breeze stirred the grasses at her feet and brought the smell of freshly plowed fields. A little brook ran over the stones not far away; a bullfrog croaked.

Footsteps came through the withered leaves of winter and through the tender grass. They stopped suddenly. Margaret opened her eyes. Hawthorne was before her, looking as if he did not know quite what to do. Margaret gave him a friendly smile and he sat down on one of the roots of her tree. They talked of trivial things: of the woods in autumn and the woods in spring; of crows and linnets and song sparrows; of the impressions of childhood and the tenacity of youthful memory. Margaret was in a melting mood. She had been in the woods almost all day and she felt the mellowing influence of the trees and birds and drifting clouds; she felt radiant with faith, love and life. All somber thoughts of her unfulfilled destiny, of the obstructions which kept her from realizing her ambitions seemed to be taken up by the breeze and dissolved in the air; the past was negligible, the future was a pleasant mystery....

She had a happy talk with Hawthorne, who, when he went home, recorded the experience in his Journal.

Once she went with Emerson to see Fanny Ellsler dance. She was completely charmed. She leaned over and whispered ecstatically, "That is poetry, Waldo." Emerson, in an equally ecstatic whisper, replied, "No, Margaret, it is religion."

She found, as she grew older, that such experiences, though fewer in number, were greater in intensity. It seemed that the more discriminating she became, the greater became her ability to enjoy. . . .

But such enjoyments were rare. She wrote, "I have no belief in beautiful lives. We are born to be mutilated; and the blood must flow till in every vein its place is supplied by the Divine ichor." She thought that she would live a long time for she saw in herself "much rude matter that needed to be spiritualized."

The world was becoming less and less aware of her rebellious times; for she was learning how to curb her caustic tongue. When she considered it necessary to call attention to a fault, she did it so charmingly that the recipient of her acid favors felt doubly chagrined. There was the time when, at a concert, she was bothered throughout by the giggling and whispering of some girls in front of her. At the end of the program, Margaret leaned forward and with a gracious smile said, "I'm sure you did not realize how plainly your voices carried and how much they interfered with the enjoyment of all those around you. I just tell you that you may know for a future time."

The springtime called to her from across unknown spaces—from prairieland and mountainland, from chasms and declivities where waters boomed, from Indian encampments. The springtime used James Freeman Clarke's voice: He and his sister Sarah were planning a trip West. At Chicago their brother William would join them. Would not Margaret come too? After some deliberation, Margaret agreed:

Then James did a friendly thing; he sent her a check for fifty dollars and a poem that he had written.

Fearing lest Margaret might feel diffident about accepting money from him, he wrote her a friendly and persuasive letter in which he said, "Goethe says that some things cannot be concealed.... Fire cannot be concealed for the smoke will betray it by day, the light by night; love cannot be concealed, for if it be not spoken in words, it is betrayed by the looks of the eye."

Margaret accepted the fifty dollars. And one day when the orchards were a blur of blossoms and the laburnum trees were fainting under their weight of gold, the three adventurers set forth.

The West was at that time the source of much interest and much curiosity to New Englanders. The new settlers went back and forth carrying seeds from the East and planting them in the West. One man had taken a boat-load of apple-seeds from Pennsylvania and now the plains of Ohio and the fields of Indiana were full of spriggly trees....

Margaret wrote to Emerson from Chicago. They had gone through lovely woods where they had stopped to gather lupines and moccasin flowers; they visited Indian encampments and smoked the pipe of peace; they saw the new settlers on their way to market at Milwaukee—a Hungarian count who had a large tract of land in Wisconsin and who lived like a feudal lord; an Irish nobleman, who brought his garden stuff in before cockcrow.

The Indians interested Margaret more than the immigrants; they seemed a nobler race than the noblemen, for they did not look at the land merely to utilize it. There was already germinating that spirit of efficiency which to-day is the god of the "go-getter," wherever he may dwell. Margaret looked into the years and saw the turn that things would take; and she deplored the fact that the new republic, from all signs and portents, was building for itself a stronghold of mere material prosperity. She saw in the Indians the relics of a different age, where the trees and the rivers and the hills were symbols of a greater Power. She talked to them and won their confidence; and learned many of their legends and their sacred symbols.

They crowded around her curiously. She wore a locket around her neck, which they regarded as a talisman to keep her safe from illness and ill-fortune. Her parasol fascinated them; it was the first that they had ever seen. She talked to the women by signs. The children ran about half-naked, the young girls cut wood. Their wigwams were not clean; there was a peculiar, unpleasant smell about their bodies.... Margaret saw them as a downtrodden race forced to accept a religion they could not understand, forced to accept a life which was unnatural to them.

She went to a Christian church which they attended; their faces were blank, impassive. "Better their own dog-feasts and bloody rites than such mockery as this," Margaret thought.

An Indian said to her, speaking of the slave-owners of the South, "You say that Christianity is pleasing to God. How can that be? Those men (the slave-owners) are Christians!"

She found some difficulty in explaining to them the difference between Christ and Christian....

Ellery Channing wrote her characteristic letters, which made her smile. He thought it well to remind her of a festive day still held in much respect in the East—Bunker Hill day.

"Such crowds of ugly women and ugliest men! Such sucking of candies and sham patriotism! All Boston in black coats and white breeches. One sees a Daniel Webster paraded on a scaffold, the President of the United States in his rear and a range of cracked or at least moldy, ineffectual Continental soldiers drooping in un-easy chairs.... Whether the eloquence was cataract-style or after the flood or antediluvian I cannot say. The Mayflower figure of never-to-be-forgotten Washington ... stalked in and out of the oration like a ghost.... O thou unfortunate Generalissimo Washington, one could wish thou mightest have died in thy infancy...."

Margaret made notes everywhere; and occasionally she found time to write an article. She was eager to put all her experiences, all her observations, into a book.

VIII

APOLLO AND DIANA

IN SEPTEMBER she was back in Cambridge. Work on her new book now began in earnest. It was a book on her travels through the West and it was to be called simply, *Summer on the Lakes*. Before she was very far advanced in it, she realized that she must consult many books of reference. The most natural place to go was to the Harvard library. It was not very difficult for her to obtain permission to use the library and every day she went there and read for hours.

She was a pioneer in new territory, a strange, unusual figure in those sainted rooms. Never before had a woman ventured into them to consult their books. The students, as they passed back and forth, gave her sidelong and sometimes hostile looks. Margaret knew that they resented her intrusion, not because she was who she was, but because she was a prophecy of what, one day, would be a common practice. She showed them, by her presence there, that it would not be very long before they would lose their masculine prerogative of assuming absolute sway in this, their particular domain. Margaret smiled to herself at their discomfiture. She had moments when she would have liked to say to them, "Don't be so worried; you might as well accept us as colleagues. When woman has a fair chance, her work will vie creditably with that of the ages. Don't fear that she will become too masculine. When she learns to use her intellect, she will show that use of it need not absorb or weaken, but rather refine and invigorate her affections."

Whole days she spent in the college library; whole nights she wrote. When she finally went to bed, she could not sleep, but lay tossing about, racked by headache and by twitching nerves. She grew weary to death of the book and longed to have it off her hands. It did not please her; she felt that she had not done justice to the over-rich materials at her disposal.

Her Conversations were resumed, her pupils eagerly returned to her. But she was tired of teaching; she felt that she must have a change of occupation, must burst into a life of action. The sameness of things bored her beyond measure.

Her book went to press in the spring. What a relief to see the last of it! Soon came the proof sheets. Margaret corrected them in the evenings. And all night a procession of pages passed before her in her sleep, and their contents assumed the most grotesque shapes, dancing up and down, making hideous faces. She saw painted Indians and heard their weird chants; she heard the bark of prairie dogs, the baying of wolves.

At last the proofs were corrected and bundled off to the publisher.

Every cent that Margaret could spare she gave to Ellery and Ellen Channing. Thanks to the generosity of a friend, Samuel Ward, Ellery had succeeded in getting his poems published. His chief activity now was walking. Emerson often went with him, and Thoreau went when he had time. He was no longer Emerson's "working-man," but was working at his family's business—manufacturing pencils. These three were known as the Concord Walkers. Concord did not take them very seriously. The word "genius" was somewhat loosely used at the time and doubtless the Concordians regarded a genius as some one not to be considered as belonging to everyday life. Ellery Channing, for example. They did not know what to make of him; sometimes he said the funniest things, at others he was as gloomy as a crow among a flock of eagles. Then there was Alcott, another genius. He had carted his family off to Fruitlands and kept them half-starving because he believed that human beings should not eat anything that belonged to animals. The cow's milk was for calves, he said, and eggs should be used to bring forth chickens. (In regard to the wholesale production of chickens from eggs, Alcott undoubtedly had been misinformed.) He even hesitated about including apples in the daily diet, because he maintained that apples should be kept exclusively to feed the worms that made their homes in them! Of course the colony at Fruitlands almost starved. And one day in mid-winter Alcott borrowed an ox-sled, bundled his four little women up and the family trekked back to Concord. There Alcott shut himself up in his room, declaring that he would remain no longer in an ungrateful world. "And his poor wife at her wit's end, not knowing which way to turn!" said the unlettered Concord housewives, packing up meat-pies and preserves and sweet-cakes to take to the unfortunate family.

They were a little in awe of Margaret, who, however, was always pleasant to meet, in spite of her haughty way and her great learning. Emerson they considered a little queer....

One day Margaret received a troubled letter from Ellery. Ellen was not well. "Every morning and every night she is dragged down to the ground with tending the baby." Ellery asked Margaret if she would undertake to find a servant for them—"a really good person, at $1.50 a week"! He had grown weary of dish-washing and scrubbing and helping with the meals.

So Margaret looked around for a reliable woman who would be a help to Ellen.

She was planning another book, the book which was to deal with woman's status as compared with man's. She had written an essay on the subject for the *Dial*, but this was not enough. She was passionately concerned with the frustrations, the disappointments, the narrow lives of women, was an ardent feminist, though she did not call herself by that name....

Writing was hard labor to her. Emerson said that her pen was a nonconductor. Conversation was different; and in conversation women were superior to men, she thought. "While they (men) tramp on in their clumsy way, we wheel and fly and dart hither and thither." She knew that she would never write as well as she talked. "My voice excites me, my pen never."

When the summer sun came more slantingly and the moon rose more red, she went to Fishkill, to spend seven idyllic weeks with her friend Caroline Sturgis. They took long walks along the Hudson, they explored the woods and fields. One day it rained. And that day Margaret started her book about women. It went well; and when she put it aside for the day she did not have the racking headache which had always followed a day's writing. Rather she felt all aglow, as if she had been in communion with mystic forces. Now she wanted to stay at Fishkill long enough to finish the book; for the moment she got home, there would be a thousand other things for her to do.

There was something in the air—a proposition which, if she accepted it, would take her away from Boston. It was an offer from Horace Greeley to become the literary editor of the *Tribune*. Mrs. Greeley was responsible for this. She kept urging Horace to ask Margaret to join his staff; she pointed out to him that it would be a distinct acquisition to the paper to have such a woman connected with it. Greeley secretly agreed with her, but took the occasion to sneer a little about all the woman-worship that went on in Boston. Wifelike, Mrs. Greeley listened, knowing very well the jealousy that most husbands feel for women whom their wives admire. It was not very long, however, before he made Margaret an offer. After careful consideration, she accepted it.

She finished her book with a flourish and returned to Cambridge in high spirits.

It was a sad time. Mrs. Fuller, who had grown increasingly dependent on Margaret, could scarcely visualize life without her. She had many worries, and always felt strengthened when she could talk of them with Margaret. Ellen was not happy, neither was she well; Eugene, her eldest son, was far away; her youngest son, Lloyd, was insane. Of all these things Mrs. Fuller thought as she followed Margaret from room to room while she gathered up her trinkets to take with her to New York.

Margaret thought how life seemed always full of conflicts; how the individual was constantly torn. She knew that a change would be good for her; for too long she had been the burden-bearer at home; for too long her creative energies had been stifled by too many responsibilities. All this she realized clearly, yet felt infinite depression now that the opportunity had come by which she was to be released. The heart was an unwilling servant to the mind, she thought; the heart refused reason and did not countenance logic.

She wished that she could take all her family with her to New York. She knew that this was impossible. The younger boys had left college and were entering on their professional lives. Indeed it was a question whether the family would ever again be united except for short, snatched visits. Their mother felt that henceforth she should divide her time among all the children.

Margaret longed to have Ellen more happily situated. This she might help to bring about. It was obvious that what would bring Ellen the greatest relief would be to escape from

Ellery for a time at least. Margaret had already made up her mind to approach Horace Greeley on the subject of Ellery. It might be possible to find some work for him on the *Tribune*. It was high time that Ellery should assume some of the responsibility into which he had so precipitately plunged by allowing his passion to run away with his reason.

Gathering up her various trinkets, Margaret tried to argue away the tears which fell upon them as she placed them neatly in her trunk. "Such tears are childish tears and belie a deeper wisdom. It is foolish in me to be so anxious about my family."

But her heart said, "There is a mystic thrill betwixt children of one mother, which can never cease to be felt until the soul is quite born anew."

Mrs. Greeley had written her that she was to make her home with them.

She found them living in a spacious, old house set in eight acres of land which ran down to the East River at Turtle Bay, opposite the southernmost point of Blackwell's Island. This was like a country residence to Horace, who had always lived a few rods from his work. The silence of the night was so oppressive to him that sometimes he could not sleep. For thirteen years he had been a city man; he liked lights and hurry and noise, he liked to feel that he was in the very heart of the city's work. At the end of the presidential canvass which had sent Polk to the White House, Greeley was so "thoroughly used up" that he was glad enough to take the advice of his wife and of his friends and moved far away from his work.

The house was sparsely furnished, too sparsely, Margaret thought. Those grounds with the wooded ravine, with the sloping lawns and the magnificent trees deserved a sumptuous house, with exquisite crystal and beautifully wrought silver in the dining-room, warm rugs on shining floors, precious ornaments of old pottery and old brass here and there, some rare bindings and a case of engraved gems. All these things she pictured, as she walked slowly up from the ravine or paced back and forth on the broad piazza which ran the whole length of the house in full view of the sails which seemed to greet it as the boats swam round the bay.

She was very thoughtful as she went back and forth; she had lost some of that buoyancy which had made Emerson laugh so immoderately when he first met her. Sometimes her eyes would flash with the old pagan fires and sometimes her tongue would utter an old, quick retort. But not as often as formerly. The fierce fires had been brought under control, the wild, impetuous paganism had been transmuted into vigorous arraignment of hypocrisies and shams. "O that my friends would teach me the simple art of not too much!" she exclaimed once and wondered how they could go on bearing the "ceaseless eloquence of my nature." Then came a prayer for moderation—the cold, Puritanical reproof administered to the passionate ardor of the South.

Always this Puritan that was in her looked on at the pagan that was in her and tempered it. This was her greatest safety. Had the pagan part been dominant, she doubtless would have run her bark against many a shoal of excess ... and would have suffered when the pagan part retired and gave way to the Puritan. Repressed she doubtless was; but not as disastrously as one unable to direct the course of her creative energies into other channels....

Mrs. Greeley was inclined to pamper her; did not allow her to go to the office when she had a headache. Horace, slaving away at his ten columns a day, thought she drank too much tea and told her so. Often he went home and found her holding court to a dozen women instead of writing a review of a book which had waited days for the right mood. This irked him. The fact that she could write only when in the vein was absurd to him; he was a "hack-horse of the daily press," accustomed to turn out copy almost as automatically as Henry Thoreau's shop at Concord turned out pencils. Often Margaret's story arrived at the office a day late. That it was well written was no compensation for its tardy arrival; a newspaper is primarily a paper of news and belated brilliance is valueless.

Greeley considered Margaret inconsistent in her ideas about women. She believed whole-heartedly in their emancipation. "It is a vulgar error that love—*a* love—is to woman her whole existence." She would have Minerva as much esteemed as Venus: "Fellow pilgrims and helpmeets ye are, Apollo and Diana." For her there was no *belonging* of the one sex to the other; immortal souls should be free; and women's souls were as immortal as man's. She demanded for women the fullest recognition of social and political equality.

Greeley was large-minded about this; he saw no reason why women should occupy subservient positions if they were capable of filling others. "But," he argued, "if women are to be equal, always treat them as such; do not exact a deference from men; do not set them on pedestals and expect men to worship and deify them. If woman is man's equal in the office, let her be his equal in the drawing-room."

Margaret expected this gallant attitude; equality of intellect and of opportunity need not do away with chivalry, she argued. Let chivalry remain as long as possible; there was little enough of it; and it was one of the badges of beauty in social life. . . .

So they argued. Greeley did not sympathize with the fanciful, fantastical, exaggerated, colorful side of Margaret. He was a plebeian in taste and in manners; Margaret was a patrician. There were many subjects it would have been well not to dwell upon; it might have been better if Margaret had met her employer only during working hours; then she would not have had so much evidence of his plebeianism.

But she was more tolerant of uncouth excellence than she once had been. She had a genuine liking for Greeley: "With the exception of my own mother, I think him the most disinterestedly generous person I have ever known."

Greeley was large-minded enough not to judge Margaret by her mannerisms. He appreciated her ability as a critic no less than he admired her nobility of character. He called her "the most remarkable woman that America has yet known," "the loftiest, bravest soul that has yet irradiated the form of American womanhood."

Her articles were widely read and the circulation of the *Tribune* increased.

"My business life" Margaret called her life in New York; and wrote, answering Richard's somewhat petulant complaint about the scantiness of her correspondence that she expected him to understand, as did most of her friends, that from now on she was obliged to act in her public career rather than toward them personally. "I have given almost all my young energies to personal relations. I no longer feel inclined to this, and wish to share and impel the general stream of thought."

Was she challenging her fates when she said this? It would seem so. For, very soon afterwards she met some one with whom her relations were extremely personal.

IX

THE LITERARY LION

JAMES NATHAN was a Jew who came from Hamburg. He was a sensitive soul, somewhat younger than Margaret, and he was doomed to spend part of every day in a New York office. He hated his work and longed for an Arcadia and a congenial spirit therein to whom he could confide his dreams and aspirations. The life of buying and selling, the vulgar traffic of the market-place, was anathema to him. His was no plebeian mind; not for him the utilitarian life where leisure was considered a waste and graceful indolence the pastime of fools and women. He felt a little out of place in the industrial world of lower Broadway.

Margaret who was as Southern in temperament as she was Northern in character, was charmed with the gentle Jew. They walked among the fallen leaves of autumn, they stood on the river bank and watched the sails pass; they went to concerts and heard Ole Bull play on his beautiful Stradivarius. Coming home, they loitered along the narrow paths leading to the big old house and watched the shadows that the moon etched from tree to tree. They had fancies about themselves: They were in an Eastern country where the sun shone long on ancient temples; the birds were in full song, the trees in full leaf....

Margaret said, "You have a mysterious power over me. Sometimes it causes awe; and yet, I feel deep confidence in you."

He answered her by saying that he had to escape from her at times, he was so conscious of a similar influence from her. There was more talk of themselves, their instincts and intuitions, their advances and retreats. Margaret felt that this man knew her better than did any one else; he even revealed her to herself. She felt vibrant and more alive than she had ever felt.

And that night she lay awake for a long time, looking out through her window at the baring branches of the trees which started up between her and the stars. And she wondered if, this time, she was to know the secret which had transformed Psyche the mortal, into a daughter of the gods.

She was thirty-four, her step was not as buoyant as it had been, she could not summon merriment as frequently as she had. What matter? What matter? If she was to know this secret, this ecstatic, life-giving secret of sexual love, the years would fly away from her and something much deeper and more abiding than merriment would come to her.

She began to be oblivious of the bare walls and of the sparsely furnished rooms of the big, old house. Something of joy appeared in her steps; her eyes glowed anew with their old pagan fires. There was an added richness about her, which brought more and more callers up the graveled paths....

Her contributions to the *Tribune* were more fluent, more vigorous and were full of wiser comments. Then came her book, *Woman in the Nineteenth Century*. She was the subject of every periodical in the country; the country was divided into two camps, the one friendly to the point of hysteria, the other equally hostile. The first edition was exhausted in a week and Margaret received a check for eighty-five dollars!

She sent some money to her mother, she sent a check to Ellen. Thanks to her powers of persuasion, Ellery was working on the *Tribune* too, but she avoided meeting him whenever she could. When she saw him she saw Ellen and the change that life with him had wrought in her. Ellen's light-heartedness had vanished; she had no energy; a cloud seemed to have settled on her spirit.

New York gave Margaret the opportunity of seeing again her old friend Lydia Maria Child, with whom she had studied metaphysics in her petulant, youthful, bluestocking days. They talked of the march of their souls and of Pythagoras' theory of metempsychosis, which was so little understood. They talked of more simple, homely things like gloves and clothes and carriages drawn by fine, high-stepping horses. "They are all needed in the social life," said Mrs. Child, "and they cost money. That's why I am a hermit. I can't afford all the social requisites."

Margaret argued about this: "A hermit's life is not right, particularly for a writer. You should not keep too much apart from the common stream of things; there is a stimulus in crowds which you do not receive anywhere else. Of course a certain amount of solitude is necessary to the creative artist, but I find my mind stagnating after *too much* solitude. And greater ones than I have had the same experience."

The greater one whom she had particularly in mind was Emerson. She had recently received a letter from him in which she had detected a shade of restlessness. He had been for too long dependent on himself, he said; had no regular daily task, no office to summon him from his dreams. At his lectures his audiences no longer stimulated him; there was no challenging in them; they were mentally lazy; they accepted everything too readily, were too easily satisfied. Thinking that increased physical activity might give him what he needed, he had bought fourteen acres of field and pine grove on the shore of Walden Pond, where he spent long days working like a squire, with hatchet and pruning-hook. He cut away dead shrubbery, he made paths between the trees, he piled up underbrush in open spaces where it would be safe for firing. He grew warm from his labors and felt physically invigorated; but the inner restlessness remained.

"Even he," Margaret thought, "even he needs the occasional novelty of scene or association."

She went about a good deal and met many charming people. One evening at a party she was particularly witty and seemed in excellent spirits. A group gathered around her as usual and sat eagerly listening to such conversation as they afterwards declared had never before been uttered by any woman. Anecdotes sparkled through it, tragedies heightened its portent, myths and legends demonstrated modern tendencies. At length Margaret got up to leave. As she went to the dressing-room for her cloak, she sighed deeply. An acquaintance heard her. "Why the sigh?" Margaret shrugged. "Alone, as usual," she answered. And asked herself if it must always be so, if she must always feel this deep, spiritual loneliness and feel it most poignantly in the midst of a gay, light-laughing throng.

Going home, she thought of James Nathan. There might be a letter from him awaiting her. And she hurried up the path between the trees.

There was a letter. She took it to her room to read. Her hand trembled when she held the match to the gas-jet.

She stood in her cloak reading; color came into her cheeks and spread in patches over her neck. A nerve in her lower lip began to beat; she could have seen the pulsation had she looked in the mirror. The letter was cold. It wounded her. She thought her demon must be at work again, devising ill against her. Why, otherwise, could Nathan, who was most noble, write such words to her? That there was in him a lower as well as a higher nature than she was aware of; that the "man of the world" in him had recognized the "dame" in her and had been filled with strange longings. . . .

Margaret threw the letter down and stood for a moment irresolute. Her cloak slipped from her shoulders. From the trees in the ravine came the shrill and eerie hoot of an owl. Was it a portent?

She went to the window. Spring was beginning to walk among the trees and to freshen the fragrant earth. A light shone from a river-boat moored in the bay; the waves stole in among the fissures in the rocks and stole out again, making little sucking sounds; countless stars were out.

The magnificent poise of Nature! Margaret stood looking out upon it, tormented and tortured more than she had ever been.

The next day was Sunday. Margaret woke with a headache, but she could not remain in her room. She went out into the March wind, hymn-book in hand. She went to church, and as she walked through the solemn streets, she felt something burning the backs of her eyeballs and rising uncomfortably in her throat—some obstruction which prevented her from sharing the Sabbath calm.

The service was not soothing. She felt herself removed from all the other worshipers, who seemed at one with themselves and with their God. The words of the minister had a hollow sound and the organ was mournful. She left church unsatisfied.

The day dragged; and the next day dragged at work. In the evening, Margaret went to see a performance of *Antigone*. This tragedy of the ancients did what the minister and the organ and the anthem had failed to do: In looking on the woes of Antigone, Margaret forgot her own. And she went home feeling that life was not as hopeless as she had supposed.

The next day she answered Nathan's letter. She told him frankly of the suffering it had caused her; and made honest confession of her love for him: "The time has passed when I could protect myself by reserve. I must now seem just as I feel.... I feel as if the joyous sweetness I did feel in the sense of your life, might revive again.... It lies with you."

There was a reconciliation, and for a time all was well. Margaret went to work with vigor in her step, she went to rest singing. Things were prospering; her *Summer on the Lakes,* the account of her western travels, had sold better than she expected; her new book was fulfilling its purpose: It was making people think of the destiny of man. "By man I mean both man and woman; these are the two halves of one thought. I believe that the development of the one cannot be effected without that of the other. My highest wish is that this truth should be distinctly and rationally apprehended and the conditions of life and freedom recognized as the same for the daughters and the sons of time; twin exponents of a divine thought."

So she wrote in her introduction. The tongues still wagged: She was called bold and strong and brilliant, ahead of her time; she was called a mystic, a prophet, a fantastic visionary.

Greeley was becoming more satisfied with her work, which he said was steadier than at first. While not as elaborate as her articles in the *Dial,* it was better journalism; and journalism was what he required of her.

Sometimes he insisted on having a book review finished within a certain time. Against her better judgment, Margaret complied; it was not natural to her to write under pressure. And usually the articles written under these circumstances brought adverse criticism.

Sometimes her critical remarks were taken as the expression of her own conceit. There existed a large public who could not discriminate between literary frankness and personal self-assertion. It was the day of "tomahawk revenge." And a displeased author retaliated by dashing off a vitriolic diatribe against the too candid reviewer. Poe's incidental writings were full of this kind of thing, and for even fuller and franker expression of pique, there is Lowell's famous *Fable for Critics.* Margaret agreed with Emerson that America was too easily satisfied and when she stated that Lowell was lacking in the genuine poetic gift—that she must give this as her honest opinion in spite of "the grief of many friends and the disgust of more"—the sheep-like portion of the public, who had allowed themselves to be led by other opinions, began to bleat about her bumptiousness and self-conceit.

She postponed for as long as she could, the reviewing of Longfellow's poems. Greeley brought the book to her one day and said that he was anxious for her criticism of it. Margaret begged to be let off. "My views of poetry are so entirely different from his, I'd rather not undertake this."

"But who is to do it, if not you?"

"Why not you, Mr. Greeley?"

"H-m! Well, we'll see."

Greeley took the book back to his office. Days passed, still the volume remained unread. Greeley took it back to Margaret. "I can't find time for this, you'll have to do it," he said.

She could evade the issue no longer. She knew that she would be very severely censured for what she felt obliged to say about Mr. Longfellow. She knew that a vigorous vein of sentimentality ran through the vitals of her country and made detached, impersonal judgment impossible. Minds were so clogged with sentimentality that they could not freely function. Not freely functioning, they were easily influenced by mediocre art, mediocre literature, mediocre music. It looked as if the whole standard would be a mediocre one. Margaret, reaching toward the stars, yearning to cleave her channel straight through all mediocrity, drove her hatchet deep into the heart of shams, deep into the heart of comfortable hypocrisies and too easily apprehended platitudes.

She knew that she could not spare Henry Wadsworth Longfellow. His goodness, his placidity, his unquestioning faith all stood up before her and challenged her to say what she had to say about his superficial thought, his false images, his academic flourishes in the face of poetry.

Let them challenge! And let her pen say what it must.

Her article raised a terrific tempest. A cyclone of letters struck the office of the *Tribune:* The critic was jealous; she was piqued because she was not herself, successful as a poet. She had a caustic tongue, which was the spokesman of an ill-natured mind. So said the majority of letters. The minority said, "All hail to you! You are courageous; you have convictions and the stamina to express them fearlessly. We need you if this country is not to sink into a mire of mental and cultural stagnation."

From the length and breadth of the land came this storm of letters. They moved Margaret deeply, particularly those from those readers who glimpsed her purpose. On such as these depended the salvation of the country. And Margaret saw herself as an armed knight on a white horse riding at the head of a troop with flying banners bearing the words, *Los Exaltados, Las Exaltadas.* The redemption of the world from ignorance! This was their mission—men and women marching side by side, heads high, eyes turned toward the stars! Thus did Margaret glimpse the pilgrimage for which she was already mustering her forces.

She was soon a literary lion in New York. Strangers came up the paths to the Greeley house and left cards. Margaret had no time to return such calls. The strangers called again, and this time asked if they might see her. If she was in the mood, she saw them. She was like a queen giving audience. Through half-closed eyes she scrutinized her visitors. If they were merely idly curious, she dealt with them summarily; her manner was haughty, frigid, aloof; her voice was steel-like. These merely curious did not know quite how to respond to her, and after a few minutes of hopeless floundering, got up and left. Those who came seeking sympathy and advice, received all they came to find and more. They soon found themselves telling Margaret secrets which no one else had ever heard.

Often she shut herself up from every one. "Why do they want me personally?" she exclaimed. "I give them all I can in my work. I must conserve my strength." And she sat in a darkened room with a cold cloth on her forehead.

But a certain amount of social life was necessary to her, and after a few days of isolation she was out again at a party. Miss Lynch was somewhat celebrated for her soirées. All the wits gathered at her house—the authors, artists and journalists, and the dilettanti, who often make more amusing conversation than those whose profession it is. Margaret was *persona grata* at these gatherings. And when she entered the room, the room immediately became more alive.

She stood out in a crowd. She had a splendid head, which she held regally; her expression was now one of a person who, through experience, through self-discipline, through aspiration, has become deeply spiritualized. She dressed well, she walked proudly. People turned to look at her when she went down the aisle of a theater or concert-hall.

There were times when the slapdash life of the Greeley household was obnoxious to her. She, a breaker of conventions, was, compared with her eccentric host and hostess, highly conventional. She loved little Arthur Greeley, who was called Pickie. He was only eight months old when she became a member of the household, but he soon grew to know her and to look for her. Margaret carried him around, talked to him, tossed harmless balls at him. And he responded with ecstatic gurgles and sudden shrieks of mirth.

Horace Greeley looked on indulgently and tried to read the riddle of this extraordinary woman with her extravagant fancies, her clear-headedness, her ardors and her reserves. There was something Oriental about her, Greeley thought, and something masculine. She never, for example, allowed personal feelings to enter into an abstract argument; she was logical, clear, precise. A strange combination; a human paradox; a mystic, a fatalist, a believer in signs and omens; a believer in immortality; one who loved luxury and ease, but one who could renounce them readily.

At first Greeley had thought that Margaret was spoiled by all the woman-worship and all the extravagant eulogies of her men friends. But as he grew to know her better, he realized that he, hard-headed Philistine that he was, was being drawn into the general current: "I learned to know her as a most fearless and unselfish champion of Truth and Human Good at all hazards.... She probably knew the cherished secrets of more hearts than any one else.... She responded to the essential brotherhood of all human-kind."

Margaret knew that she was repressed, and longed at times to be completely absorbed in a great activity or a great love. Failing this, she feared that she might become bitter. She had low moments when the viper came back into her tongue; she dreaded them. And she prayed, "Father let me not wound ...

let my touch be light and gentle ... let me not fail to be kind and tender when need is."

She knew the danger of appearing self-righteous; she loathed a patronizing attitude and cried, "I would not assume an overstrained, poetic magnanimity!"

Yet she knew herself to be superior. And she prayed that she might free her fellowmen "from the conventional bonds whereby their sight is holden."

Was she doing this? Was her work fulfilling this purpose? She did not know. Sometimes she failed to understand the reason of her being—she who could talk so brilliantly about the general destiny. But there she was, "a wandering Intelligence, driven from spot to spot, that I may learn all secrets and fulfill a circle of knowledge."

And she repeated "To what purpose?" "Of what use is knowledge if it must be kept treasured inside one, as one shuts up a precious gem, allowing a visitor to see it at rare intervals?"

X

ENCHANTMENT

MARGARET WAS GROWING WEARY of her imaginary heroes. It was all very well to pour out her heart to Beethoven, to commune in secret with Goethe and to whisper confidences to Novalis, if such communings were of any satisfaction. But never was there any answering word, such as she now longed to hear. She was not enough of a mystic to find satisfaction in unending visualizations; she was no Saint Theresa whose imagination was able to transmute her physical longings into spiritual ecstasy. For she believed in the *threefold* expression of man and she knew that much of her despair came from her failure to realize this expression in its entirety.

A hungry soul will clothe a beloved person in resplendent garments. Illusion comes quickly to the side of passion and glamour supplies certain necessary attributes.

Margaret loved James Nathan. He was of a somewhat melancholy turn, and he had nice discrimination in speech. These pale, melancholy natures are often very attractive to women. Nathan pictured vividly his uncongenial surroundings and the unhappiness that they caused him. Who better than Margaret knew the tortures of a sensitive spirit obliged to adjust itself to the horrors of a commercial life? Because of his sensitive nature, Nathan had been the victim of countless misunderstandings. But he had borne abuse in silence. He was very subtle; he did not placard himself with his self-righteousness. On the contrary, he managed to mask it so cleverly that Margaret saw in him a beautiful humility. That is what illusion does when one is attracted toward another; it supplies the characteristics which one especially admires.

So she yielded herself to this love, assured that, this time, it was reciprocated. They met, they walked, they listened to good music; they sat for hours in a little cove among the rocks....

And when they parted, Margaret went to her desk and wrote, "I do so long for childish rest and play, instead of all the depths which never will go deep enough."

Those unquenchable fires of her spirit! In her youth she had prayed that the experience of love might not be denied her; now that she loved and felt her spirit still athirst, she prayed that she might revert to simple happiness such as children know. The mystery of life was tantalizing to her; and in her lack of experience she appeared sometimes naïve. She, who could point out errors in some of Emerson's allusions, she who denied to Lowell the true gift of poetry and who called Longfellow artificial and secondhand, might have learned this mystery which was so tantalizing to her, from any of the unschooled, degraded throng who dwelt across from her, on Blackwell's Island!

Once when Nathan was indifferent and remote, she sent him two poems written to her by two admirers, one of whom was her brother-in-law Ellery Channing. We can imagine Nathan smiling a little when he read them. There was something so wistfully childish about the act!

She trusted Nathan implicitly; to her he was all honor, all truthfulness, all loyalty. Did he seem brusque or irritable, it was her fault, she said; some unpleasant trait in her had called out the brusqueness or the irritability. If he allowed an unusually long time to go by between his visits to her, something had happened to cause his worry and he stayed away that he might not communicate the worry to her....

He wrote explaining his absence: He had been placed in a false position, a very unpleasant situation. He could not make excuses; that seemed cowardly; so he allowed himself to remain in the false position, feeling that he would prefer heroic silence to justifiable speech. This time, he asked her to destroy his letter....

She carried it next to her heart; and when she answered it, assured him that no circumstance could alter their relation. "I am myself exposed to misconstruction constantly from what I write." As soon as she could, she would destroy his letter, she said, but not just yet.... And she urged him to come to her soon.

She wanted to be light-hearted with him but she could not. "Now this deeper strain has been awakened . . . will the strings ever vibrate to the lighter airs again?"

It was not a happy love. When she was separated from him, she thought of him with longing as the one mortal whose presence could give her absolute repose. Her love deified him; he had unlocked for her "all the treasure-chambers of the universe." There were times when she feared that "the enchanted doors must close again." For she feared she was not wise enough to go with him through all the devious turnings of the temple.

Infinitely pathetic are her words to him, "Perhaps it is that I was not enough a child at the right time and now am too childish; but will you not have patience with that?"

She knew that she had missed her childhood; and now in the maturity of her years, little, frank simplicities kept coming up, which should have been disposed of long ago. Perhaps they irritated him? But if he truly loved her, he would be tolerant of them. Would she not be tolerant of any conceivable weakness he might display?

By the depth and purity of her own love she judged his, and never once did she allow her faith to falter. "You have approached me personally nearer than any other person and have said words to me most unusual and close, to which I have willingly listened."

He had a flowery tongue; and he played on the guitar. A romantic figure, with his lustrous, oriental eyes, his attractive pallor and his guitar! What thoughts Margaret had, as she lay on her couch rapturously regarding him and listening to the music which came from his slender fingers and from his lips!

He sent her heartsease and moss-roses; he gathered the blossoms of the blackberry and poured them into her lap. There was about him something mystical, which moved her deeply; she felt her will running away to become absorbed in his; often he read her thoughts. He was well aware of the power he exercised over her; and Margaret was all submission, all passively feminine.

It was a relief to rest after all her years of masculine managing; it was a relief to lie on the couch and have him read to her or sing to her while the sun slanted in through the half-drawn curtains and the thrushes called from the sycamore tree. She said that he was like red tulips, whose petals glowed like gems. . . .

Sometimes when she sat before her desk writing to him, she suddenly became powerless and could write no more. She was sure that he was thinking of her at these times. Even at a distance he was able to absorb her will so completely that she became weak and incapable of thought or of action.

This was alarming. She wrote to him, "You attract beings so much that after a while it is too much for their good or pleasure. Then comes the painful retrograde motion. But I feel confident that my angel will not let it be so with me." She had faith in her protecting angel. . . .

Had she been less trusting, she might have asked herself if it was not her demon who had led her into this strange relation, which was so devastating.

Nathan told her that by and by she would be stimulated by his love and through it would grow to be more herself. She prayed that this might be so, for she did not understand the relation, which was not as she had imagined a great love to be. She had pictured love as a vitalizing force, a wondrous joy which irradiated a communion of souls. She found it exhausting and unsatisfactory. She felt that there were depths in her which should be reached, but which always failed to be reached. It may have been that, lacking fulfillment, she was weakened.

And what of Nathan? He seemed to thrive; to him the ultimate fulfillment seemed not to be necessary. Doubtless Margaret gave so much when merely sitting in the room beside him or when walking with him among the shrubbery, that he needed nothing more. Her nature was so bounteous, her love so deep that she could not help strengthening him who was the object of it. Did not every one feel the force of her magnetism? How much more then would he not feel who was the sole recipient of it!

And so he talked to her of their great *spiritual* affinity.

While he drew more and more vitality from her extraordinary magnetic power, he proposed that they should become related from within! The well-fed man preaches a sermon on moderation; Crœsus goes among the tenements exhorting the housewives to be careful of their pennies!

Margaret was increasingly the victim of ill-health. She found that she could not go to so many parties; she was so exhausted at the end of the day that she had to go to bed soon after supper. And in bed she could not sleep. She came down in the morning weary and heavy-eyed. Greeley growled that it was tea-drinking that kept her awake.

She knew very well that it was not tea-drinking. But what was it? What in her relation with Nathan was it that was so exhausting? It should not be so; of this she was convinced. Love was a force, the *only* force which could invigorate; this was a philosophical, not merely a sentimental fact. It was hourly demonstrated in nature.

Nathan began to be critical of her: He was sure she did not understand him; she misinterpreted some of his simplest remarks; she was too sensitive....

Margaret listened... and upbraided herself: She was awkward, unschooled in the delicate nuances of life, incapable of any lightness of touch.... (She who had made Emerson laugh so immoderately!) Of late, an oppression had taken all her buoyancy from her. But it would return....

She prayed him to be patient: "You shall upbear me to the stars... and I feel sure that you will not find me incompetent."

Her submission was distasteful to him. Had she been capable of small deceptions, had she feigned indifference, he doubtless would have been better-minded. In love, Margaret had no caprice; she who was of so many moods in her ordinary life, in love was static. Always her *motif* remained the same, though her key was constantly changing: She loved him;

she trusted him, for she knew that his love was equally deep, equally wide....

An extremely unwise assertion to make to a lover. No lover wishes to be taken so much for granted. Where then is the mystery, the stimulating uncertainty which keeps one forever on the *qui vive* lest he do something which may prove displeasing to the one he loves? When a man is certain of victory, he begins planning new attacks.

A little knowledge of the world would have taught Margaret these obvious facts. The trouble was she was not of the world; she had lived for so many years in fantastic realms created by her own imagination—ideal realms where artifice was unknown and where honor and sincerity were answered by honor and sincerity—that she regarded her world of fact as her world of fancy incarnate. And yet, in her world of fancy, love was something more than it was proving to be in her actual world.... This was perplexing.

The strange thing was that she was able to counsel Richard in his affairs of the heart. When he wrote her that he did not know what to do to please his "friend," she advised him to stay away a little longer than usual, and not to be too impetuous. If only she had heeded this advice herself!

But she did not; she urged Nathan to come to her; she told him of her illnesses and her lack of sleep. She sent him poems she had written about armed knights who were her champions, and about the mystery of the sun and the solace of spring rains.

The Greeleys did not accept Nathan and often he and Margaret planned their meetings in town. Margaret usually made the suggestions: "I will walk toward Bowling Green and back again"; "next time we must go to Hoboken—it is not so confined there."

She had unusual spells of inarticulateness, which worried her: "My dearest, I feel a deep desire to utter myself, to answer you from my inmost soul, but I cannot. The easy powers, the superficial eloquence all fail me.... You would have to take me to heart and read my silence ... and I believe you will."

She demanded attentions: A little note to ease the disappointment she had felt the day before when no note came; a little visit even of twenty minutes; a meeting with him when she left the office....

Their meetings became more and more unsatisfactory. "Oh, it was a waste of this heavenly day to walk upon the terrace and talk about these barriers that keep us apart!"

She cries out to him that it is an unfair fight, he has so much more energy than she; she feels she cannot combat his arguments....

He became so pettish that he argued about the simplest things; asked her if she ever told Mrs. Greeley of their confidences. Margaret was amazed that he could suggest the possibility of such a thing. He told her she was proud, that she had been spoiled by flattery. And she accepted it because she had such reverence for his judgment!

She would not quarrel with him, but always "turned the other cheek" and thanked him for showing her to herself: "I will now kneel and laying thy dear hand upon my heart, implore that if pride or suspicion should hide there again, the recollection of this day may rise up and make them flutter their wings."

Nathan realized that he had been too ardent in his protestations; now he wished to withdraw, as he had no desire for Margaret's influential friends to think ill of him. He took the occasion when they were out walking to use the word "hope"; he trusted that she was not building up too much hope.

And that time Margaret did not turn the other cheek. She went home and wrote him her answer, for as always when with him, she felt unable to express herself. And here is a strange anomaly: It was her nature to be inspired to speech when with some one with whom she felt in sympathy. With Emerson, who said, "They"—her conversations—"interested me in every manner—talent, memory, wit, stern introspection, poetic play, religion, the finest personal feeling, the aspects of the future—each followed each in full activity and left me enriched and ... astonished by the gifts of my guest."

It was likewise her nature to find writing laborious. Yet, in her relation with Nathan speech came falteringly and her pen flew. She reproved him royally after he had humiliated her by the use of the word hope. "If Margaret dared express herself more frankly than another," she wrote, "it is because she has been in her way a queen, and received her guests as also of royal blood."

As a queen she continued to bestow her favor. She took him to church with her one day, and afterwards wrote this to him, "I do not think any human being ever felt a lovelier confidence in the pure tenderness of another than I did when I left the church."

She cherished the feeling, but it was not to last. Nathan was irritable on the way home; her exaltation was hateful to him; he spoke harshly. Away flew the cherished feeling. Margaret thought, "Nothing but perfect love will give a man patience to understand a woman." The day was spoiled.

She went home and spent the rest of the day playing with Pickie who was now a year old. But she could not still her thoughts: "To think that anything could enslave my heart short of perfect love such as I myself am born to feel, and shall yet, in some age and some world, feel for some one that can feel it for me!"

The mutiny had begun. Her mind at last stood challenger to her heart. But her heart was courageous; tried to tell her that the fault was hers—she was not good and pure and sweet enough. This prevented the absolute *rapport* which she so earnestly longed for. Nathan was noble, said her heart, and it pained him to tell her the harsh truths about herself.... "If you do not mend your ways," her heart said, "he may meet some one to whose will he will be as subservient as you are to his."

An unthinkable idea! She flew to her desk and wrote a long letter: "Your heart, your precious heart that I did long for ...you have cruelly hung it up quite out of my reach.... For no price! There is something I am not to have at any price.... You must not give it away *in my sight,* at any rate."

Poor inexperienced Margaret!

For a few days she had repose. It was spring and the world was beautiful. The trees in the Greeley garden were ready to burst into blossom; in the park the flowers were awake; the wind was soft, the sun danced. Margaret loved such days and from them drew great spiritual strength.

Nathan wrote her that the last harsh words he spoke to her had made him ill.

Away went Margaret's feeling of repose! Now she was all fire again: "I have a rush of feeling that seems like the passage of a spirit through me and ought to flow to you like a blessing. This is the most beautiful feeling I have ever experienced; it is indeed divine and can never, I fear me, be expressed."

XI

"AS MELANCHOLY AS A LOVER'S LUTE"

NATHAN WROTE AND TOLD HER THAT HE was contemplating a trip to Europe. Alarming news! What did it portend? Would he return to her or would he not? She read on; at length the motive of the letter was revealed to her: He needed money. He was ambitious to explore the East; he wanted to be the first to navigate the Dead Sea; he wanted to make minute examination of the mosque el Aksa in Jerusalem. It might be that she had some rich friends of disinterested generosity who would contribute toward the work. There was no question as to the success of his venture provided that the necessary funds were forthcoming. He asked her to acquaint Mrs. Greeley with his intention. And another thing—Would Margaret take care of Josey, his Newfoundland pup, while he was gone, and might he leave his guitar with her?

A subtle touch—that mention of his guitar.

Margaret wrote at once to some of her friends in Boston and told them about the proposed enlivening of the Dead Sea. She went out across the terrace, down the slope under the blossoms, past the bed of myrtle to the rocks overlooking the bay, where she had sat so many times with Nathan. She felt sad; she could not conceive of life without him. She sat on the rocks till shadows fell upon them and the sun sank; then she went back up the path.

Now she had no repose. She longed to show her love for Nathan "in a thousand sweet ways"; she grudged the passing of a day which did not bring him to her. . . . Soon there would be many such days.

Nathan remained away, pleading work—the hundred things which must be done before one sails. She believed him. She could not do otherwise.

Her days were fatiguing, her nights brought but little sleep. One day Josey arrived; and that evening Nathan came with his guitar. He sang to her; he talked ardently; he told her he was going to take her letters with him when he went away. He was charming.

Only a week remained. Margaret felt incapable of any action. "The fact of an approaching separation presses on my mind and makes me unable to make the best use of the hours that remain. . . . Feeling keeps one from doing."

She sent him a book; she sent him a poem and asked him not to smile at it. "I am a little afraid of your smiles, *Liebster*." And she sent him some money she had collected for him from her friends.

He wrote and told her he was sad and she found happiness in the confession. He asked her to go sometimes on a beautiful evening to the cove where they had sat so often, to remain very quiet and call on him and he would come to her, defying space. He said he wanted to be certain that she was conscious of him occasionally.

Conscious of him! Would the time ever come when she was not conscious of him?

She sent him her pen with which she had written all his letters; she sent him a silver pencil and asked him to have his initials put on it. She said she had a book of Shelley's poems for him, but she wished to put that into his hands herself and point out to him some passages which she particularly liked.

May drizzled its way out and June came in with clouds. Mist hung over the harbor. Nathan was gone.

And now there came a succession of beautiful days. Margaret, believing in omens and the mystical significance of everyday events, found something ironic in this: "I do not think fate smiled upon us; how much cold and storm there was, how little warm, soft air!"

The roses came out and the "enchanting magnolia and oriental locust"; the fruit was red on the vines and all of nature full and lustrous. "But through all breathes to me a tone of sorrow, for I have lost my dear companion, the first I ever had who could feel every little side of life and beauty as exquisitely as myself."

Letters were poor consolation when the world was radiant and the heart so sad. Margaret spent a good deal of time in her room. She dreaded the daily trips into town, she shrank from entering her office because she knew there would be no smiling messenger boy awaiting her with a letter.

Her mother came to visit her. Her presence was comforting. Margaret took her for walks. Josey went with them, bounding along ahead. He was not an obedient pup and he seemed to have an aversion for water. Margaret, who had decided opinions about the salutariness of bathing, did not tolerate this aversion and called on some boys who were passing, to give him a ducking.

She avoided the places where she and Nathan had walked.

When her mother returned to Boston, Margaret prepared to face her first summer in a city. It was very hot. She came home exhausted and lay in a darkened room.

The first sharp sadness of separation was dulled a little by the number of things to be done. But in the evening, when the sun had gone and the moon had not yet risen, she experienced the anguish of utter loneliness. One evening Nathan suddenly came to her. She was in her room, the lamp was not yet lit. She lay looking at the moon making its way between the branches of the trees. Suddenly she was conscious of great happiness. "I lay in a sort of trance as on evenings when you used to sing to me." He was everywhere, completely filling the room with his extraordinary personality. . . . That night she slept.

Writing was difficult in the midsummer heat. She escaped as often as she could and went to stay with friends, the Springs, who had a delightful place called Eagleswood, a short way out of town. There was a small boy in the family, whom Margaret loved. Frequently when she went to her office she found a pink rose waiting for her, from him.

She wrote long letters to Nathan, telling him the many things which she had left unsaid when they were together; and she secured letters from influential persons and sent them to him. The memory of their "dissonances" now seemed superficial to her; they were "but tuning of the breast, to make the music better." She told him what was going on in the country: The great procession to pay honor to General Jackson who was dead; the movement which was astir against the annexation of Texas. And she told him some of the things that she was doing; she had written an appeal to the public to help released female convicts, and the public had responded generously.

Sometimes she had a presentiment that she might not see him again. She wrote, "We have been much to one another and should we never meet again in bodily presence, precious realities must ensue to both of us from the past."

The miles of space which stretched between them seemed to glorify him. All the unpleasant dissonances were gathered up and dropped into oblivion, and all that remained were happy memories of days under the trees with the birds singing overhead, of times without number when she lay and listened to his voice and watched his slender fingers draw music from the guitar....

She waited two months and then she heard from him. A beautiful letter. It spoke of their sacrifice at parting from each other, but trusted to the preciousness of their "spiritual connection, which will bear the test of absence and *various influences*." A noble letter, which called on all the gods to witness to its sincerity; a melodramatic letter: "Let me lie down and die rather than by my presence abet falsehood!" Afterwards came the requests: Would she secure for him a letter of recommendation from George Bancroft? Would she see that the travel articles he hoped to send from time to time, reached Mr. Greeley?

Margaret would not have asked a favor for herself of George Bancroft who was now Secretary of the Navy. Only a few days previously, the *Tribune,* which was the chief organ of the opposition party, had published a ludicrous story about him. Although Margaret had been a frequent guest at the Bancroft home, her relation with Mr. Bancroft was not one which made her feel free to ask favors. Furthermore, she knew that the Secretary of the Navy had plenty of more important things to occupy his attention just then. He was anxious for the annexation of Texas and was planning the establishment of a naval academy at Annapolis; he was in constant consultation with the Secretary of War as to the advisability of sending Zachary Taylor and his troops into the debatable land between Mexico and Texas.

For many years Bancroft and Margaret had been friendly enemies. Their first clash had taken place when Margaret at twenty-four took exception to his article in the *North American Review* on "Slavery in Rome." Both of them had advanced considerably since then. Margaret had organized "the most formidable party of literary iconoclasts yet brought together in America," had introduced Browning to the American public, had gained the reputation of being the best conversationalist of the age, had published a book which caused a commotion throughout the land and was literary critic of the leading newspaper of the day. Whatever may have been Bancroft's personal feeling toward her, there is little likelihood that he had anything but admiration for her intellectual gifts.

She would not have asked a favor for herself, but she asked the favor for Nathan. Within five days she received a gracious reply and the requested letter. This she sent off immediately, with the hope that it would not fail to reach Nathan. "If it should by any chance, Fate must have determined to leave you entirely to the impression made by your personal presence."

The letter reached its destination.

The heat was almost unbearable. Margaret had a hammock slung on the piazza and there she lay listening to the hiss and drone of insects and the rumble of far-off traffic. She did not go to the office so regularly now, but did her writing at home. It took Greeley some little time to accustom himself to this idea but he finally managed to persuade himself that the work was more important than the place of its production. He was pleased with the attention that Margaret's articles were attracting; many letters of approval and some of disapproval came to his desk. He liked the provocative touch; Margaret's articles abounded in such touches.

Nathan's first articles arrived. Margaret took charge of them, edited them, corrected them. They appeared in the *Tribune* under the heading, "Wayside Notes Abroad." Margaret kept six copies of each issue in which they appeared and sent them across the sea.

She experimented with Nathan in thought transference. "We shall see if you do not comply"—to some request—"without being asked in words."

August brought Emerson to visit her for a few days. His presence gave the house a serenity it had not had since her mother left. Mrs. Greeley had been ill; a gloom hung over the place. Emerson dispersed it; he was "full of free talk and in as serene beauty as ever."

William Henry Channing was living in New York now. His work took him much among the poor. Margaret often went with him to visit the sick and to encourage those who needed encouragement. Among such people she was her most loving; there no pretense was needed, no game was to be played. She looked on them as friends and talked with them as one friend talks to another....

And so the summer passed. The maple trees in the garden began to turn red, the air grew more crisp. A profound melancholy came to dwell at the Greeley house. Margaret was ill, she was discouraged; it seemed at times that she could not endure her loneliness any longer. She began to have regrets about her relation with Nathan; it seemed to her that they had wasted time, had played with living but had missed life. "I should have been so much more happy in real than in the ideal intercourse," she cried in a letter at the summer's close.

She did not hear from him for months, and when at length his letter came, she found it "cold and scanty." She wrote, "What I needed was to feel the warmth of your heart; it would have enlivened me at once."

She could not shut out doubtful questionings from her mind. She detected evasions in his tone; and he made excuses for not writing more warmly—travel was tiring, it dissipated one's energies.... She reminded him that she expected from him truthfulness above all things, and tried to tell herself that the coldness of his note was caused by disappointment in not receiving one from her when he expected it.

Again the fear of new attachments: "I know if you give yourself to other influences, it is not likely to be lightly or suddenly, for your nature is not light or shallow." She could not escape from the thought of these other influences; it pursued her to her desk, it met her when she took Josey for a walk, it stood waiting for her to wake from fretful sleep. She began to think of the unpleasant hours they had had, when he criticized her.... And she wrote, "Heaven alone has brought us near; no earthly circumstance favored it at all." Surely, surely then, if the gods desired the meeting, things must be well between them. With touching frailty she wrote, "You will love me as much, as long and as carefully as you can, will you not?"

He no longer spoke of their spiritual affinity; his letters were full of facts of his travel and of the articles he sent back—"such crude fare as was not agreeable to her delicate taste," which he had had a share in forming. Daily she grew more hungry and the line on each side of her mouth deepened....

Then unexpectedly came a gift from him, a book, Foscolo

on Petrarch. Once more she was happy and could reconcile herself to his absence. She wrote him joyously: Now that the summer had gone, she could accept his absence more philosophically. She gave him suggestions about his letters to the *Tribune*, "Mix more personal life in them...."

Then she told him of a long-awaited event which at last gave promise of happening. Her friends the Springs were going to Europe the following summer and had invited her to go as their guest. It would be too ironic if this, her greatest desire would be realized just as he was returning to America. She could not think that it would happen so... surely her angel would see that it would not happen so....

She awaited the next event; from it she would draw conclusions as to her angel's or her demon's ascendancy.... She received a cheerful letter from Eugene. His prospects were better than they had ever been, he said; he was able to be co-editor of a paper and a little later, part-proprietor.... He was in high fettle....

Margaret was exuberant. Her angel was looking after her; her confidence in God came back again.

XII
"SIGHT OF PROTEUS"

SHE SPENT OCTOBER in Massachusetts and had scarcely a moment to herself. Richard was rather difficult; he resented the fact that Margaret gave him so little of her time. His suit with the fair Anna was not prospering; he wanted to talk about it. Once he managed to steal Margaret away for an hour; they walked beside the river where the willows were beginning to look careworn. Richard talked and talked: He could not endure the suspense much longer; he had to know how things were; it was much better to know the worst than to be kept dangling in mid-air. . . .

The sun was blood-red in the West, the clouds were fire-laden. Margaret thought of other walks she had taken and of other conversations she had had. *Her* willow trees which were so exquisite when Nathan went away, were beginning to look careworn too. As she listened to Richard she thought, "Is his position very different from mine? Am I so sure that I am really loved?" She pushed the thought away from her, and gave all her ears to Richard. . . .

There was no letter awaiting her when she returned to New York. She plunged into her work, but every little while, an image rose up out of her subconsciousness and interrupted her. . . . She remembered something she had read of Goethe's mother: "When my son has a grief, he makes it into a poem," she had said. Margaret sighed. Should not the world ring with poetry?

She wandered through the garden which had a bedraggled look. The first frosts had hit the dahlias and they hung limp and lifeless as if they had suffered some disgrace. The willows, as they swayed their branches back and forth, had an idiotic look, the fruit trees had put up their shutters for the season.

Margaret was going to spend the winter in a boarding-house and rejoin the Greeleys in the spring. This meant packing, which was a bore; and it meant saying good-by to Pickie, which was much more than that. He was a beautiful child, was running about everywhere and babbling his first words.

One day she received a package from England. It was a copy of her book *Women in the Nineteenth Century*, which had just been published there in Clarke's Cabinet Library. She was much pleased. She wrote to Richard, "The republication will bring me no money, but it will be of aid to me here, as our dear country folks look anxiously for verdicts from the other side of the water." She was by no means blind to the little foibles of her fellowmen.

By Christmas she was established in a boarding-house in Warren Street. What a menagerie it was! She felt quite foreign in it. Although some of the inmates were amusing, and although some made great efforts to be friendly, none of them was of Margaret's essential world. There were business men who seemed to her more like machines than human beings. She found them wearisome. There were business women who made overtures to her. She respected them.

One thing she enjoyed about the place was its comfort and order. After the slapdash life in the Greeley household, this was restful. Occasionally she went to spend a day or two with Lydia Maria Child, who gave her frank criticisms of her books. When Mrs. Child saw an article of Margaret's which appealed especially to her, she always sent its author a gift of appreciation.

No word from Nathan for more than two months. The anniversary of their meeting went by, apparently forgotten by him. Margaret did not forget it.

Another month. And then a letter came from Rome; it was "full of soul and sweetness" and it brought a rose from Shelley's grave. When Margaret opened the envelope the rose fell out and lost itself, leaving only the dried leaves. Where it went Margaret could not imagine, but she never found it. The incident was significant to her, was disturbingly portentous.

She did not answer this letter for six weeks. She had moved from the Warren Street establishment and was living in "the prettiest, little room imaginable" in Amity Place. She had a fireplace in her room, and her curtains were airy and cheerful. Naturally she was much happier than in the stodgy boarding-house, and apparently was in high spirits. She went about a good deal, was much courted. . . .

She decided definitely to go to Europe with the Springs in August. This meant borrowing five hundred dollars from some one. But what of that? She would be able to repay it soon; Europe was rich in writers' raw materials.

Before August came, there was much to be done. She was to bring out her *Miscellanies;* her work with the *Tribune* must go on.

The constant worry of her family went on too. Ellen was increasingly unhappy, for Ellery was becoming more impossible to live with. He was irritable, he flew into rages, he seemed unable to control his temper. "He is driven by fate or his genius or both," Caroline Sturgis wrote to Margaret. Margaret was intolerant of this rack and tear of "genius." Genius was made the excuse for far too many weaknesses. Every individual had an obligation to himself and to those with whom he came into contact; it was to bring his passions under the control of his will. "Make the emotions the servant, not the master of the mind," was an axiom she kept constantly before her. The world too easily made allowances for lack of control, she thought, particularly that lack of control which had to do with the sex relation. To her it was unthinkable that Ellen should go on bearing children to a man with whom she lived in such disharmony. Such a state of affairs was contrary to the divine principle of human life. "Union is only possible to those who are units," she wrote in her *Woman in the Nineteenth Century*. Each day brought her added proof of the truth of this. But the world did not see it, or if it did, it closed its eyes and closed its lips, smugly content to be blind and to be silent because certain liberties were accorded to man and it was woman's lot to bear them in a spirit of spineless fortitude. This was Christianity, this was one of the principles of the church; not Christ's church, but the church of those who called themselves His followers.

"It is to the pagans we must turn to learn the secret of a happy and virtuous life," Margaret exclaimed many times.

She was intolerant of the half-truths preached by "awakened men." One of these was the stress which was laid on the necessity of keeping the body physically clean. All very well as far as it went. "Cold bathing and exercise will not suffice to keep a life pure without an *inward* baptism and noble, exhilarating employment for the thoughts and the passions." She feared for her country; she saw it marching down the years making a god of physical well-being and material prosperity, saw it striving to perfect the form of things, complacently oblivious of the actuating spirit which created form. She saw a race of physical giants with the souls of dwarfs; saw a race of full-grown men with the minds of children; and the most disconsolate thing she saw was a smug rejoicing in the general immaturity. And she cried, "It must not be! Human beings are not so constituted that they can live without expansion. If they do not get it in one way, they must in another, or perish."

March blustered in, whirled the dust about, brought the snowdrops up out of the ground, brought spears of tulips and tipped the lilac bushes with the first suggestion of leaves. Margaret left the prettiest room in the world and went back to live in the big, old house where Pickie's laughter now ran from the roof to the mysterious regions where preserves and pickles stood in colorful rows.

How the place brought memories back to her! The curving paths, the cherry tree outside her window, the spreading sycamore, the willow trees, which made her think of graceful ladies dancing a minuet, the cove made by the rocks ... everything throbbed with memories.

Margaret sat beside her window and looked out at the boats which seemed to balance on the tops of the waves. She could not bear to go down to the cove made by the rocks....

For seven weeks she waited for a letter; then, when the cherry tree was smothered in blossoms and when the lilacs made one giddy from their scent, she wrote, "Hast thou forgotten any of these things, hast thou ceased to cherish me, O Israel! Where are you? What are you doing? I have not heard from you for more than four months!"

There was commotion in the old house above the bay. Mrs. Greeley was going to take Pickie up to Vermont for the summer, was leaving soon. Margaret had taken a room in Brooklyn till the first of August, when she was to sail for England. She counted the weeks.... At the end of September she expected to be in Hamburg, where Nathan was.

What was to become of Josey, the Newfoundland pup, all summer? Mr. Greeley could not be responsible for him; Margaret could not take him to Brooklyn with her. She made this the excuse for writing another letter....

May came in with hot breaths, steamers arrived from the East, unloaded their cargoes, tossed their mail-bags into wagons. But none brought word from Nathan....

The air was charged with the murmurings of war. George Bancroft had given up his post as Secretary of the Navy to become War Secretary. Zachary Taylor had an army in the Southwest, where there had been peace for more than a hundred years. A raw-boned, square-jawed, uncouth product of the Middle West was going to Washington as the only Whig representative from Illinois. He did not appear to be ambitious about leadership, but he had decided opinions about slavery.

Interesting events. But closer actualities claimed Margaret—trivial things, but important to her. The new occupants of Greeley's house found Josey a nuisance; Greeley kept asking her what she intended to do with him. She wrote again and asked Nathan what his wishes were. And she told him that she would not write again unless she heard from him.

Two months more. Barely a fortnight before the date of her sailing, she received a letter from Nathan. It was a long-winded dissertation on himself; he had recently arrived in Hamburg, where he was the object of countless "dinners, salutations, parties and congratulations." ("Why congratulations?" Margaret thought, and read on.) More about his lionizing and the general rejoicing at his return.... Finally she read that his funds were exhausted.... A change of tone here. One would have thought that through Margaret's fault his funds were exhausted. He had relied on her to get his articles published, he said; he had no idea, when he planned his trip to the East, that she intended leaving New York; only through the sale of his articles could he finance that trip; he was sure that he could continue to make them increasingly interesting, as he intended to make explorations which were not often made. But now ... his plans were upset. He did not know whether his articles would still be welcome, when Margaret was not there to take charge of them; he did not know where to undertake the publication of a book of travels he was contemplating. Might not Mr. Greeley undertake it?

Regarding the disposition of Josey he wrote, "If he is too much trouble and if Mr. C. C. March cannot keep him for me and you know of no other person that will, just have him sold at auction or let him run loose away or what he may do. A kind Providence will have a care of him."

He closed his letter with a reference to his own essential righteousness and to the lack of understanding to which he was constantly subjected.

Not two weeks remained till Margaret had to leave for Boston. There were a thousand things to be done. Her headaches were continuous. "The sense of having a great deal to do seems to hurt my head and unfit me for doing it." But she did all that Nathan had asked her to do, and a few days before the first of August, she took the boat to Boston, to spend the remaining time with her family.

Her mother would have liked to keep her quiet, to soothe

her aching head and calm her overwrought nerves. But there were so many persons to see! There was Emerson, who was giving her letters to Carlyle and Tennyson. She already had one to Elizabeth Barrett through whom she hoped to meet Browning. There was President Everett of Harvard who had important letters for her; and there were many others.

She managed to see them all. July melted away and a blistering August came up out of the harbor. The *Cambria* stood waiting to set sail. The last good-bys were said, the last handkerchiefs fluttered. Margaret's lifelong desire was passing from imagination into something much more concrete.

PART III
FULFILLMENT

I

DELIGHT; DISILLUSIONMENT

Margaret hated the days at sea; the sudden relaxation made her lifeless, she could scarcely bear the bracing air and the brilliant sun; she hated the boisterous promenaders who boasted about the number of miles they walked each day. The smell of food made her sick. She longed for the sight of land. She spent most of the time in her cabin; the stewardess brought her orange juice and garrulous optimism. The *Cambria* was breaking all speed records, said the stewardess. Never had they made such time; she was sure they would be in Liverpool in ten days. The weather was perfect, she said; any one who complained of it tempted the Almighty.

When she could assure Margaret that they would be in Liverpool in two days, Margaret ventured out on deck. She was soon surrounded. Some of her friends were on board and there were others who knew her name and who now took the opportunity of knowing more. There were a few distinguished persons on board; they had titles and they were going home to England after service in the wilds of Canada. Margaret liked their voices.

One morning she looked out of her porthole and saw a gull

following the ship, then she saw another, then another. She dressed as quickly as she could and went on deck.

Ah, there it was! The first shadowy outline of land! Margaret knew how Columbus felt when he sighted a bit of seaweed tumbling about in the waves, and when the first faint darkening appeared above the line of the horizon. She sat for hours watching that shadowy outline. It took form—austere crags with breakers beating against them, then banks of green, finally gray knobs jutting up here and there, which were houses. A rapturous sight!

They disembarked and went to the Adelphi Hotel. It was midday and the sun was high. Carts cluttered over the cobbles of the narrow streets, strange North-country voices reached Margaret's ear. A jocular good-humor seemed to be everywhere; people were not as serious as in New England. In the hotel Margaret noted the difference in the men she saw—they had greater mental range than American men, were more widely read, more cosmopolitan, more courteous.

One of her first callers was Alexander Ireland, a liberal-minded man who had read and approved of the *Dial* when she was editor of it. He was public-spirited and he did not believe in intoxicating drinks, but found no difficulty in disposing of four or five cups of very strong tea. He talked of Emerson and said he hoped to be able to persuade him to come over on a lecture tour before the year was out.

They all went sight-seeing, the Springs and Margaret; they heard the hum of Manchester and walked the Roman walls of Chester. Margaret was enchanted with the place, and with the luxuriant green of the countryside. "It is as exquisite as I had hoped." She felt that there was a bond between man and nature in England which there was not at home; the mellow cordiality of the landscape was apparent in the people, who were hospitable in an easy, unruffled way, who accepted strangers at their face value and assumed that their motives were friendly. They had no affectations, for the simple reason that they did not need any; the great game of bluff is not an English occupation, nor was it eighty years ago....

In the canal-boat from Lancaster to Kendall were two men, one an Englishman, the other a German. The Englishman was charming, the German smirked. He tried to draw little Eddie Spring into conversation, and the result was ludicrous. Eddie was an intelligent child not accustomed to being patronized by those older than he. The German talked to him as if he were a simpleton. Margaret looked at him and thought of Goethe, his countryman. But Goethe was universal, she concluded, and could not be regarded as typical of any nation.

They passed a field of blue-bells. Up rose now and then a lordly campanula, up rose a clump of foxgloves. They slipped through a shadowy woods where they disturbed a whole community of rabbits who took to their heels and flew for cover as if there were no safety above ground. They went past cottages with flaming fuchsias in their gardens. Margaret made a note in her little book, "Must send directions for culture of fuchsias to Mother."

They went from Kendall to Ambleside through the beautiful lake country where Wordsworth lived. A friend had found lodgings for them in a stone cottage which looked out over the mountains, not far from Harriet Martineau's home, the Knoll. The district was alive with literary associations; just over there in Greta Hall in Keswick, Robert Southey had spent twenty years driving his pen hard to support his family and that of his brother-in-law Samuel Coleridge. De Quincy had lived at no great distance from him, but was now in Edinburgh. The widow of Dr. Arnold was a neighbor of Miss Martineau's and Rydal Mount, where Wordsworth sunned himself, was but a mile away.

They met interesting people—landed gentry, manufacturers, professors. A charming Scotch gentlewoman, seventy-six years old, animated and intelligent, was a revelation to Margaret. Margaret recognized in her a living, vibrant demonstration of what she meant when she wrote in an essay, "It is time indeed that men and women both should cease to grow old in any other way than as the tree does, full of grace and honor. The hair of the artist turns white but his eyes shine clearer than ever, and we feel that age brings him maturity and not decay. So would it be with all, were the springs of immortal refreshment but unsealed within the soul."

She had little patience with the increasing deification of youth in her own country. If this were to continue, it would mean a national intelligence hopelessly immature. Margaret wished her country to have its share in producing some of the elect of mankind. It had produced Emerson. "But it is yet a European babe; the soul that may shape its *mature* life scarce begins to know itself."

There were reasons for the preponderating indifference toward the cultivated life in America. Margaret realized this and made allowances.

She was surprised at the knowledge that Englishwomen had of politics, of literature, of art. They were at home in any conversation; they were familiar with Emerson's writings and had read Margaret's *Dial*.

Harriet Martineau had told them many things about the new republic which had made the pleasant British beverage an excuse for war. Margaret was eager to see Miss Martineau again. Indeed she was the chief reason for Margaret's lingering in the Lake District—she and Wordsworth, who lived a few miles from her.

Almost immediately they called on Miss Martineau. She was very cordial. Although she looked better than when Margaret had said good-by to her in Cambridge more than ten years before, she seemed to be in a highly nervous state, and her deafness had increased. They asked about Wordsworth who lived at Rydal Mount and learned a few of his quirks and foibles: He went for a walk every day, rain or shine, winter or summer. In the winter he wore a long cloak, a Scotch bonnet and green goggles. Usually a score of children ran along after him, coaxing him to cut ash switches out of the hedge for them. A curious combination of economy and generosity he was. If you dropped in for tea, you were likely not to have enough cream to put into it, and yet Wordsworth gave away all the milk the household did not use to cottagers perfectly well able to buy their own. If you dropped in for any other meal, you were greeted with, "You are very welcome to have a cup of tea with us, but if you want any meat you must pay for it."

Miss Martineau spoke sparingly of the Coleridges, who were a painful subject to her. There was young Hartley, the son of the poet, who had died from drink. De Quincy just managed to keep the wolf at a not altogether comfortable distance from the door. "When he lived at Keswick," said Miss Martineau, "he drank five or six wine-glasses of laudanum a night. Coleridge was to blame for that, of course, for de Quincy ran across him shortly after he came down from Oxford, and Coleridge was then drinking his tumblerful a day."

Miss Martineau prepared her for the meeting with Wordsworth—"He does all the talking and never knows the name of the person he is addressing. He talks mostly about his poems and he is pretty sure to take the visitor to see the terrace where he has composed so many."

Margaret understood very well how he might easily forget names. The older one became and the more absorbed in the general stream of life, the less important became small incidents; and a name was only a label, made only superficial distinctions between one person and another. What was important was the personality beneath the name.

She anticipated with great eagerness her meeting with Wordsworth. In her mind's eye she saw him dwelling in a somber, isolated place—in a stone cottage set upon a moor where at times the wind moaned and where tales were told of witches riding by on thunderclaps. A wild and melancholy beauty must surround him; there must be stately trees whose branches held phantoms of æolian harps; small, wind-blown clumps of shrubbery must raise their stunted forms above the hardy gold of gorse, the unyielding brown of bracken; untamed, romantic stretches must spread their mysterious scrolls before him when he looked out from the windows of his study.

The next afternoon she started out with the Springs to pay the momentous call. They passed Rydal Hall, the ancient seat of the Flemings. This promised well; it was a romantic place. They stopped for a few minutes before a small stone church, got out of the carriage and went in. Margaret loved old churches. All the persecutions of the early Christians, all the martyrdom of the saints came vividly before her as she wandered over the cold, stone flags, as she paused before the altar with its mystic symbols. She thought of the simplicity of the Great Teacher and of the complexity that subsequent interpreters had made of his teachings. For a moment she lost herself in a maze of parable and allegory. The sun came in through a blue and gold window and fell on a small brass tablet commemorating some one no longer on the earth. Margaret raised her eyes; she looked up at the gold and blue window; she worshiped the sun.

Silently she passed out of the little church, silently climbed into the carriage which was to take her to Wordsworth's home.

They came to a modest stone house set in a short distance from the road. Well trimmed trees surrounded it, a row of laurel bushes sloped down toward the terraces which ended in a bank of sycamore and cypress trees. Margaret stood looking at all this cultivated symmetry, at this carefully tended luxuriance of green, conscious of extreme disappointment. Where were her sweeping moors, her wind-blown clumps of shrubbery, where the weird and melancholy beauty which should surround William Wordsworth? A dozen places she had passed which were much more fitting for him than this place where he lived! She sighed. Slowly and with majestic grace she went in through the little gate and knocked on the door.

And now she is shaking hands with the splendid, old man in the shabby, black coat. His eyes have great kindness in them as they look at her. Almost immediately he speaks of his sister Dorothy, the tragic member of the household—his "better angel," his "dear companion," his counselor.

For nine years Dorothy's mind has been afflicted. She sits by herself in an upper room in the modest, stone house; she looks out upon the trim lawns and upon the gentle terraces, and in her fancy she is once again among the Cumberland hills and Coleridge is alive. Or she is walking with her brother across the Scottish moors.

Margaret is much moved by the old poet's love for Dorothy. He leads her to a table where Dorothy's picture stands. Tears come into Margaret's eyes. The old man sees them and begins reciting the poem he dedicated to his "dear companion" half a century ago. His voice is vibrant as he recites:

"Five years have passed; five summers with the length
Of five long winters!"

On and on he goes, through the whole solemn length of the poem. Sometimes his voice breaks a little, retreats into a high-pitched tremolo, sinks into a whisper. Then, moved by the memory revitalized by his immortal lines, he summons again the deep resonance, the pulsing passion:

"For thou art with me here upon the banks
Of this fair river; thou, my dearest friend,
My dear, dear friend, and in thy voice I catch
The language of my former heart, and read

My former pleasures in the shooting lights
Of thy wild eyes."

Listening to him, Margaret wonders what strange, mystical relation between brother and sister could bring forth such passionate words. And her mind goes to the only explanation which seems logical to her—that life in its manifold manifestations passes through a series of experiences varied and yet similar, and two souls that love can never lose each other. In its long journey, the human spirit meets its earthly complement many times; now she is wife, now sister.

The poet reaches the final lines. Calling forth all his strength, he recites them with sonorous grandeur, as if he would summon back those wandering wits, that rare intelligence, that lustrous mind. He does not see his sister as the old lady in the room upstairs, but as the joyous girl, resplendent in vitality, who gave her thoughts so freely to him when he first attempted to change the trend of poetry:

"... nor wilt thou then forget
That after wanderings, many years
Of absence, these steep woods and lofty cliffs,
And this green, pastoral landscape were to me
More dear, both for themselves and for thy sake."

He has finished. A hush is over the room. Only a curtain stirs, blown gently by the autumn breeze. Margaret holds out her hands to the old poet. He grasps them.

After a moment he says, "Now you must see my hollyhocks."

There was a long avenue of them. They stood up like two rows of sentries in their most colorful uniforms, waiting to be reviewed. Wordsworth was particularly proud of them and spent much time wandering the country trying to persuade the natives to grow more of them.

Margaret was sincere in her admiration. She had never before seen such luxury of color in any border of hollyhocks. With the poet she walked between the two rows of them and finally reached the famous terrace where so many of Wordsworth's poems had been written.

Suddenly the old poet began to talk politics. He spoke of the Corn Laws which were then agitating all of England; he spoke of Peel and Bright and Cobden. He spoke knowingly and with intelligence. This was a little surprising to Margaret, who knew that he refused to read any current news and was, therefore, not regarded as an authority on any subject of the day.

She was eager to know what the neighborhood thought of him and, the next day, made inquiries. She learned that he was considered a little queer; he went for a walk every day and on his walks declaimed his poetry with no small amount of fervor. She heard the story of the stone-cutter who, one day, heard a vigorous voice chanting. He looked up from his work and saw the old, familiar figure in the long cloak coming between the hedgerows. "Ald Wudsworth's brocken lowce ageean," he said to himself, and went on with his work.

"Do the people value him because he is a poet and universally celebrated?" Margaret asked.

"I think not, madam; I think they value him because he is so kind a neighbor."

Margaret was more at peace than she had been for months. She had shortened the distance between herself and Hamburg by three thousand miles; she was within a few hours of London, where a letter might be waiting for her. She was, moreover, in the most magnificent country she had ever been in— where old manor-houses told of chivalrous days and where moss-covered walls re-created history for her. Every stick and stone was history-laden, and the people all reflected the richness of an ancient civilization. She went through rooms where queens had lived and where courtiers had knelt seeking royal favor. There were times when she could not quite believe that her long dream had become a reality and she expected to find herself presently back in Nassau Street with Greeley in his shirtsleeves shouting orders....

She dined in a North country farmhouse with floors of stone flags and with cheerful china ranged on the open shelves of an old, carved cabinet. She saw rows and rows of cheeses set in a cool dairy and she ate oaten cakes, which made her think of Burns and Walter Scott.

Edinburgh gave Margaret de Quincy "for some hours." He was then seventy years old and his brain was not as retentive as it once had been. He kept harping on events which had happened long ago, when his faculties were more alert. He spoke well and he was polished and urbane.

There were other times when it did not seem in the least strange to her that she should be visiting places she had so often visited in imagination. She always had lived in stories which touched her deeply; and so, when she visited Carlisle where Mary Queen of Scots had stayed, the wonder was not so much her own being there as it was the beautiful Mary's not being there.

One day, the long looked-for letter from Nathan reached her. She opened it with nervousness and with some trepidation....

And this time she read what she had long feared to read— that he was engaged to be married. Unbelievable words! And yet, had she not known? She shut herself up in her room and drew the curtains. Why allow light to mock at her whose light had gone?

But moping only accentuated her grief, her humiliation; it was much better to remain active, to climb high mountains, to rattle along on the top of a coach. So they all started for Perth. The sun shone full on the meadows, a breeze stirred in the stiff heather on the moors. They visited all the obvious places—Drummond Castle where Queen Victoria occasionally went to stay, Kinfauns, the home of Lord Grey; they rambled through the "Lady of the Lake" country and stood on the shore of Loch Katrine.

A six-mile pass connects Loch Katrine with Loch Lomond. Margaret walked the distance and felt that she could have walked ten times as far, so exhilarating was the air. There was another reason; walking was an outlet for her feelings. What those feelings were may be easily imagined. She was proud, fiery, sensitive; she had responded to Nathan as to no other man: "You have touched my heart and thrilled it at the center." She had been led to think that he had similar feelings for her. True, he had talked of spiritual affinity and high brotherly devotion, but not until he began to fear that he had talked too much in another strain. He had sent her gifts accompanied with tender messages, had used a lover's language to her. He had accepted gifts from her and had called on her for help—of money, of influence, of a superior mentality. Margaret had refused him nothing, and when he had the effrontery to criticize her, she had accepted his criticism and had said that she would try to do better for his sake.

It is more than possible that Nathan saw how the wind was blowing long before he went abroad; it seems equally more than possible that he would have asked her to marry him, had she been more free from encumbrances. He appears to have been somewhat of an adventurer; he was self-centered. This is evident in his letters, it is even evident in Margaret's answers to his letters. He was probably very much disappointed when he learned the exact state of Margaret's finances and the number of her obligations.

That she was unable to see him clearly and completely was due to two things—her inexperience with life and her inability to think uncharitably of any one who had touched her so deeply. Her knowledge of human nature was gained from intercourse with persons as high-minded as herself. Her experience with Samuel Ward should have taught her a lesson, but it did not. The truth is that she was weary of being a sibyl, a high priestess, a seer; she wanted to come down from her pedestal and have the experience of being the human being that she felt she was; she longed to meet some one who could be to her what she had been to many. The intensity of her longing must be taken as her reason for believing so implicitly in Nathan. She could not conceive of any one making such a confidante of any one as he had made of her, unless there was a rare bond of sympathy between them. And she had gone on, making her deep desire the father of her thoughts, her great heart-hunger the begetter of her hopes....

And now, trudging along from Loch Katrine to Loch Lomond, she went over a thousand incidents and tried to think wherein she had caused herself to become the object of such unbearable humiliation. She remembered that the Greeleys had never liked Nathan; she recalled the letter she had received from him, in which he had cautioned her against certain hopes. The warmth flew into her face when she thought of that letter, and she felt glad that she had answered him as she had. She recalled other letters; and now saw them in a different light; she saw now that Nathan had been playing with her and that he was vain and shallow....

No ... she *would* not have such thoughts of him, no matter how much he made her suffer; she would not allow bitter thoughts to come.

She reached the shore of Loch Lomond, and saw her friends waiting to take her in the boat with them across to the little inn of Rowardennan which looked up to the towering heights of Ben Lomond.

The Scottish boatmen were sturdy fellows with great muscles showing through their shirts. One of them sang Gaelic songs—wild, plaintive melodies of love and tragedy. He sang a song of a girl whose lover had deserted her and married another. It had a hundred verses....

Would she ever forget? It seemed that she would not; for no sooner had she schooled herself to smile and chat than something came along and brought her grief's memory back to her. She supposed that it would always be so—that when she saw a flaming sunset or a bed starred over with blue myrtle flowers, or when she heard the little sucking sounds of water running under rocks—when she saw or heard a thousand different things, she would be reminded of Nathan. ... She sighed, as she watched the big Highlander become tearful over his song.

The evening was perfect. Margaret's room looked up toward the rugged peak of Ben Lomond, the highest point of that high country. The September shadows were growing faint between the trees, the mountains were climbing toward the sun. Of a sudden a bird called from somewhere—two plaintive, questioning notes. The sun sank.

All night Margaret was conscious of oppression, she had strange, tormenting dreams from which she woke suddenly with palpitating heart. She lay awake and looked out toward the mountain. The crisp breeze stirred the curtains, now and then a wild thing called from the woods. She woke late and saw a glowing day. "The day of all days for climbing the mountain," said every one who seemed to know about such things. Evidently all the world had thought so too, for a large party had arrived at sunup and engaged all the horses. This meant that the normal sleepers must go on foot.

II

COMPENSATION

Mountains are deceptive. Although it had seemed, the evening before, that Ben Lomond was only a stone's throw distant, it was in the bright sunlight—and in reality—much further; and the ascent was at least four miles long.

Mrs. Spring did not want to take the long walk, so it was decided that Margaret and Mr. Spring would climb the mountain alone. They started off bravely without a guide; they went at a good clip, but gradually slackened their speed that they might enjoy the surrounding beauty. It was not very long till they reached the mountain and began the long ascent, which, of necessity, was slow. While they rested, they looked about in wonderment at the rolling range of hills, green-shadowed with climbing trees. Ben Lomond, the giant of the community, seemed to keep a watchful eye on all the rest.

At length they reached the peak. Margaret stood transported. Miles and miles of purple heather, with many lakes glistening "like eyes that tell the secrets of the earth."

About four o'clock, before the sun's rays began to slant too much, they began the descent. Looking above them at the changing sky and around them at the darkening hills, they strayed from the narrow path. They did not discover this till Margaret's foot sank into the soft bed of a spring. But no matter; it would be simple enough to find their way back to the path, Mr. Spring said. Margaret had her doubts; these spongy places were likely to occur every few yards. On the regular path they were bridged over; at other places they might wander too wide and too deep for comfort if not actually for safety.

Mr. Spring went back up the mountain to look for the lost path. Margaret waited, with an eye on the quickly changing heavens, on the quickly darkening hills. Soon came Spring's voice saying he had found the path. Margaret answered and started in the direction of the sound. She walked for ten minutes then called to him. No answer. She called many times; her echo came back to her—a maniacal, mocking voice. She became alarmed, she glanced at the sun, which was now a fiery circle with a thin mist moving across its face.

Margaret decided that the best thing she could do was to try to find her way down alone. Doubtless she would meet Marcus at the foot of the mountain. She went cautiously to avoid secret springs. Wild things darted in front of her, strange birds went through the air leaving behind them strange, unhappy cries. She felt that the hills were closing their doors against her; she was remote and alien. . . .

At last she came to the foot of the range of hills. She hurried. And stepped on spongy earth and sank to her knees. With great difficulty she managed to scramble out; she sought firmer footing. It seemed as if all the springs of all the range of hills had met there and formed a great bog, which cut off all access to the road. Margaret climbed higher, tried another descent. The sun went down. A wind came over the hilltops and ran like a darting devil through all the trees. Quickly the sky changed from rose to amber, from amber to green, from green to sullen gray.

Margaret climbed and skirted and debouched. Twilight came with its somber shadows. She reached an open space and looked down. There was Loch Lomond and there was the inn, looking so much more comfortable than it really was. How Margaret longed for its open fires and for its steaming tea!

She was cold, her feet were wet, her skirts were wet. She had only a light shawl to put around her.

She looked longingly at the inn. If only she could jump from where she was into its friendly courtyard! If she could learn from the rooks that flew screaming over her head, and sail through the air across those trees, those treacherous springs, those cavernous pools! Between her and the inn stood another hill hemmed in on three sides by a watercourse. Perhaps the watercourse was not deep. She went cautiously down, catching at the heather-sprays, steadying herself as well as she could, unutterably weary. She reached the edge of the watercourse, clung to a sapling and leaned over. Dark depths going down to the middle of the earth. She picked up a stone and threw it into the water to get an idea of its depth. The stone made a long, churgling, hollow sound. Margaret did not dare to venture into the water.

She started back up the hill but soon sank down, completely exhausted. Night came on quickly, a mist blew over the hills. Margaret shivered. She got up and looked for the inn. She saw a pale light, no bigger than the prick of a dagger, gleaming afar off. She listened for the sound of human voices. She heard nothing but the ceaseless gurgle of the waterfall. She was terrorized. She realized that she would have to spend the night there. To think of keeping herself warm by walking was absurd; she might stumble into a torrent or sink into a bog. She knew that she must move about; to sit still with only her light shawl around her would be to invite pneumonia.

Very cautiously she began walking around in a small circle. The stars came out for a spell and hung high above the mist; but the mist thickened, and the stars disappeared. Margaret tried to think of heroes she had met in literature— of brave women in dangerous places, of legendary knights in enchanted forests. She thought of Nathan with a full-lipped fräulein under the harvest moon. She tried to summon those well-loved friends to whom she had often talked—Goethe and Novalis and Beethoven. She saw Nathan's pale face and melancholy eyes. She tried to recall familiar music—Hadyn or Mozart or a recitative from Verdi. She heard Nathan's voice telling her how noble she was....

After an eternity, a silvery radiance showed behind the mist. "There's the moon, and that means that it is two o'clock," Margaret thought. And she reckoned how long it would be before dawn. Now and then she summoned all her courage and called loudly, for she believed that a search party was somewhere in the thickness, looking for her. But she heard no answer but the same strange echo she had heard before....

All night the torrent sounded and the wind hissed and whistled; sometimes a grouse called from the heather and a rabbit squealed.... Then came the dawn, most mysterious hour of the twenty-four, when time seems to pause, to gather force perhaps to meet the day. Then day itself marching over the hills, but with no banners flying. Diffidently it came, like a troop of nuns in long, gray garments on their way to prayer.

Through the mist Margaret climbed the hill, scrambling over waterfalls and through bogs, her clothes, by this time, bedraggled and torn. A group of shepherds on their way up into the hills with their flocks, saw her stumbling toward them and ran forward. Seeing them, Margaret collapsed. They carried her down the hill and back to the inn, where her friends were frantic and exhausted from a night of waiting. Twenty men with dogs were out among the hills, looking for her.

There was great rejoicing at the inn. And there were anecdotes about the dangers of the hills—of lost children who had gone to gather heather; of lost grown-ups whose bodies were never found.... Margaret heard the tales in silence. She was wondering why her angel had allowed her to return in safety.

For she was safe. After three days she was active again and was able to thank the kind shepherds whom Mr. Spring was feasting in the barn in acknowledgment of their kindness. Margaret sat talking with them for an hour after the meal and for her entertainment they danced the Highland Fling and the Scottish Reel and told her legends about the wild country she now felt she knew quite well.

. . . .

They visited Glasgow which Margaret declared "more resembles an Inferno than any other city we have yet visited." Naturally they did not linger any longer than was necessary in the Inferno, but went on to Stirling and put up at the inn of the Scottish Chiefs. Then back to Edinburgh, which by contrast with Glasgow, seemed a Paradise.

During some part of this time Margaret managed to write to Nathan congratulating him on his engagement. It was not an easy letter to write; for she could not help feeling that she had been deceived.

And now autumn was come to the moors and the bracken was bronze in the sun; the stone walls were garlanded with russets and wines, the woods were aflame.... A drenching rain ushered the party into the soot of Newcastle. But it did not prevent Margaret from going down into a mine. "It was quite an odd sensation to be taken off one's feet and dropped down into darkness by the bucket."

The rain had run along before them, but when they reached York, its course had evidently finished. Out marched the sun, like an aggressive, old lady who is not going to have any more of this nonsense. And behold, a rainbow was looped over the cathedral.

A moving experience! To stand in the door of the cathedral and look at the rainbow, while music poured forth from within. Once more Margaret's problems were absorbed in the beauty which encompassed her.

They stopped at Sheffield. It was Saturday. Margaret went to see the men who tended the great furnaces. Pallid, anæmic-looking men, who seemed to have thrown all their vitality into the flaming maws. She saw them line up in the evening for their pay envelopes; and did not wonder that the doors of the gin palaces swung constantly back and forth.

After Sheffield, Warwick Castle was a panacea. It was "a real representative of English aristocracy in the days of its nobler life." Margaret felt that she was a fitting guest to wander through those lofty rooms, and to linger with the charming company whom Van Dyke had created for the walls. Here was the ideal life of her childhood; here the materialization of her youthful dreams—these tapestries, these stately stairways, these rooms so pregnant with memories. More than once she wondered whether all her dreams would be as fully realized. For always they contained the great love for whom she had longed for many years.

While she watched her fancies taking form before her, while she lingered in Stratford and worshiped in the room where Shakespeare was born, remembering, a little wistfully, that far-off Sabbath when first she opened the pages of *Romeo and Juliet;* while she strolled through the fields to Shottery and visualized Anne Hathaway leaning on a stile, waiting for a lover who was also a genius—a rather crotchety and quite elderly man in Chelsea, looking over some letters, reread one he had received some weeks before from Concord, Massachusetts.... "On August 1st, Margaret Fuller goes to England ... you must not fail to give a good and faithful interview to this wise, sincere, accomplished and most entertaining of women. I wish to bespeak Jane Carlyle's friendliest ear to one of the noblest of women."

The crotchety and quite elderly man put the letter down. " 'Most entertaining and most noble,' " he doubtless thought, with a mental grunt. "Emerson sounds half-infatuated. I s'pose the woman jabbers all the time ... these 'entertaining' women always do. All but Jane. She knows when to keep her tongue in her cheek." And Carlyle turned to other letters and thought no more of Margaret just then.

Meanwhile she drew nearer to London. And on a mellow October day arrived.

She found herself not in a city but in a world which a lifetime would not be long enough to spend in exploring. She felt that the figures in many of the novels she had read had come to life and were brushing past her in the streets. A vast, mysterious series of contradictions, this squalid, luxurious, ruffianly, fastidious, miserable, joyous, agonizing London!

It was the wrong time of the year, of course. Parliament was not in session and the sun did not shine. This meant that the "pomp and luxury" were not on parade. They were instead in country places, starting off in the crisp mornings to shoot partridges or pheasants or wild ducks; or riding out to capture a panting fox with terror in its eyes. A barbarous country and a paradox—for the most highly cultivated people were those who refused an animal a sporting chance.

In spite of these country attractions, in spite of fog and smoke and October lassitude, London was entrancing. Margaret felt that here she belonged. This great, sprawling, smoke-stained, friendly city was more comprehensible to her than her native Boston. She thought it strange that this was so; she had always felt a little critical of England. But the John Bull she had criticized was the churlish, overfed bourgeois, with his hands in his pockets and his insatiable thirst for beer. Now she saw the other types—"those noble, generous and sincere beings" of exquisite manners and leisurely charm, who knew how to dally delightfully through life and who possessed the art of profitable indolence. Margaret was enchanted with them.

She sent off a letter which Emerson had given her to Carlyle. Carlyle received it, read it through, then called his wife and showed it to her; for some of it was addressed to her.

Jane Carlyle, who had a sprightly tongue and could not forbear poking sly fun at her "dear Goody" now and then, chaffed him a bit, saying that she wondered if this brilliant American whom Emerson was recommending to them, was not going to trample on Lady Ashburton's toes. For some years, Carlyle had been devoted to Harriet Ashburton. Jane had allowed her jealousy to leak out, now and then, although she declared repeatedly that she was "singularly inaccessible to jealousy." Now a new female was appearing—Jane always referred to Lady Ashburton as a "female"—but this one was different. Jane knew this from her books. Any woman who felt and thought as Margaret Fuller gave evidence of feeling and thinking in her *Woman in the Nineteenth Century,* was not one who would deliberately set out to take another woman's husband away from her. She was no "masterly coquette," as was my Lady Ashburton.

Jane read Emerson's letter and noted carefully what he said: "She is full of all nobleness and with the generosity native to her mind and character, appears to me to be an exotic in New England, a foreigner from some more sultry and expansive climate."

And doubtless Jane puffed out her cheeks and made a comment like, "A pagan priestess then! It's a good thing Emerson's countrymen can't read this; it isn't exactly flattering to them."

She read on: "She is the earliest reader and lover of Goethe in this country...in short, she is a citizen of the world by quite special diploma."

"Whew!" thought Jane, "she'll think I'm nothing but a nincompoop. I imagine it would be well to let Carlyle do all the honors."

Her eye caught these words: "I wish you to see Margaret when you are in special good humor." She laughed, then caught sight of her own name...."And I entreat Jane Carlyle to abet and exalt and secure this satisfaction to me. ...In the next place I should be glad if you can easily manage to show her the faces of Tennyson and Browning. She has a sort of right to them both...because she has made their poetry widely known among our young people...."

Into Jane's mind flew the one word, "Bluestocking!" She read further: "And be it known to my friend Jane Carlyle

...that her visitor is an immense favorite in the parlor as well as in the library, in all good houses where she is known."

Jane's beautiful eyes twinkled at the reference to the *good* houses. That was so delightfully Bostonian! "That means that she doesn't go in for 'social insipidities,' doesn't it, Your Wisdom?" Jane asked. And went on to comment on the extravagance of Emerson's language, ending up with "She's a Yankee paragon; you'll have to be your wisest and your charmingest and not your most hortatory, Goody. For this woman can talk too."

And so, one day, the crotchety Scot put on his best tie and set off to captivate the exotic New Englander. He had taken Emerson's advice; had waited till he was in excellent humor.

III

THE CROTCHETY SCOT

THE MEETING was a happy one. Being in such excellent humor, Carlyle managed to conceal his intolerance of the "Heaven-on-earth, preached forth by all manner of advanced creatures" including Margaret herself, and talked of such subjects as were sure to be congenial to her: of Emerson and Concord and Bronson Alcott. Margaret was delighted with him, was "quite carried away with the rich flow of his discourse!" She expressed herself now and then, but soon such expression was impossible. Carlyle had launched forth in his most hortatory method; his deep Scotch voice rose and fell in cadenced sing-song, "so that each sentence was like the stanza of a native ballad."

He talked on and on; he seemed to forget all Jane's warnings, seemed to forget that he was making a polite call and not delivering a lecture. Margaret began to feel exhausted, moved slightly in her chair. There were many times when she would have liked to say something in reply to him, but what chance had she? From long habit she put in a word now and then, "enough to free my lungs," but her voice was as effective as an Æolian harp in a jazz band.

At last he got up to go. He invited Margaret and the Springs to spend that evening with him and Jane in Chelsea. Being all good soldiers, they accepted. Then off went the crotchety Scot to tell Jane what he thought of the American paragon:

She was a good soul, he said, enthusiastic and high-soaring; she had a sharp intellect too, but less of the Eastern exoticism than he expected to find. But what a strange vernacular she spoke! A funny, high-pitched twang which sounded very much out of place in London. He supposed that was what was meant by the Yankee brogue.

His good humor lasted; which is to say that his greeting to his guests was most cordial that evening, and his subsequent supply of anecdotes inexhaustible. Margaret and Jane became friends at once. Jane kept in the background and allowed "His Wisdom" to carry all the flags. She charmed Margaret by her grace, her intelligence and her "sweet sadness." She was a fragile little thing, of extreme sensitiveness and when winter came, referred to herself as "a little live bundle of flannel and dressing-gowns." She had learned not to break into her one-time "Jobisms" about her wretched health and her sleepless nights, and now sat serene and rather wistful in the shadow of Carlyle's philosophizing.

That night, he was more amusing than philosophical, told a hundred anecdotes about the Scotch peasantry and about men in high places. He said he knew a farmer who read Emerson's Essays regularly every Sunday. He was very witty and he was not afraid to laugh. Margaret afterwards wrote to Emerson, "Carlyle is worth a thousand of you for that; he is not ashamed to laugh when he is amused."

One bit of disappointing news he had for Margaret: He could not show her Tennyson or Browning or Landor. Browning had recently married Miss Barrett and the two of them had flown to Italy. Tennyson and Landor were, for the time, out of London.

There were, however, many others to see. Margaret began to be inundated with invitations. Her *Miscellanies* had been recently reviewed in the English press and her *Woman in the Nineteenth Century* was considered quite an achievement.

When she had an hour's leisure, Margaret used to stroll down Piccadilly and take a lumbering omnibus to the City. She loved the quiet of the Inner Temple; she loved the lawyers in their gowns and wigs and all the pompous merchants who took their beer and mutton at the Golden Cockerel or the Cheshire Cheese. She did not love the merchants as merchants but as the representation of the John Bull idea—the bourgeois John of aldermanic proportions. Often she wandered down to the Embankment and watched the barges moving slowly up and down the Thames. And she thought of the many courageous courtiers who had been rowed down to the Tower to have their heads cut off.

Kew Gardens was a fairyland to her, where lived "the great-grandfather of all the cactuses," a solemn and superior old prickly gentleman said to have lived at least a thousand years. Her eyes were dazzled by the flaming green; even in October the trees were luxuriant.

On the day she went to Hampton Court it rained, making her most precious memory *not* the stately ceilings, the tapestried walls or the historic beds and couches whereon royalty had dallied with royalty, but a spreading yew-tree which provided her with shelter!

She thought constantly of the time when she would return to London for some months. It was like sacrilege to hurry through things so—to take a peep into the British Museum, for example, and dismiss it after a visit of one day spent in the Greek and the Egyptian rooms. There was so much to be done, there were so many things to be seen! "I am bewildered by the riches of existence," she cried. "O were life but longer and my strength greater!"

One evening the Carlyles gave a dinner party for her. Only two of the guests made distinct impressions on her. One was a "witty, French, flippant sort of man, author of a *History of Philosophy* and now writing a *Life of Goethe,* a task for which he must be as unfit as irreligion and sparkling shallowness can make him." He, however, had his points; he told stories admirably and he was able to interrupt Carlyle, who, as ill-luck had it, was in his most tiresome mood— acrid and pessimistic, fault-finding to a degree, cynical and altogether insufferable. This witty fop who was able to break in on his host's maledictions, was George Henry Lewes, who, some time later, was to make literary history by setting up an establishment with George Eliot. Indeed, these two had not yet met; and the person who was to become known to the world as George Eliot was still Mary Ann Evans, an inexperienced country girl from Foleskill, an ardent, religious, wondering young woman with radical opinions on a great many subjects. She had recently translated Strauss' *Leben Jesu* but had attempted nothing really creative. She was twenty-seven years old.

Lewes was decidedly a dandy; and the ease with which he tossed off a compliment made him appear shallow to earnest-minded Margaret whose slight experience with gallantry had had such unfortunate results.

The other guest was of quite a different *genre*. He was Mazzini, "one of those noble refugees," who had been obliged to fly from Italy when he began to circulate his republican convictions. He was teaching in London in a school for poor Italian boys. Margaret was well acquainted with the work he had started in his own country, knew that he had been unable to publish any of his writings there, and that he had mastered both French and English sufficiently to use as mediums of written expression. The *People's Journal* was very friendly toward him and had published his sketches of Italian martyrs. To Margaret this sallow, melancholy man was a prophet. "He is not only one of the heroic, the courageous and the faithful...he is also one of the wise.... He is one who can live fervently but steadily, gently, every day, every hour, as well as on great occasions."

Sitting there at Carlyle's table, calm and silent in all the acrimonious rumble, Mazzini made Margaret feel that one of the saints had descended from his niche to show the company that mankind might still be divine. She burned with the desire to help him in his work. What cause could be more noble than the freeing of a shackled people? (Carlyle kept haranguing about the idiocy of the New-Era crowd and their treacly texts!) Margaret tried not to hear him but thought of Italy, oppressed by foreign and domestic tyranny; of this quiet, forceful man, who had given up his dearest wish—to write an exhaustive history of religion—and had pledged himself before God to liberate his country and unite it under a republican form of government. (Now Carlyle was off on a defense of might; if people would not behave, put collars round their necks; set them to some good, manual work, with a Titan for a boss; don't let them have time to spread abroad their "rose-water imbecilities.") Margaret glanced at Mazzini and thought of the days he had spent in prison at Savona. "But I could see the sea and the sky," he had said, "and every day a green-finch sang outside my bars." Those prison days he considered very profitable; they had strengthened his resolve and had given him the opportunity for meditation. Then he went to France and began to write his fiery documents, urging his people to bestir themselves, to throw off the yoke of tyranny; he issued a Manifesto of Young Italy and had the satisfaction of seeing its principles put into practice: Numerous organizations were formed at Leghorn, at Genoa, at many other places.... Very soon Mazzini was invited to leave France. He went to Switzerland....

In Genoa his mother watched and prayed. She knew that it was from her that the youth had inherited his radical ideas.... Youth! He was already twenty-seven. Five years later he arrived in London and began studying English. He was very poor; he was lonely; but in less than a year he was writing articles in English and was selling them to the *Westminster Review,* to the *British and Foreign Review,* to the *Monthly Chronicle.* He was closely watched. The British lion sat on his haunches, waiting to spring. The Home Secretary, Sir James Graham, thought it would be well to know what was passing between Mazzini and his continental associates, so he ordered all his letters to be opened and communicated their contents to the Neapolitan government. The most dramatic consequence of this interference had been the arrest and execution of the brothers Bandiers, who were Austrian subjects and not Italian, and who had been planning an expedition against Naples. What a flutter there was in the House of Commons! What debates about Mazzini! They proved to be as amiable time-killers as anything the walls of St. Stephen's had heard for a long time, and on they went.

Every day Carlyle read of them, and every day, growled a little more loudly at the stupidity of the asses who wrote M.P. after their names. At length he wrote to the *Times:* "I have had the honor to know Mr. Mazzini for a series of years and whatever I may think of his practical insight and skill in worldly affairs, I can with great freedom testify that he, if I have ever seen one such, is a man of genius and virtue, one of those rare men ... who are worthy to be called martyr souls, who in silence, piously in their daily life, practice what is meant by that."

That letter settled the debates about Mazzini, and the

yawning M.P.'s had to find some other question to nod and to debate over.

Of all these things Margaret thought that night at Carlyle's dinner-table, with Jane sitting silent and detached at one end of the board and Carlyle rumbling away at the other, like the great waterfall on the slope of Ben Lomond. For two whole hours he harangued the poets: Tennyson scribbled in verse simply because his schoolmasters had taught him that to be a poet was a great thing; Burns somehow had been thwarted from following a manly course behind the plow; not even Shakespeare had had the sense to see how much better it would have been to write in straight prose. And so on and so on. Every little while, Carlyle shot his chin out in a malicious way, to emphasize his words; constantly there was an unholy gleam in his eyes.

The worst of it was that the only person who seemed able to break in on his tirade was the one who had nothing to add to the conversation but smart flippancies. Jane had long since given up trying. It was extremely irritating to have to endure such an unending harangue. Margaret sat up stiffly and did her best to listen politely. Her mind was seething. What a chance for talk! What an opportunity to speak of things which waited to be spoken! And what a waste to have the talk take such a turn! To have Carlyle spend all this time declaiming his pet aversions! How she longed to rise in her majestic way, which she knew was so effective, to silence him with a caustic subtlety, to point out to him that he should not clutter the conversation with damning irrelevancies when there were so many important questions to be discussed.

She glanced at the pale, quiet man with the face of a seer. He returned her look. What understanding lay back of those fiery, shadowed eyes! What capacity for suffering, what determination, what courage! She said his name over to herself. "Mazzini!" She could scarcely believe that she had met him, that he was sitting at the table with her.

She grew desperate. Was there no one who could stop the torrent of Carlyle's reproaches? She put on all her armor and marched against him. Her strength was nothing compared with his; her voice was as the dripping of occasional rain into a quiet pool. Carlyle shouted; he boomed, he bellowed. She realized that he was too much for her; she retreated.

The harangue ended at last; at last the company rose from their cramped positions. But there was still no chance to speak with Mazzini, for Jane Carlyle was piloting the ladies up to the drawing-room. Foolish convention! Why could they not all go to the drawing-room? Why these distinctions in sex when every one was interested in the same things?

But *n'importe!* She would have an opportunity to speak to Jane, for whom she felt great tenderness—and great sympathy. There were sad depths in Jane's beautiful eyes and there was about her a sense of frustration, a consciousness of unfulfillment. "I wonder if she does not sometimes resent Carlyle's patronizing 'bonny, little woman' and 'good, little Jeannie'?" Margaret thought. "For she is very sensitive."

She talked with Jane; and discovered in her keen imagination and quick wit. When Jane spoke of dull, homely things, she had a way of illuminating them by sly, quick flashes. Housekeeping was the "universal doom of women"; housecleaning was the season when "the tables and chairs have convulsions and stand with their legs in the air." Margaret was convinced that there was a fund of ability in Jane Carlyle. She suspected that had Jane married a more ordinary man, she might have become as interesting an interpreter of the small details of life as her celebrated namesake, who drew such nice distinctions between sense and sensibility.

Jane gossiped pleasantly about the *haut monde*. It was a pity Margaret could not see London at its gayest. "You should be here in the early summer, when the great beauties of the court show themselves in the park on sunny days and the governing body assembles daily on the terrace beside the Thames, to eat strawberries and cream. I assure you, it is something to see the vanquisher of Napoleon at his tea! And it is amusing to see the way Gladstone glares at the dandified Disraeli when they happen to pass each other. Disraeli is more subdued in his dress than he once was, but he still insists on letting that lock of hair dangle over his forehead and never will he give up his foppish *boutonnière.*"

Jane was so entertaining that the time passed very quickly. It seemed but a few moments till Margaret heard the voices of the men on the stairs. And the next thing she realized was that Mazzini was in the room, was standing before her.

They sat down together apart from the other guests. Margaret asked him if he thought soon of returning to Italy. Mazzini shrugged. He did not know; one never knew one's movements. A sudden change in the papal dispensation might give a favorable turn to things, but how was one to know? One just went on quietly with one's work, one prayed for guidance and one waited. . . .

Margaret told him that she intended going to Italy in a few weeks. A month or two in Paris, then Italy which she felt that she would love, as if it were her own country.

Mazzini smiled. He would tell her some names, he said. Friends of his, and of the revolutionary party. She thanked him, and he answered simply, "One knows when one meets a friend."

Other guests were leaving. Mazzini rose. "I think it is time to go."

Margaret rose too and held out her hand. "You will come to see me before I leave London, perhaps?"

"Indeed I will."

She gave him her address.

And she went back to the little, narrow street where she and the Springs had found lodgings, feeling that new vistas were opening to her, that the future held possibilities and opportunities such as she had not imagined.

Mazzini called to see her very soon. He talked of his hopes for a united Italy. His eyes burned with the zeal of the prophet, his voice throbbed. Margaret was afire to help him in his work. She was so excited when he left that she could not remain still. She walked up and down her room and had to be reminded of her next engagement.

He called several times. She was more stimulated than she had ever been. She liked him better than any one she had ever met. "He is a beauteous and pure music." She longed to face tribulation for him, to put herself in dangerous places; she longed to suffer for the cause which meant more to him than his life. All her old ardor came back to her; she was again the fiery visionary of her youthful days; she was a heroine, a leader.

The last time he called, the Carlyles came. This was unfortunate. Carlyle immediately showed his pique at finding there some one who obviously had made a much deeper impression on Margaret than had he. At first he sulked, then he started off on one of his tirades—this time about the "rosewater imbecilities" of the reformers. He was in a hateful mood. Margaret thought how strange it was that great men are often so small in their personal lives. And she wondered if a man was really great when he allowed himself to become so petty on occasion. She wondered how many of the world's great there were who were at times small. One she knew was not. That was Mazzini.

She carried things off as well as she could, and was infinitely relieved when poor Jane rose to go.

On the day on which she left London, Margaret received a letter from Hamburg. It was Nathan's reply to her letter of congratulation.

IV

PHANTASMAGORIA

NATHAN'S LETTER was stilted. He wished to acknowledge her congratulations, but he had to admit that he had detected irritation in her tone. The rest of the letter was a defense of himself and a self-righteous declaration of his principles. He realized that from the beginning of their relation, he had been misunderstood. This had always caused him pain.

In reply to Margaret's request that he send back her letters to her, he wrote: "My love and regard for you is and was too sincere, earnest and holy as to change with any new ties or external events ... and to permit me to part with things so dear, so suddenly. Let me entreat you to let the spiritual offspring of our friendship remain in the home they were born to and intended for, until on our return to New York, we can talk the matter over more fully and fairly. In the meantime, let me assure you, they enjoy the sacredness and privacy of their birth uninterrupted and uninterfered with from any foreign alliance or relationship, and that at our meeting there, I shall do nothing but what is right, manly and honorable." Then he told her of the deep admiration he still had for her "great, superior and well-stored mind," the true regard he felt for "the integrity, profundity and holiness of your character and for the many womanly virtues and sentiments of your capacious heart and true love for the purity of your soul, from which noble source I have drawn many deep inspirations."

Margaret discounted the exaggerated praise and wrote immediately, asking again for her letters. She no longer trusted the melancholy Jew; she realized that a man who could not be trusted in word could not be trusted in act.

Those letters might prove very tempting, one day, when he found himself short of cash. She was much disturbed, although no one would have guessed the fact. As she drew further and further away from London her depression increased, and did not lift until the boat-train arrived in Paris. Hurry and confusion and a sense of perpetual holidaying! Suddenly Margaret thought, "Here is where the great Rachel is. I can see her to-night if I wish. And here George Sand lives. And Béranger and Pierre Leroux and Dumas and Leverrier!" And then her thoughts became absorbed in the shrill gabbling of porters, the hoarse gruntings of cabbies, the snapping of whips, the clattering of wheels and the whole animated phantasmagoria which is Paris.

Margaret realized that the first thing for her to do was to learn to speak French. Reading French books at home was one thing, but speaking French in Paris was quite another. And the French people spoke at such a rate! It seemed as if she would never understand them. But she applied herself; and she listened with all her ears. Very soon she found a teacher to whom she went every day.

Paris charged Margaret. "Paris the Wonder-full," she exclaimed—"Paris, the Wonder-full, where ignorance ceases to be a pain, because here we find daily such means to lessen it." The gay crowds, the laughter, the charming manners—all these atoned for the atrocious climate with which Paris greets the visitor in winter. "The Frenchmen can cheat you pleasantly," Margaret exclaimed after a shopping tour.

There were those in Paris whom Margaret desired passionately to meet. One of them was Lammenais, the apostle of democracy, who, for his convictions, had suffered poverty and imprisonment. He was sixty-four years old and had recently been chosen President of the Société de la Solidarité Républicaine, that body of ardent citizens which in less than a fortnight after organizing, had rolled the ball of its membership up to half a million souls.

Another idol of the people whom she wished very much to meet, was Béranger, the poet. This meeting, she realized, would not be easy. Béranger was getting on in years and had to conserve his strength. He never appeared at public gatherings where greatness occasionally suns itself; he seldom received any one in his home.

Margaret had a letter to Lammenais; to Béranger she had no entrée.

She applied herself to the study of French so that she would acquit herself creditably when the meeting with Lammenais took place. She was an eager student; and she loitered in public places where she would hear cultivated persons talking together. She must not commit atrocities on the delicate French tongue, as certain Englishwomen whom she met, made a habit of doing.

At last she felt that she was ready to present her letter to Lammenais.

"I found him in a little study; his secretary was writing in a larger room through which I passed. With him was a somewhat citizen-looking but vivacious, elderly man, whom I was at first sorry to see, having wished for half an hour's undisturbed visit to the apostle of democracy. But how quickly were those feelings dispersed by joy when he named to me the great national lyrist of France, the unequaled Béranger! I was very happy in that little study, in presence of these two men, whose influence has been so great, so real."

They were a contrast, those two apostles. Lammenais was pale and delicate-looking and had mystical fires in his eyes. Béranger, the poet, was bright, vivacious, scintillating, and had the mien of a bon viveur. His conversation was varied, was now serious, now gay. Lammenais was always serious.

On account of her too recent knowledge of conversational French, Margaret felt hampered. She found herself *thinking* in English, found herself translating what the two Frenchmen said, then thinking her responses and translating them. A tedious process and an unsatisfactory one.

She left them feeling that things had not gone well, and she was more than a little piqued with the idea that she had not acquitted herself with her usual distinction. This thought bothered her, made her feel that she had trespassed on Lammenais' time. She felt that she was in his debt. She wrote him a little note and enclosed it with two of her books, which she sent to him.

Dumas was having trouble with his editors. He had agreed to contribute certain articles to their periodicals and, as frequently happens, when talent is tied to time, he had failed to carry out the agreement. He was haled into court. The news spread that he was to defend himself. This was news indeed. All of Paris decided to go and hear him.

Margaret was one of the most interested. At an early hour on the morning of the trial, she set out alone, in order that she might not be disappointed in getting a place in the court of justice.

But every one else was determined not to be disappointed too. If their determination did not suppress Margaret's, their energy did. They had risen long before the milk carts rattled over the cobbles, had breakfasted before the sun was well up over the roofs, and had left home at unaccustomed hours. When Margaret arrived, every place was taken. She went up one stairway, she came down another; she waited in draughty corridors, she expostulated with a regiment of gendarmes. No use. The gendarmes shrugged helplessly, "It is a great misfortune, madame, but we can do nothing. All of Paris would like to be in that room. You can see that it is already full, so what will you?"

What would she, indeed? Try to find consolation in the Louvre, and trust to her angel to manage things better when she went to hear Monsieur Guizot make his speech on the Montpensier marriage. This alliance of Louis Philippe's son with the fourteen-year-old sister of the Queen of Spain had been a blow to the Minister's carefully nurtured *Entente Cordiale*. Margaret was eager to hear Guizot express himself about it.

But her angel managed things no better that time than when Dumas defended himself. And Margaret had to content herself with reading the speech afterwards in a newspaper.

One day she received Nathan's reply to her second request for her letters. He still temporized; when they met the matter would be "fairly and fully bespoken. But should we not meet again, I now promise and shall will that in case of death of either of us, *they shall remain unopened and unread and thus be burned by fire,* excepting only you should . . . *appoint some one to receive them for you.*"

He mentioned his letters to her—a caustic touch here: "Though they, from very obvious reasons, seem to have lost some of their original value for you, are dear as ever to me and *to a married man* perhaps *not quite unimportant.*"

Unlike Margaret, however, he had the fullest confidence in her honor. But . . . "should I herein be disappointed, I know they were given in truth and holiness and no action on your part could profane their spirit."

Margaret had allowed her pique to show itself in her last letter to him. This was unfortunate; it gave him an opportunity to reply caustically and to clothe himself anew in self-righteousness: "To that interesting portion of your letter where you say 'Mr. Nathan, you have deceived me,' I have to say 'Keep cool!' I reject with disdain the reproach that I have deceived you. I do not feel deceived in you, because I do not feel deceived in myself and in what is godly within me."

How he berated her for having destroyed one of his letters! "I call it a want of judgment and experience of life, of which want you have of late alas! proved yourself too full."

This undoubtedly was true—a fact which did not make it any easier for Margaret to accept. She was consumed with humiliation. How could she possibly have allowed herself to make so many wrong inferences about Nathan?

She read on: "When I shall have cleared from your weak and inexperienced eye the ghastly visions that falsehood, desperation, malice and treachery have raised before you, your innocent heart will make atonement for the chills, contempt and dismay you now have tried to heap upon me. Yes, Miss Fuller, *you have judged me without a hearing, you have condemned me and insulted me, trampled upon and wounded me, nay, but for the consciousness of my innocence,* would have *destroyed me!* Still, I feel you have enough of courage and of good in you to stand the truth, therefore let me tell you that within me there lies a warmer feeling and word and that only not to be obtrusive, I use as you do, the cold name and say 'Miss Fuller!' Although you seem to wish a cessation of intercourse and which heavenly sentiment you may release at your earliest pleasure, I might as well bid my heart to cease beating as to cease feeling for you a tender regard and friendship...."

Margaret tried to forget him. When she found her mind dwelling on him, she thought quickly of something else. But those letters of hers she could not forget; those naïve, impassioned transcripts of her love and of her faith in him. Why did he hesitate to send them to her? Could it be possible that he wished to make use of them in some way? But no, she must not think such things; they were unworthy of the love that she had felt for him. And had she not his word that they would remain unopened and unread—and be burned unless she appointed some one to receive them?

Yes, she had his word. But for some reason, this word was not as reassuring to her as it should have been. She looked again at his last letter. The promise was made, "in case of the death of either of us." But they might live for many years. Was he then to be the custodian of them for all these years? And for what reason?

His obstinacy angered her. There were times when she felt that she must demand the letters from him, when she must consult a lawyer who would relieve her of the unpleasant details. Her pride restrained her from resorting to such measure. Her pride was suffering grievously. But her vision was clearer than it had been. Now she saw Nathan as a vain, shallow egoist, and not an entirely scrupulous one. She was obliged to accept this idea of his lack of scrupulousness; she was pained and angered and humiliated. But she held her head high, as always; she walked with her majestic gait; she laughed, she chatted, she entertained.

When the little Spanish Infanta who had married Louis Philippe's son, was presented at court, Margaret received an invitation to be present. From the gallery she looked down through her gold lorgnette and thought of the childishness and the charm of such occasions. Her eye delighted while her mind was tolerant. She was at heart a republican, she was on the surface a snob.

The new duchess went around on the arm of the queen and gave every evidence of enjoying her party. She was only fourteen but she looked twenty. Her enthusiasm was the enthusiasm of a sheltered girl of fourteen, and not of a sophisticated young woman of twenty. She looked infinitely capable of taking care of herself. Looking at her, Margaret visualized her life in the royal household, and found herself sighing as she thought, "I fancy all her vivacity, all her young life will soon be drained out of her under the routine and constant drill of her new life."

Then off she went into a maze of speculation as to what constitutes a really royal life....

There came the great ball at the Tuileries. A magnificent spectacle, the most magnificent that Margaret had ever seen. Surely those women who so gracefully displayed their charms, were the most beautiful in the world! Surely there were no others with such dignified vivacity, such exquisite taste in clothes, such *savoir faire!* Even the ugly women among them had their charms, for they understood the art of emphasizing their best features, and their vivacity and *savoir faire* equaled the others.

Leverrier the astronomer was at the ball, "looking as if he had lost, not found his planet." It was not long since he had discovered Neptune and he was now enduring the consequent *réclame*. He attended the royal ball because an invitation to such a function is a command. Margaret thought he looked bored and ill at ease, as if he found it difficult "to exchange the music of the spheres for the music of fiddles."

She thought that she would like to hear him lecture at the Sorbonne, where he would be more attuned to his surroundings. Accordingly, one day, she set out with Marcus Spring, to hear him. At the entrance to the inner temple, they were stopped by an old guardian of the portal, who announced that Monsieur might enter if he wished, but Madame must remain outside.

Margaret the feminist was up in arms. What barbarism! Did they think that women were of no more importance than little dogs, that they were to be left on the mat outside the door? The ancient shrugged. "What will you, Madame? It is the rule."

It was vain to argue. Margaret was obliged to capitulate. The caustic comments she made about the stupid rule were but little compensation for her disappointment.

V

"LUCREZIA FLORIANI"

MARGARET WAS EAGER TO MEET GEORGE SAND, but Sand continued to dawdle away in the country, where she was trying to plan a suitable marriage for her daughter Solange, who was somewhat of a problem. Chopin was back in Paris and the gossips were busy prophesying the end of his alliance with the novelist. "What will you?" said the gossips. "They have been together for eight years; that is a long time for a genius to be faithful to one lover." And they mentioned Sandeau and Pagello, Merimée and Musset; and Sand's latest discovery, Eugène Lambert, the young artist, who had gone to Nohant during the last summer, when Chopin was coughing and irritable and altogether extremely difficult. Lambert was invited for a month but he was still at Nohant. "No wonder Madame remains in the country," said the gossips. "She hates cities anyway, and used to return to Paris only to please her Chip-Chop."

Meanwhile Margaret waited. She had read Sand's last novel *Lucrezia Floriani* which was rumored to be the story of her liason with Chopin. And she recalled what Liszt had said about Madame some years before: "George Sand catches her butterfly and tames it in her cage by feeding it on flowers and nectar—this is the love period. Then she sticks her pin into it when it struggles—that is the congé, and it always comes from her. Afterwards, she vivisects it, stuffs it and adds it to her collection of heroes for novels." Naturally, Liszt knew of what he spoke.

Shortly after the publication of *Lucrezia Floriani,* Heine wrote, "Madame Sand has treated my friend Chopin outrageously in a divinely written novel."

Winter came on, but it did not bring back the mistress of Nohant. Paris gloomed under sunless skies, chill winds cut around corners. But for Margaret there was the Opera and there was Rachel, and there were a hundred museums where one could forget the mud and the mist. The French crowds were always gay, despite the weather, were always "full of quick turns and drolleries." It was amusing to watch them in the cafés, in the shops, in the theaters.

Early in February came the announcement of the engagement of Sand's daughter to Fernand de Preauli. There came also word that the novelist was about to return to Paris to purchase the trousseau. Margaret scanned the papers for the next announcement. At last it came: Madame Sand and her family were in Paris for the carnival; once more the famous café-au-lait salon and the famous green reception-room were to receive the intelligentsia of France.

The next day Margaret wrote a letter to Sand telling her who she was and asking her if she might call. Then she waited. She waited for three days, for five days, for a week. No reply. Determined not to leave Paris without seeing the novelist, she decided that the only thing to do was make the call uninvited. She set out, more excited than she had been for a long time. She was by no means sure that she would be received, for she knew that so famous a person as George Sand must be constantly sought by the merely curious....

She knocked at the handsome oak door; it was opened by a little servant in a picturesque peasant costume. Margaret told her her name. The servant disappeared, leaving Margaret in the anteroom.

In a moment she was back. "Madame says she does not know you."

Could she retreat now, knowing that the great Sand was only a few feet distant from her? Bravely she persisted, "Ask her if she has not received a letter from me."

At that moment the door from the anteroom opened and Margaret saw a large, dark, exotic-looking woman in a purple silk dress with a black lace shawl over her shoulders. Her dark hair which was beautifully coiffed, seemed to reflect some of the purple lights from her dress; it shone with these lights. Her eyes were deep and searching. They met Margaret's eyes and they saw that she was not one of the merely curious. Madame held out her hand—an absurdly small, delicate hand for so large and so masculine a woman—

"C'est vous," she said simply and led the way into her study.

Margaret stayed for several hours. Although she could not express herself as well in French as in her own language, although she felt many times that there were thoughts "struggling in vain for utterance," she managed to make herself understood. Sand talked as she wrote—with vivacity and with a touch of the picturesque, and often with an undertone of deep feeling. She was frequently epigrammatical. They talked of abstract things and Margaret saw how much hampered the novelist was by some of her own weaknesses, how, for example, she was lacking in the freedom of those who have put passion aside or have transmuted it into their created work. Sand was now forty-two, and was rich and ardent and intense. Margaret felt that had she found a man of large enough nature, she would not have gone from lover to lover seeking the one being who could satisfy all the variations of her complex nature. She left her feeling for her a greater love than she had ever felt for any woman.

Not long afterwards, Margaret attended one of Sand's salons. She saw the famous café-au-lait room with its thick carpets, its exquisite hangings, its abundance of flowers "in superb Chinese vases," its magnificent rosewood piano. She saw the green reception-room with its paintings by Delacroix, she wandered into the notorious bedroom with its Turkish couch over which was thrown a shimmering Aubusson rug.

The guests were mostly men. They lolled about and smoked many cigarettes; they sat on cushions on the floor at Madame's feet and puffed their smoke into her face. She smoked continuously, but she did not talk much, neither did she always listen to what the others were saying. Sometimes she started up suddenly and went wandering from room to room, as if she were looking for something she could not find. If she chanced to hear any remark which interested her, she stopped and challenged it.

Chopin was not present; he never could endure George's

bohemian friends who, he thought treated her much too familiarly, tutoying her and puffing their smoke into her face. Chopin's circle was much more effete—noble Polish patriots—it was he who had introduced Mickiewicz to Sand—rich patrons of the arts who dabbled a bit at painting and at music, luxurious idlers who dawdled beautifully through life. Chopin received them in his pearl-gray suite with the pastel furnishings, which was the suite directly above Madame's.

Margaret wondered if it would be possible for her to gain admittance to that pearl-gray suite. A meeting was arranged. One day a friend of the composer's whom she had met called at her hotel and said he was going to take her to see Chopin. And almost the next thing she realized was that she was standing inside the door of that exquisite pearl-gray suite and a pale, gracious figure, almost like a smiling shadow, was raising her hand to his lips.

They sat down, Chopin asked Margaret her impressions of Paris, asked her a few polite questions about America. She noticed how often it was necessary for him to stifle his cough, she noticed the deathlike frailty of his whole body and the waxen pallor of his face. Now and then he could not stifle his cough . . . and afterwards he was shaken and spent. . . .

Finally he asked Margaret if she would like to hear him play. This, of course was what Margaret wanted most of all, knowing that she would not have an opportunity of hearing him in public. Indeed, no one would have much more opportunity of hearing him in public; his appearances were becoming fewer and fewer owing to his increasing ill-health.

He played for a long time. . . . And Margaret was amazed at the difference between his interpretation of his works and that of other pianists she had heard. . . .

She went back to her hotel feeling that there was nothing more for her to do in Paris, that any other meeting would now be an anti-climax.

VI

ROMANCE

THE TIME HAD COME TO PACK AGAIN. MARGARET had been in Paris for more than three months and had seen every one she had wished to see; there was no reason for her to delay her departure. But she would have liked to linger, for spring was not far away.

But the diligence would not wait, and there remained other places to explore.

All day the sun shone and at night the moon came out. The diligence rocked and rumbled, the driver kept cracking his whip and shouting directions as if he expected something sensational to happen at any moment. The fair fields of France lay at night like silvered plains; the windows of the cottages were golden eyes taking a last look around at the fields and orchards before going to sleep.

Châlons came. The diligence made its last stop, the passengers alighted. Margaret and the Springs took the boat to Lyons.

Lyons with its whirring shuttles, its pallid children, its serious, overburdened mothers; with its garrets and its squalor, and the blue Rhone looking on!

Then Avignon, which to Margaret meant only one thing—the tomb of Petrarch's Laura. Although the snow was still on the ground, she waded out to see this "memorial to everlasting love."

At Arles the fruit-trees were in flower and saxifrage was blooming on the steps of the Amphitheater. "An old woman sat knitting where twenty-five thousand persons once gazed down in fierce excitement on the fights of men and lions," Margaret wrote to Horace Greeley. There were marks of the ancient Romans at Arles; the women were tall, erect and beautiful, "and looked as if the Eagle still waved its wings over the city."

Now Margaret was eager to hurry on into Italy, could scarcely wait for the first glimpse of Rome. But Marseilles had to be passed, with its dirty, narrow streets, its crowds of prostitutes and strolling Orientals. And Marseilles meant setting sail again on a voyage which proved to be of thirty hours' duration instead of a promised sixteen!

Margaret was seasick and not at all in the right mood to look upon the beauties of Genoa. A pity. For all her life she had anticipated her first sight of Italy. Always she had visualized the brightest and warmest sun in the world, always had thought of soft breezes from the Mediterranean gently moving the leaves of tropical plants. The sun was bright enough but the soft breeze was a cutting wind, and so "the marble palaces, the gardens, the magnificent water-view of Genoa failed to charm."

But she recovered in time and began to take an interest in life again. The cutting wind persisted, "a villainous, horrible wind, exactly like the worst east wind in Boston!"

Reaching Naples was somewhat hazardous. The party left Leghorn in a small tub of a boat with the English flag flying from its bow. Along about midnight there came a shudder, then a crash, then a prolonged trembling as if the boat were a living thing vibrating in its first death agony. This caused great excitement—much running about, loud voices, much shouting and swearing in several languages. The passengers rushed up on deck; and learned that they had been plowed by a passing mail steamer manned by a French crew. Since the English knew no French and the French no English, the two crews found some difficulty in making each other understood. An interpreter was finally found among the passengers, and after much argument, it was decided that the mail steamer should tow its victim ingloriously back to Leghorn.

This delay made Margaret doubly appreciative of Naples when she at length arrived. Here indeed was *her* Italy! She was soon going the customary rounds; and she was thrilled— so thrilled that she felt that any moment might bring a momentous adventure which would change the whole course of her life.

It was Rome that brought the momentous adventure. It was spring again, after all the months of gloom. It was Holy Week. Crowds poured into the churches, there were special blessings by the Pope. On Holy Thursday, Margaret and the Springs went to St. Peter's, to the vesper service. Eager to see the different chapels, Margaret suggested that they separate during the service and meet afterwards at a certain place which she named. The Springs agreed. To the pleasant accompaniment of chanting voices, Margaret wandered among the tombs, among the cloistered columns. The candles threw soft shadows on the benign faces of the saints, the priest's voice rose and fell in soothing benediction.

The service finished, the worshipers rose from their pews and moved slowly out of the church. Margaret lingered before a shrine. She felt very peaceful and quietly exalted. She became conscious of a silence around her and saw that the church was practically empty. She rose from her knees and went quickly to the place where she had agreed to meet the Springs. They were not there. She raised her lorgnette and looked around. She did not see them. She walked up and down, frankly staring at each group that passed her on the way to the door. She did not see the Springs.

A young man who saw that she was evidently looking for some one, went up to her and asked her if he could be of any help. She saw that he was tall and dark and that he had a noble bearing. She managed to tell him that she had lost her friends. Together they walked through the church, looking into chapels, exploring corners remote from the glow of the lights. They lingered until all the worshipers had gone, then they went out to find a carriage.

But all the carriages by this time had been taken. There seemed nothing for Margaret to do but walk to her lodgings, which she knew were quite some distance away. But in what direction? And how was she to find her way alone? The young Italian gallantly offered his assistance. Would she permit him to accompany her to her lodgings? Very gladly Margaret permitted him.

From the Vatican to the Corso is a long walk, long enough for much conversation. But when one knows no English and the other knows almost no Italian, what is to be done?

This much Margaret understood: her young gallant was a marquis and was the youngest son of a noble but impoverished family. His name was Giovanni Ossoli.

He accompanied her to her door, and asked if he might call on her. Margaret thanked him for his gallantry and said that he might. He called very soon, and told her more about his family: the old marquis, his father, was very ill and could not live long; an elder brother was secretary of the privy council in the papal court, a younger brother was in the Roman Guard.

"And you?" Margaret asked.

"I am on the side of the revolution."

"Ah!" For the moment that was all that she could say. But she felt within her a response so deep, so vital that it seemed to come from the very center of her being. She sat looking at him, her thoughts, for the moment, lost in a confused blur of feeling. Back of this confusion an idea was trying to push itself into the forefront of her consciousness— "This meeting is eventful; it has been arranged by Fate."

She told him that she too was on the side of the revolution; that she had always raised her voice for the oppressed. She told him that she believed passionately in the divinity which illumines every human life, giving it glimpses—perhaps for only a fragment of a second—of transcendent vistas, quickening it, revitalizing it.

Suddenly she said, "If you are on the side of the revolution, you must know Mazzini!"

He had not met Mazzini personally, but he knew him. Who of the Italian youth who sympathized with the revolution, did not know him, did not reverence him? Margaret told him of her meeting with Mazzini in London; of their long talks, their questionings, their hopes for a united Italy.

The young man listened ardently to her. She felt that here was a deep, true culture. She knew that he was ignorant of book-learning—a student senses this deficiency immediately in others. But he had something deeper than mere education, more basic than acquired knowledge, more profound than cleverness. He had intense convictions, and he had a strong and loyal character.

After he had left her, Margaret remained for a long time in contemplation. She felt strangely alive and vibrant; she felt strangely excited.

He called again very soon. He told her much more about himself; he was twenty-eight years old; he knew that he was no scholar, but he would give his life to make Italy a united republic. His voice throbbed with passion when he spoke of Italy. Margaret found herself responding to him, mood for mood. She liked the deferential way he had of addressing her, as if she were a superior power to which he made obeisance. The melancholy look in his eyes was strangely appealing; she knew it came from the sufferings he endured when he thought of the sufferings of his countrymen.

The next time he called, Margaret had a headache and could not see him. He returned the following day. The moment he entered the room, Margaret knew by that psychic knowledge women have of such events, that something momentous was going to be suggested. And that day he asked her to marry him. Margaret refused.

She knew that she must consider carefully. It were best to consider alone. So she hurriedly packed her bags and took the train to Florence, carrying with her a letter to the Marchioness Arconati Visconti, from a mutual friend in France.

In Florence she was occupied with many things. Madame Arconati introduced her to every one she thought Margaret would be interested to meet. Among them were the two American sculptors, Horatio Greenough and Hiram Powers. This meeting made Margaret so homesick that she wrote to her brother Richard, "I begin at moments to have a yearning for the loved, familiar faces, but I shall not yield to it."

She *must* not yield to it, with still so many places to explore. And there was something else, something which dwelt deep in her consciousness and rose to the surface at secret times in little sudden glows of excitement, little flashes of anticipation. It was the proposition that Ossoli had made to her that she marry him. She found that she could not come to any definite decision. She tried to weigh the question of their marriage: He was twenty-eight, she was thirty-seven! She was nine years older than he; in knowledge she surpassed him by many times nine years. She had visualized the man she would marry as one to whom she could look as her intellectual superior; one on whom she could depend, womanlike, one in whose strength she could find peace. To Ossoli she was this superior person. He deified her. If she married him, she might have to continue in the rôle of counselor, of manager of the household. She would still have to be the man, the active intelligence. There would be no rest for her, and she wanted rest.

Thus said her reason.

But her heart said, "He is united to you in your zeal for a new Italy; you already feel a spiritual kinship with him;

he attracts you physically. Furthermore, he has that deep reserve which you have always admired, and that natural culture which you appreciate so much. Despite the difference in your years, despite the difference in education, there is a bond between you which fuses your two imaginations and makes other differences seem negligible."

She found as she went about seeing new places, that her perception seemed to have grown keener, her faculties more alert. She was conscious of a subtle but very decided freedom of spirit and of a lightness and mirth such as she had not felt for a long time. She applied herself whole-heartedly to the study of Italian and found it easier to master than French. She began to have a feeling for Italy which she had never had for any other country.

This feeling grew in Bologna, the bluestocking city, with its many monuments to women, its brilliant *conversazione*, where women ruled. Bologna was exquisite, was beautiful, was full of expression—a civilized city. Margaret loved it.

"A woman should love it," she wrote, "for here has the spark of intellect in women been cherished with reverent care. Here women are the soul of society."

The charms of Venice sealed her lips. She could not write of it, to do it justice. Why attempt to write of a place which "should be echoed back in music"? She stayed at the Europa and saw the leisurely life which flowed through the palaces on the Grand Canal. One night the Duchess de Beri gave a party. Margaret stared with the rest of the crowd that gathered to stare. She saw the beautifully gowned women and the gallant men glide up in their gondolas, rise majestically like mermaids and nereids in fancy dress, sweep up the broad stairs to the reception-rooms. On the opposite side of the canal, a band played, and a flotilla of gondolas lingered to listen. She saw the old Duchesse d'Angoûleme, who had come all the way from Vienna for the festivity. And she thought of all those unfortunate royalties throughout all ages, who had made history so much more readable than it otherwise would have been: the Stuarts and the Bourbons and the Bonapartes were only a few. And she could not help breathing a prayer that others with similar powers and similar heartlessness would meet similar banishment!

One day she received a letter which contained important news. It was from her brother Arthur and it told her that old Uncle Abraham was dead. Nothing was known as yet of his affairs. But Margaret hoped that at least a small bequest would come to her. And she could not help feeling relieved that this final gesture of the cantankerous old man had been so timely. Her funds were shrinking at an alarming rate.

She was about to part with the Springs who had finished with Italy for the time and were going to make a hurried trip through Switzerland and Germany, on their way back to France. Margaret did not wish to hurry through Germany. She did not wish to visit Germany at all just then; her spirit still smarted from the sting of Nathan's treachery.

So she went up North among the lakes. But this journey was not as pleasant as it might have been had she been in better health. She suffered constantly from attacks of cholera. "One time I was so ill that I was afraid I should die on the road and nobody know it but my courier, a brutal wretch who robbed me and injured me all he could under the marks of obsequiousness. He wasted a good deal of money for me before I could learn how to prevent it," she wrote to her mother.

It seemed that she was never to be freed from the anxiety about money. Daily she looked for some word from home which would tell her the amount of Uncle Abraham's bequest to her.

At last the word came. It was not consoling. The old man had not even mentioned her! Still, there was a share for her as one of sixty-three heirs who were to divide what remained of the estate after all the legacies were paid. This share amounted to a little less than a thousand dollars. She owed four hundred. "I believe if his ghost knows that any of my plans have been aided at all through him, it sighs at the thought," she wrote to Miss Rotch of New Bedford in reply to a letter of congratulation from her on the good news of her legacy.

She was becoming weary of all the ironic congratulations she received and said so to Richard in her next letter. He answered her immediately, sympathizing with her. His letter roused her; she noted a touch of bitterness in it. She did not wish him to become bitter and she hastened to answer: "It is not reasonable to expect that the world should pay us in money for what *we are*, but for what we can do for it. Society pays in money for the practical talent exerted for its benefit —to the thinker as such only the materials for thought."

She missed the companionship of the Springs, and took the first opportunity to write to them:

"I remained at Venice a week after your departure, got pretty well and tranquil again and saw all the pictures. My journey here was very profitable to the mind.... But at Brescia I was taken ill. I cannot tell you how much I suffered, in my mind especially, when it seemed to me it was affecting my head. I had no medicine, nothing I could do except entirely to abstain from food and drink cold water. The second day I had a bed made in the carriage.... I am now pretty well, only very weak....

"I find myself obliged to retain Dominico, and I cannot trust him in the least as to money. He has made it so expensive for me that I find myself obliged to curtail my journey and give up many things on which I had set my heart, for fear I shall not have enough money to get back to Florence. This is cruel to me. I know I shall regret it always. But what I most wish of you, my dear Marcus, is to write to Mr. Moshier at Florence and ask him to let me have money there if I do not receive my remittances, until I do...."

She returned to Florence feeling limp and lifeless. She went to stay with the Moshiers, an American family. Mr. Moshier was an Ohio merchant who, after having made a comfortable fortune, had come to Florence to gratify an old ambition—to become a sculptor. Unlike many who, in middle life, enter on a new profession, he gave promise of amounting to something, and showed remarkable talent.

The Moshiers were very kind. They indulged Margaret in every possible way and in a short time she was able to return to Rome.

VII

ECSTASY, APPREHENSION, GLOOM

IN HER GREAT HAPPINESS upon returning, she writes impassioned letters to her friends at home: "Italy receives me as a long-lost child!" "I wish to drink deep of this enamored cup before I speak my impassioned words." "For happiness, Rome itself is sufficient."

To her mother she writes at length: "Dearest Mother— Here I am fairly installed in a home that promises to be permanent for six months. You cannot guess how rejoiced I am! During the three months I traveled in the North of Italy and upon the lakes of Switzerland, my enjoyments were great and many, my privileges extraordinary, but my sufferings were commensurate. I made many and ardent friends of all ranks, from the very highest to the lowest. The Italians sympathize with my character and understand my nature as no other people ever did. They admire the ready eloquence of my nature and highly prize my intelligent sympathy (such as they do not find often in foreigners) with their sufferings in the past and hopes for the future....

"My mind made a vast stride in those three months and my perception of beauty was all the keener for the sickly, nervous state I was in. I had continual attacks of cholera which prostrated my strength as nothing ever did before. At present I need all that is needed for Italian travel and can never be so situated again.

"Let me thank you for your prompt attention to my wishes about money. I received the $500 in Florence where I was detained for a time by illness, the sequel of all I had in the North. But I was with good friends who nursed me with care and tenderness and saw that I had proper care and nourishment. Their name is Moshier. They were originally from Ohio. Mr. Moshier is a man of fortune who has taken to sculpture from love and shows promise of much excellence. His wife is a very good and sweet woman....

"I feel often very anxious about money. Grateful as I am for Uncle Abraham's coming just when needed to save me from a check in all my plans, it was not enough. If he had left me ten or even five thousand dollars, I should have been so happy, for money now is all I want. Firm health I see I cannot have. I am sure now that my health will never stand against shocks and difficulties. But mere money would, in a great measure, free me from them....

"Such joy came over me when I was able at last to see Rome again! To live here alone and independent, to really draw in the spirit of Rome, oh what joy! I know so well how to prize it that I think Heaven will not allow anything to disturb me. My protecting angels have been very tender of late and led me carefully out of every difficulty."

The boundless freedom of Rome! The unending joy of living in a place which knew no Puritanical repressions! Now she could give free rein to her fervent spirit—could exclaim ecstatically over a picture, a statue or a beautiful woman without being regarded coldly, without being thought strange or perverted. Margaret's spirit expanded.

She was conscious of a new awareness, of a quickening of her imagination, of rapturous freedom which showed in her walk, in the sparkle of her eyes, in increasing magnetism which flowed from her, which made the Princess Radziwell exclaim, "How happy you are! So free, so serene, so attractive, so self-possessed!" She was conscious of a strengthening of her will; she had moments of sharp perceptions, of strange, miraculous, new understandings. She had many exalted moments. "I have not been so well since I was a child, nor as happy ever," she exclaimed to herself, over and over again.

Was it the Tuscan vintage which produced this miracle? Was it the gathering of the grapes from the vines with the mild-eyed Tuscan peasants smiling in a friendly way and singing their joyous songs? Was it the contemplation of the Italian autumn of rich golds and browns, and warm, voluptuous reds?

It could not be this, for Margaret wrote to a friend, "The Italian landscape in autumn is sere and brown, so different from ours or even that of England."

To Richard she wrote ardently, "Keep free from false ties; they are the curse of life. I find myself so happy here, *alive and free!*"

She hopes that perhaps Richard will guess the cause of her abounding joy. If she can advise him against false ties, surely he will know that she speaks from a knowledge of the true! She cannot tell him how profound her knowledge is; she cannot tell him of the bond which is responsible for this new vigorous awareness, this miraculous joy. She cannot tell him that she has promised to marry Ossoli, one of the officers of the Roman Revolutionary Party. She cannot tell any one. The relationship must remain a secret till things are more settled in Italy. Ossoli is a Catholic, she a Protestant. If he is to receive any of his patrimony, he must not anger his family. Since he has espoused the revolutionary cause, he has made himself an enemy to the courts. It would be a simple matter to cut him off from his inheritance.

Often Margaret found herself wondering at the dramatic suddenness of her capitulation. And at the consequent birth of some psychic force which seemed to rise from the communion of her soul with the soul of this young man who, until a few months ago, was a total stranger to her. She did not think of her decision as a capitulation. Love to her was a divine attribute to be recognized as one recognizes a capacity for any lesser art. Of all arts, the art of loving was the greatest. To deny it was to deny one's divine birthright. The truly cultured person did not deny it, but accepted it joyously, knowing that through it he was enriched, knowing that the mystical birth of that third force which sprang from harmonious communion of two souls was as vital as the life which sprang from their physical communion. She gloried in her new life, in her added richness, which showed itself in a hundred ways—in more intense sympathy with the oppressed; in quicker discernments of character; in more immediate projections into others' points of view.

She was living on the Corso. In a letter to her mother, she described her surroundings: "I have taken charming rooms. I can see all that goes on in Rome, near the Pincian Mountains. The rooms are elegantly furnished, everything in the house is so neat, more like England than Italy, service excellent. I have my books, my flowers. . . .

"The only drawback is a little danger from the character and position of my hostess. She was formerly the mistress of a man of quality who loved her so much that she made him marry her before his death, so that she is a marchioness but not received into society. . . . This will be no objection if she lets me alone enough, but she is a most insinuating creature. ... I am a little afraid of her going too far, so that if I should be obliged to decline any overture from her, she will be angry and hate me. But if we can get along, I like her much. She has black eyes and red hair and pretty color and fine skin, very graceful manners and speaks Italian beautifully, which is good practice for me. She has introduced to me her present lover, an Italian artist, who has been devoted to her for some years. He is an officer of note in the newly organized Civic Guard and will bring all the news to the house....

"Of course I seem to ignore all these circumstances; he appears here merely as a friend and visitor ... but the ground is a little delicate."

More than a little delicate. With Ossoli calling as often as he could find time for, it was natural that such a hostess would put misconstructions on his relation—or guess his relation with Margaret. This was disturbing; for the woman was the worst liar Margaret had ever known. This might prove really alarming.

Ossoli kept urging Margaret to marry him. She hesitated. Was it wise? Her reason told her many things which proved that it would not be wise.

One day she went to see the Civic Guard maneuvering. The band played the Bolognese march and six thousand Romans paraded past the tomb of Cecelia Matella. Margaret was deeply moved. Soon perhaps other soldiers would meet the Civic Guard, the parade would be broken, the rattle of musketry would sound across the Corso.

That night she told Ossoli that she would marry him immediately.

What thoughts she had when she contemplated the step she was about to take! She could not help smiling—a little wistfully—when she remembered the wedding she had planned in her childish days—of a splendid company; of music and flowers, of envious looks and a host of congratulations. Now she must be as secretive as Juliet on her way to Friar Laurence's cell. What did it all portend?

Sometimes she had strange, contradictory visions: She saw herself a power in Rome; she saw Mazzini returning in great honor, heard him acclaimed as the savior of his people and First Citizen of a united Italy....

She saw herself perpetually oppressed by poverty and by ill health.

Ossoli was very dear to her and very tender. But he was not a wage-earner. If the revolution did not prosper, it would be necessary for him to look to some means of earning a livelihood. He was equipped for nothing. On her would fall this additional burden. Sometimes she recalled her childish fantasyings when she was a princess left by some misadventure of Fate in a strange land. She was now a marchioness; she was in her own rightful country, but how ironic was her position in that country! She could not take her place as marchioness, she had no standing as a citizen of Rome. Sometimes these thoughts came to her so poignantly that she was obliged to change her occupation at the time—to busy her hands, to go for a walk, to yield herself to some lovely scene. She would not allow them to interfere for long with the abundance of her life....

Every Monday evening she held her court. She had fresh roses in her rooms and luscious grapes on her table. The Americans who were in Rome—among them were the Storys and the Cranches—usually came, and there were several Romans whom she had met; and some English. They talked of the new Council, of the Austrians who had entered Ferrara, of the King of Sardinia. They discussed different nationalities. And the English heard how reserved they were, how cold, how insular and distant. They talked of Taglioni, who had a palace on the Grand Canal in Venice. And Margaret told of the time she had gone with Emerson to see Fanny Ellsler, Taglioni's rival. They spoke of the alliance between France and Spain, which had been such a disappointment to the young British queen. And some one prophesied that Victoria would have her alliance with Spain yet, before she finished with her reign. They laughed a little over the recent erasure of the royal lilies from the panels of Louis Philippe's carriage.

Of countless other things they talked, until the night grew strange and silent on the Corso and the owls hooted in the Coliseum. Then they left Margaret to her thoughts, her apprehensions, her delights. And after half an hour had gone, Ossoli came back again....

Enchantment was upon her. The Rome she saw was the Rome of her earliest pictures—bright sun and fragrant flowers and the magic of ancient glory. Sometimes she thought of the childish games she had played in the garden in Cambridge: Huddling against the wall, she was a hostile Greek and on the other side were the Roman forces....

Her fantasies were becoming realities; the glamour of childhood was the actuality of middle-age. If her present court was not as magnificent as the court of the child of eight who called herself a princess, it was richer in things of which a child of eight has no conception; if she did not ride forth in a glittering carriage with dazzling outriders in gold and scarlet uniforms, she went swiftly along the road of fulfillment, and her long heart-hunger was appeased. Ossoli was all that her heart desired. If her brain desired more, it could easily find satisfaction in the world around her....

The fine weather departed suddenly, suddenly the Corso was drenched with rain. The roses wilted and the fragrance that came through the streets was the accumulation of all the abominable smells the rain washed out from hidden places. The days were dark, a gloom hung over the Seven Hills.

The street sounds became almost unendurable to Margaret —the never-ending *arias,* the hand-organs whining out the Copenhagen waltz and "Home Sweet Home." In ways known only to himself, the organ-grinder had learned that an American Signora occupied the rooms above the Corso on one side and an English Signora occupied those on the other. Day after day he came through the drenching rain and offered his "obsolete abominations." The noise indoors was equally irritating. The three pet dogs of the lying marchioness being deprived of their daily walks, kept yapping and growling, jumping up into the windows and bumping their noses against the panes, storming like stunted furies at the day. Hearing their yappings and their growlings, all the riff-raff of dogdom out of doors raised their voices in response.

And this went on for forty days!

The rumblings of unrest were sharper, and were more prolonged. The "creeping sickness" of Europe was about to break out into an epidemic....

In February came the beginning of the epidemic. Paris rose against Louis-Philippe; and this time the royal carriage could not carry him through the streets, even though the lilies had been obliterated from its panels. With his queen, Louis slipped out through a back door of the Tuileries, dressed like a servant, and managed to escape to Honfleur, where he found refuge in a gardener's cottage. A little later the British consul at Havre helped the royal couple to board a boat for England as Mr. and Mrs. Smith.

In Milan and in Messina there were outbreaks by the revolutionaries. Margaret heard this news with alarm; she would have preferred a bloodless revolution. She was nervous; her old headaches came back; she could not sleep. Before very long she realized that she was going to have a child.

This miracle of motherhood of which she had thought so much, this anticipation of maternal bliss was to her "the most idle and most suffering time" of her whole life. She had no energy, she could not eat, the least mental effort was painful to her.

The rumblings in his own country brought Mazzini flying back. Suddenly war broke out everywhere, from Austria, where Metternich was crushed, to Milan where Young Italy awaited him whom they regarded as a savior.

Outside Margaret's window Austrian arms were dragged through the mud, and a bonfire was made of them in a public square. The leaders of Young Italy went wild; they danced in the streets, they embraced one another; they cried "Miracolo!" and "Providenza!"

Adam Mickiewicz, the Polish mystic, suddenly arrived from Paris. He called on Margaret almost immediately; she learned that he had no place to stay and offered him the hospitality of her rooms, which he gratefully accepted. One day Mazzini came to see her, but merely to tell her that he was not remaining in Rome. He hurried off to Milan and to Messina, where the fighting was thick.

Excitement everywhere! Ossoli brought Margaret news of the temper of the crowds he saw in cafés. The lover of the lying marchioness told what gossip he had heard; the lying marchioness repeated it to Margaret.

In Milan the citadel fell into the hands of Young Italy. Margaret thought of them—the youths she had met—and wondered how they fared. She longed passionately to take part in the struggle with them; but she was more inactive than she had ever been....

The long rains ended and the sun shone again. Surely this was a good omen, surely the cause of the revolutionists was favored by the gods.... One day the Austrian Embassy was mobbed and the double-headed eagle was pulled down from its place. Then up went another one of white-and-gold on which were inscribed the words "Alter Italia." The crowd shouted, hats and caps went flying into the air. A messenger arrived with important news: Venice, Modena and Parma had joined in the revolution and were driving the tyrants out of their high places. The crowd lost its head completely; women wept on each other's shoulders, men kissed each other's cheeks; every one began dancing and going through crazy contortions in the middle of the streets. All the youths who had not yet enlisted, dashed off to the Coliseum to enroll in regiments going to the front.

In two days Verona was added to the list of newly freed cities. Next came an official communique declaring that the whole of Italy was free! It did not look free on the Corso. Troops began to move about in Rome, out through the Ponte Molle, away from the Seven Hills. The women followed them, weeping but talking proudly about their Roman soldiers who had been at home for so long.

Margaret went out into the sun with Adam Mickiewicz. While the troops clattered through the streets, she listened to the birds singing in all the trees. Outside the Ponte Molle, the fragrance of fruit-blossoms fell upon the troops like a benediction. "Pray God it may be!" Margaret sighed. The activity excited her. "It is a time such as I have always dreamed of." Surely, surely, it held work for her. Why otherwise should her angel have led her into the midst of it. "Am I to cheer on the warriors, and after, write the history of their deeds?"

Many of the warriors she had already cheered, when she herself wanted cheering. Her funds were dwindling again, her strength was on the ebb. "My fortunes are dark and tangled," she wrote, "my strength to govern them much diminished." She realized that she could not afford to remain in Rome. She was torn between the longing to be in the center of activity and the longing for solitude. She had an idea that she was not going to live long.

It was unsatisfactory, writing to her most intimate friends and not being able to tell them her most intimate news. It was a lonely business, this hugging to herself this most profound experience of her life. She longed to confide in her mother, to ask her advice. How she sympathized with her and with all mothers! The bringing of life into the world should be an exalting experience, and not this nauseating, oppressive, disgusting thing!

She wondered what her friends would say of her when they learned her secret. Sometimes she feared what they would say. She had moods of deep depression, when she seemed unable to visualize any future for herself. She wanted a change of scene. In such a mood she went to pass a few days at Tivoli. While there she wrote to Miss Mary Rotch of New Bedford, whom she always addressed as Aunt Mary:

"Tivoli, May 29, 1848.

"Dear Aunt Mary:

"... You must always love me, whatever I do. I depend upon that. And this thought puts me in mind to ask whether you are not aware that I am as great an Associationist as W. Channing himself? That is to say as firm a believer that the next form Society will take in remedy of the dreadful ills that now consume it, will be voluntary association in small communities. The present forms have become unwieldy. But what I think on this subject I hope to have force and time to explain in print; not in the *Tribune*....

"I am now hoping in the silence and retirement of the country to write more at length on the subjects that have engaged my attention for some time back. But who knows? The disturbances of the times or an unfavorable state of my health may mar my purpose, as has happened before.

"You will have seen my account of the measures by which the Pope has lost all substantial influence in Europe. There is something fatal in a priestly environment. He remained a layman to so late an age one might have hoped he would not get stupefied by the incense, but would remember how things looked beneath the open heavens. But the influence of the crafty priests that surrounded him, was unhappily too much for his strength. However, God has blessed his good intent, and a work has begun which his failure cannot check.

"I hear often from Waldo. He sees much, learns much, but loves not Europe. There is no danger of the idle intimations of others altering his course, more than the moving a star. He knows himself and his vocation."

The days at Tivoli steadied her. She went back to her rooms on the Corso, feeling restored in health, in spirits strengthened. A letter from her brother Richard awaited her.

VIII

FULFILLMENT

RICHARD WAS DISILLUSIONED. He wrote that he had decided never to marry; perhaps Margaret would plan to live with him when she returned? He was lonely without her.

The letter perplexed Margaret. How could she answer him? There were times when she longed to tell him about her marriage and her present difficult situation. But letters were dangerous newsmongers; they might fall into the wrong hands before they left Rome. She dared not tell.

And so she wrote: "I should like to live with you where Nature was beautiful, and only occasionally to see cities or men.... But I have no idea you will be content without marrying, nor am I so selfish as to wish it."

Quickly then to change the subject: "I liked and loved George Sand, but should not care particularly to know her more, now I have the true picture of her. She is a woman who, except by her lovers, may be as well-known through her books as any other way. I have lately seen a good deal of a very celebrated woman the Princess Belgiojoso.... She is a woman of gallantry, which the Sand is not. She also has had several lovers, no doubt, but her public life has been truly energetic and beneficent." She knew it was an unsatisfactory letter, but it must suffice.

She wrote to her small niece, Ellen Channing's daughter, and sent her trinkets—"a little cross made of coral and gold . . . and a little heart made of Roman stone" for her sister Caroline. Whenever she heard that an American was returning home, she sents gifts to her family and to her friends. Friends wrote to her asking her to buy them engravings and choice *objets d'art*. Unfortunately they did not always remember to enclose the price, or they said that they would send the amount when the articles arrived. Margaret used her own money to make the purchases. Her bank account grew smaller and smaller; she had terrifying visions of herself stranded there with no place to turn for help. The Old World seemed heartless to her at times. She wrote feelingly, "Amid the corrupt splendors of the Old World, I begin to pine for the pure air of my native land."

Richard was not satisfied with her answer to his suggestion that they live together when she returned. He dashed off a prompt reply to her, urging the question. Margaret was a little more frank in her answer the next time she wrote: "There are reasons why I cannot answer positively till the autumn. . . . There are circumstances and influences now at work in my life not likely to find their issue till then. If you still wish it, I think I shall be able to answer by October."

She had dark thoughts when she thought of October: "Maybe I shall die then, when my baby is born. Then Richard will understand why I could not answer him more frankly." And she counted the months which must intervene. . . .

There was movement of troops everywhere; it looked as if all the youth of the country now wanted to have a thrust at Austria. It looked too as if the Pope meant to sanction such a war. Then suddenly, he proclaimed papal neutrality. That was the signal for trouble; the Roman storm, all ready to break over Austria, was deflected to the Quirinal. Mobs ran through the streets crying, "Morte ai Cardinali, e Morte al Papa!" Stones flew through the sacred windows of the palace, the great door through which thousands had gone at one time and another, to receive a blessing, was torn from its hinges and burned. Deep within the protecting sanctity of his citadel, the Pope waited. Outside, there were mutterings.

Pius IX waited. In the outer rooms of the palace, deputations from the people came and went, presenting bills of reform. After two days Pius yielded and the power passed from his hands into those most opposed to him.

Stirring times. Mazzini, now in seclusion in Lugano, kept on the *qui vive* for each tick of the clock. Soon the hour would come for him to hurry to Rome as the acknowledged leader of Italy.

Quiet for the moment, in spirit more serene, Margaret watched the march of events. As spring advanced she felt better. The beautiful weather allowed her to go for many walks through the grounds surrounding the villas, which were charming "in the music of their many fountains and the soft gleam, here and there, of sarcophagus or pillar." In such places had she wandered many times in imagination when New England snows walled up the world and sharp winds blew in from Boston harbor. How remote was all that life now! How simple it seemed, how free from complication, how innocent!

Mickiewicz had left her rooms and was now in Florence at the head of a squadron of troops. He had a great reception there; deputations of citizens went to his hotel and brought him forth for the people to see. Fervid speeches were made, in which he was called the Dante of Poland, "who hast received from Heaven sovereign genius, divine song, but from the earth sufferings and exile."

He responded with an equally fervid speech. The crowd listened, rapt, for Mickiewicz was an orator with a superb voice and great personal magnetism. His words flew out among the people like sparks from a giant dynamo, electrifying them. At times they broke into wild applause, and Mickiewicz waited, tense, prophetical. He ended by asking every one to go into the church of Santa Croce and give thanks to God for the opportunity that had been granted the leaders of the people to overthrow tyranny. He led them into the church. A great crowd followed him. And never was the Benedictus Dominus sung with more fervor than on that day.

This was all deeply moving. Margaret, watching the scene around her and listening to the drum-beats from further off, thought of her own country, and in the ardor of her sympathy for the struggling peoples, wrote: "My country is spoiled by prosperity, stupid with the lust of gain, soiled by crime in its willing perpetuation of slavery.... In Europe, amid the teachings of adversity, a nobler spirit is struggling—a spirit which cheers and animates mine... the spirit of our fathers flames no more, but lies hid beneath the ashes."

She had been only a lukewarm abolitionist at the time the Alcotts were offending the "best people" by visiting William Lloyd Garrison in jail. She had been inclined to think that all the fuss about slavery was a little *infra dig*, was a pastime for cranks and fanatics. She knew that she had grown since then.

She knew that she had grown since coming to Europe, where she did not have to play the sibyl, the prophet, the seer, where she was accepted naturally as one of God's creatures, with weaknesses and strengths, the same as every one else. She was softer now, more mellow, more tolerant. And she was thirty-eight.

Only about three months till her child would be born. She must leave Ossoli; she could not remain in Rome and have their secret guessed. The old marquis had died but the estate was not settled; and the two older sons were trustees. Margaret must go very carefully.

She decided to bury herself in the mountains, where living was cheaper and the air less invigorating than the air of Rome.

On her last day in Rome she wrote to Madame Arconati: "I sit in my obscure corner and watch the progress of events. ... Everything confirms me in my radicalism, and without any desire to hasten matters, indeed with surprise to see them rush so like a torrent, I seem to see them all tending to realize my own hopes."

She went up into the mountains of Abruzzi, to the little town of Aquila, which in more affluent days, had boasted a baronial residence. Now its splendor was less artificial; it looked down the mountainside to almond-groves and vineyards connected by winding bridle-paths with a golden valley aglow with saffron flowers. Off in the distance were fields of grain and beside them crimson fields where poppies grew and fields starred over with blue cornflowers.

Remnants of the artificial splendor still remained in ruined marble and in crumbling stone crescents which once marked noble doorways.

The Passionists and the Capucins had monasteries on the other side of the poppy fields. One looked down the mountainside across the valley and saw the brown-robed monks pacing back and forth with bowed heads; or one saw them coming slowly up the bridle-path, their rosaries moving gently as they moved.

In this little town Margaret found lodgings and settled down to rest and to write the story of her European experiences. She went for walks each day—down the path between the olive-trees, through the poppy fields and past the monasteries. She interested herself in the peasants who blessed her and called her *simpatica*. Sometimes she rode on a donkey, sometimes found a quiet corner among the trees where she sat for hours with her books. She tried to write, but found difficulty in getting started.

The post left the mountain town only three times a week; letters arrived no oftener. Margaret felt isolated and alone. She had thought that Ossoli would spend most of his weekends with her; she saw that this was impossible; Aquila was too inaccessible.

He told her that his brothers had suspicions about her, that they feared that she would influence him against the Pope. They had heard that he often called on her in the Corso; they may have heard more. Margaret was the least mercenary of mortals, but she did not want Ossoli to lose any of his patrimony because of her; and she wanted their child to have the advantages of whatever inheritance should come to him. Secrecy then until the revolution prospered!

She wrote a great many letters, for she did not want to lose touch with her friends. But letters to Ossoli did not suffice. And after a month she had to admit that she could bear the loneliness no longer.

She went to Rieti, another mountain town, but more accessible to Rome. Now it would be possible for Ossoli to spend a Sunday with her when he had the time. He would travel by coach all Saturday night and be with her for breakfast. "I will have your coffee ready," she wrote. And she would have fresh fruit on the table and flowers everywhere. He would see what a good housewife she was!

She was eager to finish her book before her child was born. But it did not go well; there seemed always to be some obstruction, usually the worry about money. Now, for example, she had only enough to last her a month. She had written to Greeley to assure herself that she would have no worry during these trying weeks, and he had answered, saying that her remittance had been sent. She waited. It did not arrive. If it did not arrive before a month passed! She could not bear to think of such a possibility and much against her inclination, she wrote to Richard for a loan. "In the trouble I am in, it seems as if I could rely on no friend but you," she said.

The days dragged; her writing did not go well. Margaret suffered constantly from headaches, and had to call on the local doctor to bleed her frequently. Never had she known such melancholy as she felt now. In her desolation she lost her faith. "If there be a God who takes a paternal interest in human affairs, something might be hoped from Him, it would seem," she cried.

Time marched along. Daily she heard the little bell tinkling up from the convent, the river rushing over the stones, the peasants singing at their work in the fields.

She wrote to Emerson, Rieti, July 11, 1848:

"Once I had resolution to face my difficulties myself and try to give only what was pleasant to others; but now that my courage has fairly given way and the fatigue of life is beyond my strength, I do not prize myself nor expect others to prize me.

"Some years ago I thought you very unjust because you did not lend full faith to my spiritual experiences; but I see you were quite right. I thought I had tasted of the true elixir, and that the want of daily bread or the pangs of imprisonment would never make me a complaining beggar. A widow, I expected still to have the cruse full for others. Those were glorious hours and angels certainly visited me; but there must have been too much earth—too much taint of weakness and folly, so that baptism did not suffice. I know now those same things, but at present they are words, not living spells.

"I hear at this moment the clock of the Church del Purgatorio telling noon in this mountain solitude. Snow yet lingers on these mountain-tops, after forty days of hottest sunshine.... It has been so hot here that even the peasant in the field says, *Non porro piu resistere,* and slumbers in the shade. I love to see their patriarchal ways of guarding the sheep and tilling the fields. They are a simple race. Remote from the corruptions of foreign travel, they do not ask for money, but smile upon and bless me as I pass—for the Italians love me.... I never see any English or Americans and now think wholly in Italian; only the surgeon who bled me the other day, was proud to speak a little French, which he had learned at Tunis! The ignorance of this people is amusing. I am to them a divine visitant—an instructive Ceres—telling them wonderful tales of foreign customs, and even legends of the lives of their own saints. They are people whom I could love and live with. Bread and grapes among them would suffice me."

August came. Margaret's money was almost spent. Beside herself with anxiety, she wrote again to Richard: "I do not know what will become of me if I do not, in the course of September, receive some money either from you or from Mr. Greeley.... Sometimes it seems to me I have no friend, or some one would divine how I am placed, and find the means to relieve me. Yet I know I have friends. Mr. G. shows no disposition to further my plans. Liberality on the part of the *Tribune* would have made my path so easy... and I could have made at least a rich intellectual compensation.... The want of a few dollars prevented my seeing the birthplace of Ovid! Hoping I may be relieved by September 2, I try to keep my mind tranquil and make as much use as possible of the present moment."

It was not easy to be tranquil, not easy to face her ordeal without fear. She was thirty-eight, she was alone in an ignorant district where medical help was of the most primitive kind. She was without funds. It was doubtful if she could see Ossoli again before the child was born, for he had written that the Civic Guard was ordered to Bologna. This news was almost the worst that he could impart to her; it meant that he was to be far from her when her greatest trial came. Passionately he wrote to her: "My state is the most deplorable that can be; I have had an extraordinary struggle. If your condition were not such as it is, I could decide more easily, but in the present moment I cannot leave you; I cannot remove myself to a distance from you, my dear love; ah! how cruel is my destiny in this emergency."

Margaret answered him immediately, consoling him, counseling him.

"Rieti, 18th August, 1848.

"I feel a profound sympathy with your torments, but I am not able to give you a perfectly wise counsel. Only it seems to me the worst possible moment to take up arms except in the cause of duty, of honor. The Pope being so cold, his minister undecided, nothing will be well or successfully done. As the intervention of France and England is hoped for, it is yet uncertain whether the war will continue. If not, you will leave Rome and the employment with your uncle for nothing.

"If it is possible to wait two or three weeks, the public state and mind also will be decided, and you can make your decision with more tranquillity. Otherwise, it seems to me that I ought to say nothing, but leave it to your own judgment what to do. Only if you go, come here first. I must see you once more.

"It troubles me much that I can tell you nothing of myself, but I am still in the same waiting state. I passed a very bad night, my head is, this morning, much disturbed. I have bled a good deal at the nose and it is hard for me to write.

"Do not ask permission of your uncle if it is so difficult. We shall know how to arrange things without that. If you do not come, I shall expect a letter from you on Sunday; also (if there are any) from the banker's, and also, the last of those Milanese papers. Poor friends, shut up there—I wish so much for some certain intelligence of their fate.

"Adieu, dear; our misfortunes are many and unlooked for. Not often does destiny demand a greater price for some happy moments. Never do I repent of our love, and for you, if not for me, I hope that life has still some good in store. Adieu. May God give you counsel and help, since it is not now in the power of your Margherita."

She tried to be tranquil, but she could not help starting nervously when any sound reached her from another part of the house. She tried not to think of her financial worries, but she could not avoid such thought. Daily she waited for Richard's answer to her appeal for help. It did not come; her funds grew less. She could wait no longer and in her desperation, wrote to an American in Rome and asked him for a loan of a hundred dollars. He agreed to let her have it. For the moment, her worst worries were assuaged. She waited now for the climax of her physical suffering; and while she waited she prayed that Ossoli would not have to leave Rome.

One day she saw an answer to her prayer. She read in the papers that the Pope had suspended the departure of the troops.

The last week in August. Only a short time now till the terrifying ordeal. Writing was almost impossible. Her mind felt as weighted as her body; her spirit was oppressed; she was full of grave apprehension. If only Ossoli would come to her!

She appealed to him: "... You do not say whether you are to come Saturday evening or no, but I hope for it confidently. I cannot wait longer.... Nothing comes for me yet. I do not know what to think.

"There is a beautiful spot near here where we can go together if I am still able to go out when you come. I shall expect you on Sunday morning and will have your coffee ready again. Nothing more now, because writing is really difficult...."

How she waited for him! How she watched! Every morning she awoke when the first long fingers of the dawn stretched up over the hills. She rose, she went to the window, she looked down the winding road to the corner where the diligence stopped. She felt so helpless and so utterly alone. She could trust no one. She realized quite suddenly that every one around her was robbing her. Small sums—a bit here, a bit there; small, mean deductions. Every tradesman demanded a few soldi more when he learned that the commodities were for the foreign signora; the landlord added extras to his weekly bill.

What could she do? If she questioned anything, the landlord and the tradesmen would fly into a rage, would refuse to serve her. She could not afford to antagonize them—at any rate, not just at present.

In came September with cooling breaths. Margaret woke early, as usual, got up and dragged her cumbersome body to the window. One day, she did not get up. She could not; her will was the slave of her body that day. She could not move. And that day Ossoli came.

He crept quietly up the stairs lest his footfall wake her; quietly he opened the door of her bedroom. She had managed to raise herself up on her elbow, for she heard him coming up the street. She was waiting for him when he entered.

All that day he sat beside her bed, and all that night. He stroked her fevered forehead, he soothed her; he was very tender.

Margaret was racked with pain; she was sure she would not live.

She lived. And on the following day, on September the fifth, 1848, her son was born. Never had she suffered as she suffered then. The doctor who took care of her was a crude, brutal creature, not used to dealing with gentlefolk. Margaret shuddered when he went near her. But Ossoli remained beside her and gave her all the comfort that any one could give.

He could not stay long. Early the next morning he had to return to Rome. In deep faith—for he was a devout Catholic—he commended her to God, then stole down the stairs, down the winding road to where the diligence waited at the corner.

God alone sustained her, for certainly she had no other care. She was racked with fever and could not nurse her child; she was surrounded with dishonesty; finally, she was obliged to send her servant away because she was having an affair with the master of the house. She must find another; and she must have a wet-nurse for Angelo Phillip Eugene who lay on his pillow and vociferously exercised his lungs.

The wet-nurse was found. Margaret knew that the price she demanded was exorbitant, but again, what could she do? She must submit to her fate. A little grimly, she thought, "There must be some old sin I have to work out of my karma, and this life is my hell, following my last incarnation."

But none of these thoughts to Ossoli; nothing but love and tenderness and cheer to him! The very day after he left, she dictated a letter to him and signed her name to it:

"Rieti, Thursday, 7th September, 1848.
"Dear Husband—
"I am well, much better than I hoped. The baby also is well, but cries much yet, and I hope he will be more quiet when you come. For the rest, I desire that you should be without anxiety about me, and I will send you frequent accounts of myself, writing again very soon...."

Two days later she managed to scribble a note to him herself. And now the mother writes, as well as the wife:

"The baby is very beautiful. All say so. I take much delight in watching him. He sends you a kiss, as also does your M."

Convalescence was slow; but she was patient. She had her baby, Ossoli was safe, her funds for the time, were sufficient. The beautiful autumn days brought peace to her. Up in her sun-swept room, with the wind bringing to her the soothing sound of bells from the Capucines' convent, she sat looking at the new little life that had been entrusted to her keeping and she prayed that her good angel would guide her aright. It was difficult to believe that there was bloodshed in Milan and in Naples and that many of the young men she had met the year before, were no longer living.

She wrote regularly to Ossoli, who had had a spell of sickness.

"Rieti, 28th September, 1848.

"I have seen more bad people this last year than in all my life before, and I fear not to have ended yet. I think of your letter which came on Sunday morning. How much I wish to see you! The baby does not grow much, but he is always so lovely, has really delicate little ways, like a dancer. For the rest, I can speak so much better than write that, anticipating your visit, will say no more.

"Your affectionate M."

"Rieti, 7th October, 1848.

"Mio Caro—

". . . I am sorry that I cannot explain myself better in writing in Italian. It is too difficult for me. The dear baby seemed to look for you, the night after your departure. Before morning he woke, sought, refused his milk, cried much, and seemed to seek something that he could not find. At last I rose, took him in my arms, talked to him and finally he was consoled. He is well now it is fine weather. I think of going out with him. Adieu, ever dearest. God protect thee."

"8th Oct...
"Sometimes the baby is naughty....I have given him your kiss, but he does not deserve it. He is naughty now, and I am very weary with tending him...."

"Sunday morning (undated).
"I received your note; I am consoled. I love you much more than in the first days, for I see by trial how pure and good is your heart. When we meet again, I will tell you all my reasons for being disturbed. You will not be surprised. I cannot be very tranquil, for I find that if I do not follow, do not insist, do not play the spy over all these people, they deceive me....I can no longer go out with the baby. I thought myself safe in taking him to the bishop's garden, but a child died there of smallpox the past week. Thus I am prisoner here and I know not for how long.

"Giovanni seeks to *seduce* Clara, and she is enraged and wishes to go home. But she will not leave me before my departure. She has told Giovanni that if he speaks to her again, she will go away from me. She is in great fear lest her husband should know it...."

Ossoli thought it best that she leave the baby in Rieti. Necessity demanded that she return to Rome. Rome was rich in copy. And copy she must have, for now, more than ever, she must earn money. Furthermore, she was beginning to weary of her life of idleness; she was restless; she felt that she was wasting time. And she was sick to death of the cow-eyed peasants, whose ignorance could be endured for a time, but who became very boresome after constant association.

She would not leave until the baby was inoculated against smallpox. The doctor delayed. She was beside herself with anxiety. She entreated him to come. At last he came.

About the first of November she was ready to leave the sun-swept room, the olive groves, the little, tinkling bells from the Capucines' convent; to leave Angelo her dearly beloved to the care of a wet-nurse who swore that she would look after him as tenderly as if he were her own child.

IX

RUMBLINGS

THE DILIGENCE left Rieti between three and four in the morning. The nights were cold in the mountains and autumn rains had swollen the rivers. Margaret lay awake listening to the ceaseless rush of water, and prayed that before her night of starting, the torrent would quiet itself.

One day the director of the diligence sent word that the Marchioness Crispoldi had engaged a special coach for herself and her family, and would not leave till daybreak. If Margaret wished, she might take passage in that. Margaret accepted the offer gratefully.

Evening came on. A high wind howled from the mountain, rain began to fall in sheets. Margaret went to her window. The river was more than twice its usual size and was rushing and roaring like a mad thing. Margaret drew the curtains and turned away. "At any rate, I don't leave for several hours. All may be calm by then." She stood looking down at Angelo asleep in her bed.

All night she listened to the roar, and when dawn came she got up and dressed herself in her warmest clothes. The first streaks of light came over the hills, smoke rose from the chimneys of all the cottages—but no coach arrived. Margaret went downstairs. It might be possible to learn something from the master of the house. He shrugged.

While they talked together, a messenger came. The regular diligence which had left two hours earlier, had been swamped some miles below the town and all the passengers had had to swim for their lives. Naturally, Madame Crispoldi's coach would not leave that day. Margaret thanked God for her escape and went upstairs to try to get some sleep.

But sleep was difficult to coax. Margaret's mind began its questioning and its deducing: Why had she been spared? Why, at the last moment, had the fates intervened to prevent her from going on the diligence? Evidently there still was work for her to do....

For several days the river kept up its rushing and its roaring, for several days the wind howled from the mountains. The leaves fell from the trees and gave the red roofs a chance to show themselves, now and then lightning flashed. The children of the village danced through the streets and clustered on the bridge which spanned the roaring stream, leaning perilously far over and uttering shrill cries of delight. Some of the larger boys brought armfuls of straw which they lighted and threw down into the water.

At last the long rumble was subdued and the sun came out across the snow-capped hills. Word went about the village that the diligence would leave the next morning. Once more Margaret got her things together and lay awake waiting for the dawn.

Two large diligences left that morning, drawn by all the horses on the route. The going was very slow—down the slippery mountain roads into ravines where snow lay on the withered grass, reminding Margaret of New England. All day they crawled along and when night fell drew up at an old inn erected on the site of the home of the Sabine Virgins. The innkeeper bustled out; he was very chatty: The Tiber had overflowed its banks, he heard; he did not see how the diligence could reach Rome.

There was some consternation among the passengers. What to do? Could they perhaps spend the night at the inn? Things would look more cheerful when the sun shone. The innkeeper threw up his hands. What to do indeed! His hostelry could not accommodate thirty persons—no, not even if he and his wife were to sleep in the kitchen. There were no other houses near. Might they not, in a pinch, spend the night in the diligences, he suggested.

A raw wind blew up from the marshes; the passengers shivered. Margaret took things in hand: To spend the night in such rank, damp air would be worse than to attempt crossing the Tiber. Hearing a voice which sounded positive and convincing, the others agreed to continue the journey. With a creaking and a grinding, the diligences started up again. Soon the moon came out and silvered all the ancient grandeurs; a thin mist hovered over the valleys, as if the spirits of many nuns were waving their gray veils gently in salutation. Every one watched eagerly for the first glimpse of the Tiber.

Up rose the towers and the domes of Rome, but between them and the travelers lay plains and meadows shining in the moonlight like sheets of molten silver. The water from the Tiber!

The drivers stopped, considered. The road before them was likewise overspread. Finally they decided that the water was not deep enough to endanger any lives.

Fortunately it was not. The horses had known much harder journeys than that. They went cautiously, the water flew up on each side in glistening spray....

At last the gate was reached. Margaret, relieved and excited to be again in Rome, got out while the diligence was being examined, and walked through the moonlight to the grounds of a large villa with "its rich shrubberies of myrtle and its statues so pale and eloquent in the moonlight."

The room which Ossoli had engaged for her looked out on the Piazza Barberini. It was large and airy and had "the most delightful view all around imaginable." For neighbors Margaret had a Prussian sculptor; a good priest who made her fire for her when the landlady happened to be out marketing; a "frightful Russian princess with mustaches, and a footman who ties her bonnet for her," and an Englishwoman of ample proportions who had made for the household a beautiful terrace of flowers.

The spirit of the place was a happy one. The proprietors were a delightful old couple who immediately began to mother Margaret. Many times she sat with them and heard unbelievable stories of the friendship which existed between their singing-birds and their enormous black cat.

To such a place Ossoli could come without question and without spies. Margaret found him paler from his recent illness, and more melancholy. He was worried about his affairs. He had learned that his father's estate was encumbered with debts; he doubted if anything would remain for him after they were paid. He still wished their marriage to remain a secret, for one never knew what strange, sudden turn the wheel of fate might take.

Margaret told him in detail about her last trying weeks at Rieti. She never wearied of talking of Angelo, who had his father's slim hands and feet but was fair and blue-eyed, like Ellen Channing. "I cannot remain long from him, *caro mio*, he is so very dear, and life seems so uncertain."

Her windows gave her a look at the Quirinal. Tragic happenings there! Only a few days after her arrival in Rome, the Pope's minister Count Rossi, on descending from his carriage to enter the Chamber of Deputies, was stabbed in the back. The next day, as Margaret sat by her window writing a letter to her mother, she saw several regiments followed by a large crowd of citizens, marching toward the Quirinal. They found the Swiss Guard drawn up before the palace.

One of the leaders requested an audience with the Pope. It was refused. They rushed to the door and attempted to force it. The guard fired. Margaret saw a man fall, heard the sudden beating of a drum. That meant that the National Guard was being called out. From another direction she saw a carriage dashing through the streets. It turned in to the Palace Barberini. A liveried servant got down from the box and barred the gate of the courtyard.... The Prince of the palace was seeking the safety of his high walls.... A prophetic incident.

For several hours the noise kept up outside the Quirinal. Suddenly an upper window flew open and a man appeared armed. He fired into the crowd. His shot was answered; he fell backwards....

This was the Pope's confessor.

Inside the palace there was great consternation. Deputies hurried into the secret room where Pius IX sat in his robes of state. They told him that his confessor was dead. Pius crossed himself and bowed his head.

Outside, the crowd overcame the guard and threw itself against the door of the palace. Deputies kept coming and going between the secret room and the corridors which led to other parts of the palace.

"They demand an audience with Your Eminence." Pius did not move.

A special deputy hurried in. "They have set fire to the palace."

The Pope rose. "Tell them I will see them."

From her window Margaret saw the great door of the palace swing open and the leaders of the Revolutionary Party enter. They demanded of the Pope a new ministry under Galetti, the withdrawal of the Swiss Guard and the substitution of the Civil Militia. In other words, the Pope was to consider himself their prisoner.

Pope Pius was obliged to agree to all that they suggested.

Regarding all these happenings, Margaret wrote to her mother: "... Never feel any apprehension for my safety. There are those who will protect me, if necessary, and besides, I am on the conquering side. These events have, to me, the deepest interest. These days are what I have always longed for—were I only free from private care! But when the best and noblest want bread to give to the cause of liberty, I can just not demand *that* of them; their blood they would give me.

"You cannot conceive the enchantment of this place. So much I suffered here last January and February, I thought myself a little weaned; but returning, my heart swelled even to tears with the cry of the poet, 'O Rome, *my* country, city of the soul!' Those have not lived who have not seen Rome.

"I have been through what is called the grape-cure, much more charming, certainly, than the water-cure. At present I am very well; but alas! because I have gone to bed early and done very little. I do not know if I can maintain any labor. As to my life, I think that it is not the will of Heaven it should terminate very soon....

"If I came home at this moment, I should feel as if forced to leave my own house, my own people and the hour which I had always longed for. If I do come in this way, all I can promise is to plague other people as little as possible. My own plans and desires will be postponed to another world.

"Do not feel anxious about me. Some higher power leads me through strange, dark, thorny paths, broken at times by glades opening down into prospects of sunny beauty, into which I am not permitted to enter. If God disposes for us, it is not for nothing. This I can say, my heart is in some respects better, it is kinder and more humble. Also, my mental acquisitions have certainly been great, however inadequate to my desires.

"Of circumstances which complicate my position, I cannot write. Were you here, I would confide in you fully, and have more than once, in the silence of the night, recited to you the most strange and romantic chapters in the story of my sad life. At one time when I thought I might die, I empowered a person who has given me, as far as possible to him, the aid and sympathy of a brother, to communicate them to you, on his return to the United States. But now I think we shall meet again, and I am sure you will always love your daughter, and will know gladly that in all events she has tried to aid and striven never to injure her fellows. In earlier days, I dreamed of doing and being much, but now am content with the Magdalen to rest my plea hereon, *she has loved much.*"

. . . .

The name of Mazzini began to be shouted in the streets. A Republic must be formed at once and the exiled patriot recalled to Rome. Masses were said in all the churches for the souls of the brave fellows who had fallen in Naples, in Venice, in Milan for the cause of the revolution....

Meanwhile, the cardinals who had been chased from Rome, met daily to talk of electing an anti-Pope. Pius remained shut up in the Quirinal with a hostile guard around him. He prayed in his closet and incense encircled his head like a halo. In close communication with him were the French and the Bavarian ambassadors, the duc d'Harcourt and the Count Spaur. They had been very busy of late, getting their countrymen out of Rome. Most of the English had gone home, too, and the population which lived by the trade of foreigners were complaining because their means of livelihood were taken from them.

One day the leading comic paper appeared with a very bold caricature in its pages: Pius IX with the body of a plump, well-plumaged bird sitting on the perch of a cage with folded wings, while in the background a young Republican stood holding in one hand a match and in the other his watch. Below the match was a barrel of gunpowder.... Pius saw the cartoon and sent for the duc d'Harcourt. And that day a courier left for France with a dispatch which requested Louis Napoleon's help.

Priests went to the Quirinal unmolested. The militia thought nothing of the movements of priests; they were harmless, ineffectual creatures, of no more importance than women.

One night, nine days after the bombardment of the palace, a priest walked out through the great door and the guard thought nothing of the incident. But the next day they learned that the Pope was not praying in his closet. His two friends from France and Bavaria had arranged his escape.

He issued a manifesto protesting against the sacrilege which had been practiced on him and on those in his service. The revolutionaries carried this manifesto through the streets of Rome, mumbling false chants over it, and deposited it "in places provided for lowest uses." Then they went to all the hatters' shops, took from them all the cardinals' hats that they contained and threw them into the Tiber. The orators of the Republican Party climbed up on barrels and boxes in public places and addressed the crowds from balconies overlooking public squares. One of them cried, "Jesus bade them feed his lambs. If they have done so, it has been to rob their fleece and drink their blood."

The rumblings in the streets grew louder, the Civic Guard paraded in the morning sun, their swords flashing.

From her window Margaret watched the gathering storm. On warm days she and Ossoli went for picnics to unfrequented places outside the gates. They took roasted chestnuts which they bought in the streets and a small flagon of sweet wine. Ossoli was very tender with her, and his deference amounted to adoration.

They talked of little Angelo. Sometimes Margaret felt that she could not wait another hour without seeing him. Motherhood calmed her restless craving. "In him (Angelo) I find satisfaction for the first time to the deep wants of my heart." They talked of their future and of the consequences which would follow knowledge of their marriage. A dark subject. "My brothers are hateful to me now because I sympathize with the rebellion. What will they do when they know that I have married a Protestant and a friend of Mazzini's?"

Margaret cheered him, "Come, let us enjoy to-day while we have it. The sun shines, we are well, we have each other and our dear one is taken care of." And she tried to be merry and to make Ossoli smile...

She wrote more hopefully to Richard than she had written for months: "How much I should like to pass a week walking about Rome with you! Have patience, have obstinate patience; we may yet be here together. You may come as United States Ambassador and I will be your cicerone. Should my hair then be white, don't be anxious. It is still brown and with the admiration of the Italians... my soul will still be young...."

Her optimism has come back again and she can say once more to him, "I have found that this life, if full of unexpected conflicts and strange agonies, also never ceases to open up founts of joy and new great occasions for those who are fitted to use them."

So she told herself; and set herself diligently to her task of writing. She was a history-maker and her world was all about her offering her momentous occasions to make use of. Soon she might have a more active part to play....

Just before Christmas she went up into the mountains to see Angelo. He appeared well but she noticed that he had not grown much in two months. When she saw him undressed she knew the reason; he had had smallpox. His little body was scarred, though his face and hands were uninjured. In consternation, Margaret called the wet-nurse, and learned, bit by bit, that the doctor, though sent for, had refused to tend the child.

"But why?" the mother asks.

"His family told him that you were avaricious."

"What has that to do with it? Did he not think it was worth his trouble to try to save the child's life?"

"Maybe, Signora."

And the mother clasped the child to her and asked heaven how long this separation must continue....

She discovered a hundred things which made her all the more anxious to take Angelo back to Rome with her: The looseness of the house which allowed the wind to come in at all sides; the number of persons who played with Angelo; the fact that although he was fat, he did not seem to have grown since she had left him.

But she could not take him back to Rome with her. Apart from Ossoli's wish for secrecy, there were other reasons why the child was safest out of Rome. The mumblings of voices might grow into the rumblings of cannon. At any moment, that Republican soldier pictured in the comic weekly might set alight the barrel of gunpowder.

Stifling her anguish, Margaret returned to Rome.

On clear nights she and Ossoli made excursions to places she had always wished to see. Sometimes she spent whole days out of doors, for the sun shone that winter. But she missed the associations of the winter before, she missed the Monday evenings when everything under the sun was discussed. She longed for an intelligent exchange of ideas. But she contented herself. "I try with all my force to march straight onwards—to answer the claims of the day."

From his retreat at Gaeta, the Pope issued periodical protests, forbidding participation in the elections for a national assembly, which were soon to be held. These protests were as effective as the hooting of the owls in the Coliseum.

The elections were held, the Assembly convened. A great

procession of troops marched from the Campidoglio; the bands played the Marseillaise.

Margaret watched proceedings from a balcony in the Piazza di Venzia, where she had been advised by the American Consul to move. She was struck by the difference between the deputies of that election and those of former times. Now they marched without any badge of distinction but a tricolored scarf. Only a year before they had assembled in magnificent carriages and behind them were their liveried attendants carrying escutcheons.

Where were they now, those nobles, those proud princes of Rome who had made the ecclesiastical court a thing of such pomp and pride? Shut up in their palaces with the gates of their courtyards safely barred, or fled to some distant place where troops did not parade and where they could still wear their royal uniforms.

A few days after this assembly, Rome was declared a republic. All at once the bells on all the churches began to ring, all at once a thousand tricolors appeared in the streets. The people, as usual, wept, shouted, danced for joy. "Our day of deliverance is at hand," they said to one another.

To Richard she wrote:

"... I have led rather too lonely a life of late. Before, it seemed as if too many voices of men startled away the inspirations; but having now lived eight months much alone, I doubt that good has come of it and think to return and herd with others for a little. I have realized in these last days the thought of Goethe:

> He who would in loneliness live
> Ah! he is soon alone;
> Each one loves, each one lives
> And leaves him to his pain.

"I went away and hid all the summer. Not content with that, I said, on returning to Rome I must be busy and receive people little. They have taken me at my word and hardly any one comes to see me. Now, if I want some play and prattle, I shall have to run after them. It is fair enough that we all in turn, should be made to feel our need of one another...."

X

ANGUISH

ONE SUNDAY, Margaret and Ossoli went for a walk past the Quirinal, past the Capitol, into the Corso. A large placard attracted them. They stopped to read it. It was a summons to the city to invest Mazzini with the rights and privileges of a citizen of Rome.

Wherever they went they saw similar placards. And that day, Ossoli was more cheerful than he had been for a long time. If his cause should prosper and Rome remain a republic, the affairs of his family would automatically be transferred to the power with which he was allied. There could be then no question of his obtaining his rightful heritage.... Then too, he might receive a good post under Mazzini, and they would live openly as husband and wife, he and his Margherita, and little Angelo would have a good nursemaid....

A few days afterwards, all the bells began to ring again and banners to fly from all the windows. Doors opened and women flocked into the streets. A guard of honor was drawn up outside a large building; bands played....

Presently there appeared walking from the direction of the Ponte Molle, a tall figure in a long cloak. A shout went up, "Mazzini!"

After seventeen years of exile he had come back to be

made an honorable citizen of Rome. He was almost forty-four years old, his cheeks were lined, his eyes were sunken. But the strange, fanatical fires still glowed in them.

Now the weeping was general, now youths lost their swagger and brushed their eyes with the backs of their hands. Old men threw themselves on their knees, crossed themselves and gave thanks that they had lived to see that day; old women drew close to Mazzini and reached out their bony hands to touch his cloak. Their faith was absolute.

For some minutes Mazzini could not speak. The guard of honor waited, rigid. At last he said a few simple words; he thanked the people for their faith and thanked God that things looked brighter. "I feel a spring of new life in me," he said. He did not say much more, but went quickly into the large building.

The next day he took his place in the Assembly. First he appointed a Committee of War and increased the Roman army from 16,000 to 45,000 men. He sent word to his friend Garibaldi to come as quickly as he could from Milan.

And one day Garibaldi arrived with his motley band of fifteen hundred men, he and his staff on horseback. Their scarlet blouses and the nondescript uniforms of the soldiers gave the procession the appearance of a circus parade.

One evening when Margaret was alone in her room writing, she heard the doorbell ring, heard some one speak her name. She got up and opened her door. Mazzini was coming up the stairs. How changed he was! His face showed "all his new sufferings" which had been transmuted into a spiritualized splendor, so that he now looked "more divine than ever."

He stayed with Margaret for two hours, but this was scarcely long enough to talk of all the things there were to talk of. When he left he said that he would come often.

There was no more writing for Margaret that night. Her

desire to do something to further the cause of the republic flamed up again. She loved Mazzini with all the fervor a religious devotee has for a saint. "Freely would I give my life to aid him," she thought.

This might become necessary. Mazzini was in great danger. In a short time he sent troops against the Piedmontese whose minister Gioberti was working zealously to reinstate the Pope. The skirmish did not last long; the Piedmontese were defeated. Rome rejoiced.

And now the Assembly replaced the Executive Committee by a Triumvirate with Mazzini at its head. Twice he sent tickets to Margaret to hear him speak. She listened rapt. Mazzini had a commanding voice, a fine delivery and a magnetic personality. But speaking exhausted him so that when he sat down he seemed merely a wraith of a man, "sustained only by the fire of his soul."

In March Margaret went to Rieti to see little Angelo. She found him vigorous and healthy and altogether delightful. She carried him into the olive grove and there they stayed for hours. She thought that he was going to be a precocious child. This pleased her, as she wanted him to resemble her. She had forgotten that among her childish scribblings there had been found a scrap of paper containing words strangely prophetical. They were written when she was ten years old and had been found among her father's papers: "On the 23rd of May, 1810, was born one foredoomed to sorrow and pain and like others, to have misfortunes. She had feeling which few have, which is the SOURCE of sorrow." The last thing she wished for little Angelo was that he should be "foredoomed to sorrow." If he could be like her in other respects—if he could have her quick wit, her keen perceptions, her sensitiveness, her passion for truth—she felt certain that he would become a well developed personality. And so she played with him in the olive grove and tried to visualize him as a man.

About the middle of April, she returned to Rome. Events had moved swiftly. In France, Louis Napoleon who was President, thought it would not be a bad idea to send help to the Pope. It would win to his side all the priesthood of France and would give the army a new adventure and thus conciliate it for a time. Consequently, he ordered General Oudinot to go South with an army of ten thousand picked men.

While there was stirring talk in Rome of making Mazzini President of the New Republic, this army steadily advanced. On the last day of April it crept unmolested into Civita-Vecchia, in the shadow of the very walls of Rome. Within those walls were only eight thousand soldiers, most of them citizens in arms for the first time. The French officers, anticipating immediate capitulation, swaggered around in full dress and joked about the ragamuffin brigade that huddled on the other side of the wall.

Out came Garibaldi with his motley troops, who showed remarkable spirit. This was a surprise. Before they realized what was going on, the French found themselves seriously threatened on two sides. What was there for them to do but retreat?

Retreat they did, to reform their regiments and take counsel together—but not before they had lost a thousand men.

Now there were serious doings inside the walls of Rome. Rumors came that the Austrians were on their way and that Bomba was coming from Naples with a large force. The news of Bomba was not believed; the last picture that he gave of himself was one of hurry and consternation and the ardent desire to remove himself as far as possible from the republican artillery.

On the day that Oudinot appeared outside the walls, Margaret received this letter: "Dear Miss Fuller: You are named *Regolatrice* of the Hospital of the Fate-Bene Fratelli. Go there at twelve, if the alarm bell has not rung before. When you arrive there, you will receive all the women coming for the wounded, and give them your directions, so that you are sure to have a certain number of them, night and day. May God help us. Christine Trivulze, of Belgiojoso."

This was Margaret's opportunity. Now her longing to participate in the struggle was to be realized....

The roads leading into Rome were filled with carts and improvised ambulances moving slowly along, with blood dripping through their floors. At the Hospital of the Fate-Bene Fratelli, Margaret received the loads of wounded and saw that they had immediate attention. She thought of Ossoli fighting on the walls; she thought of Angelo alone in the mountains and wondered if, one day, he would be brought in mangled from the field of war. And she thought of all the mothers of these boys whose wounds she washed... and of the others, whose wounds were beyond washing... and she felt herself a *Mater Dolorosa* and was consumed with grief.

Every day when the hour came for her to get a breath of fresh air, she went to the post office and waited under the burning sun for word of little Angelo. All the others seemed a long way off now—Richard and Ellen and her mother. Richard had married quite suddenly, some one whose name Margaret did not know. Ellen was no happier than she had ever been these last few years. Arthur was an ordained clergyman.

Margaret thanked God that they were all safe in America; she thanked God that she was in Italy doing something for Mazzini. She saw him often; and each time he seemed more melancholy and more haggard than the time before.

She had but little opportunity for writing. Sometimes she was at the hospital all day and all night. She had as many moments with Ossoli as she could, but they were few enough. The Princess Belgiojoso, whose fortune was in the possession of the papal authorities of Milan, went from house to house soliciting funds for the hospitals. The Americans contributed two hundred and fifty dollars. The Storys were among those who helped, for they were now in Rome.

Suddenly there was a cessation of military action, suddenly an armistice was declared. But Oudinot remained outside the gates, and the Civic Guard kept its arms in order.

There came rumblings: A Spanish expedition of 4,000 men was on the march; the Austrians were coming with 28,000, and Bomba was actually at the head of 25,000 troops. Garibaldi decided to make an attack before all these troops united. One night about the middle of May he went forth to meet Bomba. Only one thousand soldiers remained within the walls of Rome.

On the way he met the friendly garrison from Bologna, 10,000 of them. They marched together and sighted Bomba near Palestrina. They engaged them. Bomba was defeated and sent flying across the frontier. Garibaldi returned to Rome.

There he found a French army of 35,000 strong, with great field guns and a corps of skillful artillery officers. Opposing them were 15,000 Roman youths. Oudinot had just issued this manifesto: "To afford French residents the opportunity of leaving the city on demand of the French Minister, I agree not to attack Rome before Monday morning, June 5th."

An hour before dawn on Sunday, June 4th, the sudden booming of cannon and the rain of musketry told the citizens that Oudinot's manifesto had been but a ruse to throw them off their guard. And while his lips had moved in dictation of the gallant promise, his eyes swept over the ramparts of Rome to detect the most undefended places.

On these his attack was made. Garibaldi's soldiers, weary from their long march, jumped again into action. Four times they recaptured the Villa Corsini. At length Oudinot withdrew. But throughout all that Sabbath day, cars moved along the streets, carrying wounded men to hospitals....

Early the next morning, Margaret went to headquarters and asked for Ossoli. He was not there. Where was he? She prayed God that his regiment had not yet been called upon. She hurried away. Perhaps he had gone to her....

But he had not been to her lodgings.

She managed to send a little note to him:

"Monday, June 5th, 1849.
"Mio Caro—

"This morning I went to the garden of the Vatican at half-past eight; they sought you and said when they returned that you had gone out. I returned immediately home; but as you have not been here, I think it was a mistake. This evening I hope to be in the house at eight; if you come first, wait, I beg of you. Thank God that you are yet living. How much I suffered yesterday you can believe. Till we meet again, caro consorte, as that wicked Ser. Giovanni always wrote. I go out because I ought to go to the hospitals."

She went off to the hospital; but her mind was not on her work. She thought constantly of Ossoli and prayed that he was safe.

Along toward noontime, word came from him. He was safe! But his place was just inside the walls; and the walls offered but little resistance to the thundering field guns.

The next day Margaret wrote a letter to Mrs. Story, who was in Florence:

"Rome, 6th June, 1849.
"... On Sunday, from our loggia, I witnessed a terrible, a real battle. It began at four in the morning; it lasted to the last gleam of light. The musket-fire was almost unintermitted; the roll of the cannon, especially from St. Angelo, most majestic.... I saw the smoke of every discharge, the

flash of the bayonets; with a glass could see the men. Both French and Italians fought with the most obstinate valor. The French could not use their heavy cannon, being always driven away by the legions of Garibaldi and ... when trying to find positions for them. The loss on our side was about three hundred killed and wounded; theirs must be much greater. In one casino have been found seventy dead bodies of theirs. I find the wounded men at the hospitals in a transport of indignation. The French soldiers fought so furiously that they think them false as their general, and cannot endure the remembrance of their visits during the armistice, and talk of brotherhood. The cannonade on one side has continued day and night (being full moon), till this morning. ... The French throw rockets into the town; one burst in the courtyard of the hospital, just as I arrived there yesterday, agitating the poor sufferers very much; they said they did not want to die like mice in a trap."

The siege began in more measured fashion. Oudinot changed his tactics to a wearing-down method of fighting. Mazzini ordered that church bells be taken from their high places and cast into cannon. Every old musket that had hung on Roman walls for generations was rammed with gunpowder. ...

Day after day the boom and rattle, day after day the slow-moving carts with their loads of wounded. The statues which stood up in the gardens against the dark trees were shattered; the birds huddled in the pine trees or took to quiet country shelters.

Margaret lived in anguish. On the days when she heard no news of Ossoli, she went to where his regiment was stationed. Once she saw blood dripping from the wall where, an hour before, he had been fighting. She knew that at any moment a shell might whistle through the air and fall in front of her or behind her as she went from hospital to hospital.

And one night she wrote to Mrs. Story and told her of her secret marriage and the birth of her child. She asked Mrs. Story to care for Angelo if she should die.

At the same time she wrote to Ossoli: "In the event of the death of both of us, I have left a paper with a certificate in regard to Angelino and some lines, praying the Storys to take care of him. If, by any accident, *I* die, you can revoke this paper if you will from me as being your wife. I have asked Nino to go to America, but you will do as seems best to you.... If you live and I die, be always most devoted to Nino. If you ever love another, think first of him, I pray, pray, love."

The writing of these letters gave her melancholy relief. She schooled herself to live only by moments. And when the sun went down on a day which still saw Ossoli alive, she gave thanks....

Day after day the anguish of seeing fair youth mutilated ... Margaret wrote their letters for them, to their mothers, their wives, their sweethearts.... Her soul was sickened by the frightful cost of war. She began to wonder if Mazzini was right in the means he used to gain his great democracy. Her heart ached for him. He had aged; his eyes were bloodshot, his cheeks parched as if all the life-force had been drained out of them. But he was calm and gentle and "of a more fiery purpose than ever."

She wrote a long letter to Emerson:

"Rome, 10th June, 1849.

"I received your letter amid the round of cannonade and musketry. It was a terrible battle fought here from the first till the last light of day. I could see all its progress from my balcony. The Italians fought like lions. It is truly a heroic spirit that animates them. They make a stand here for honor and their rights, with little ground for hope, they resist, now they are betrayed by France.

"Since the 30th April, I go almost daily to the hospitals, and though I have suffered—for I had no idea before how terrible gunshot wounds and wound fever are—yet I have taken pleasure in being with the men; there is scarcely one who is not moved by a noble spirit. Many, especially among the Lombards, are the flower of Italian youth. When they begin to get better, I carry them books and flowers; they read and we talk.

"The palace of the Pope on the Quirinal is now used for convalescents. In those beautiful gardens I walk with them—one with his sling, another with his crutch. The gardener plays off all his water-works for the defenders of the country, and gathers flowers for me, their friend.

"A day or two since, we sat in the Pope's little pavilion, where he used to give private audience. The sun was going gloriously down over Monte Mario, where gleamed the white tents of the French light-horse among the trees. The cannonade was heard at intervals. Two bright-eyed boys sat at our feet and gathered up eagerly every word said by the heroes of the day. It was a beautiful hour stolen from the midst of ruin and sorrow; and tales were told as full of grace and pathos as in the gardens of Boccaccio—only in a very different spirit—with noble hope for man, with reverence for woman. . . .

"Should I never return—and sometimes I despair of doing so, it seems so far off, so difficult, I am caught in such a net of ties here—if ever you know of my life here, I think you will only wonder at the constancy with which I have sustained myself; the degree of profit to which, amid great difficulties, I have put the time, at least in the way of observation. Meanwhile, love me all you can; let me feel that amid the fearful agitations of the world, there are pure hands, with healthful, even pulse, stretched out toward me, if I claim their grasp. . . ."

As she lay at night in that shadowy land between sleep and wakefulness, she had strange incongruous visions: She saw herself as a child studying Horace and Virgil; she saw Ossoli walking in the fields around Groton; she heard the river thundering down from the mountains at Rieti. The white peacocks from the gardens of the Vatican passed before her; Richard appeared suddenly, and Eugene her best loved brother.... She woke suddenly with the cannon booming in the heavens.

The bombardment became heavier. Refugees ran distracted through the streets. They swarmed into the house where Margaret lived. They told her gruesome tales....

The heat was stifling. Provisions were almost out of reach, so high had prices gone. Shopkeepers shrugged. "What will you? There is scarcely any food left in all of Rome."

The end of June. The city was an Inferno. How could any one possibly live another day? Margaret sent an urgent note to Lewis Cass, Chargé d'affaires of the American Embassy. He hurried to her lodgings. He found her lying on a sofa, very pale, completely exhausted. Her relief at seeing him told him that she had something of great importance to tell him....

She told him of her secret marriage, and about Angelo. She gave him a bunch of papers which she asked him to keep and if she died, to send them to her family and her friends in the United States.

She said, "Ossoli is now in command of a battery on the Pincian Hill. You know that is the most exposed position in Rome and directly in line of the French fire. It is not reasonable to think that he can escape another such night as last night. So to-night I shall go to him and share with him whatever happens. He is to come for me at Ave Maria. ... It is now almost that hour."

Cass took the papers, tried to hearten her, said good-by and hurried away. Just outside the gate he met Ossoli....

He watched for them and in a few minutes saw them going together toward the Pincian Hill.

Night drew on, the stars came out. Margaret and Ossoli watched them from the Pincian Hill. Hour after hour went by, beating up against the stars from a clock-tower the French bombs had not reached.

All was quiet outside the walls.

All night long, they waited for the bombardment to begin. It was not recommenced. In the early morning they walked back through the torn streets to Margaret's room where they breakfasted together and talked in half-whispers as if they listened for something....

On that day the French army entered Rome. The siege was over; Mazzini had failed.... And Ossoli's fortunes were more precarious than ever....

XI

EXILES

MARGARET'S THOUGHTS now flew to her family. In all probability she would see them again. This was comforting. But close beside it ran the other, ever-present racking thought about the means of living. What would Ossoli do in America? She could not visualize him there; he did not speak a word of English, she doubted if he would ever learn the language. She would have to be the breadwinner. That was all very well if her health held out. But would it? At present she felt that she could never earn another cent. She was unutterably exhausted.

She tried to write to Richard but could not make much headway. "I feel indisposed to write; my heart is too full. Private hopes of mine are fallen with the hopes of Italy. I have played for a new stake and lost it. Life looks too difficult."

She knew that she could not remain in Rome. For the priestly retinue had all come back from Gaeta and marched triumphantly through the palace doors. French soldiers paraded up and down with bayonets fixed. When they saw little knots of citizens gathered together, they leveled the bayonets at them and ordered them to disperse.

Margaret was anxious to see little Angelo; and as soon as she could, she went up into the mountains. Her heart leaped joyously when she saw the rows of red roofs ablaze in the summer sun, when she saw the grapevines trailing over the trees and heard the little bell from the Capucines' convent. She wondered if Angelo would recognize her immediately. Would he snuggle his head against her shoulder in the dear, confiding way he had? Would he break into smiles, the moment she appeared?

She hurried from the diligence, up the narrow, little street. The woman in whose charge Margaret had left the child seemed to turn away from her when she opened the door; she was slow in answering Margaret's questions. Margaret went past her. "But quick! I must see him! Take me at once to him."

He was lying in a miserable cot; he was worn to a skeleton; he looked like a faded, little corpse; he could not smile, he could not even raise his hand.

"How has this happened?" the mother asks and wonders how she can keep her hands off the cringing creature before her.

With whines and complaints, the woman makes her excuses: Her milk left her; she was ill.... What could she do? It was not her fault?

"But was there no other milk? Why did you not get other milk for him? You were well paid for it."

Milk was hard to find. Besides, he would not take it.

"What did you feed him then?"
She had fed him on bread dipped in wine.
"The sour native wine!"
"Si, signora."

It took a month of tender nursing to bring the smiles back to Angelo's face. How Margaret loathed those lying, thieving people! But now they could not rob her, for she knew their language; and she bought things herself....

While in Rieti, Margaret wrote her mother of her secret marriage and of little Angelo.

"... Receiving a few days since, a package of letters from America, I opened them with more feeling of hope and good cheer than for a long time past. The first words that met my eyes were these, in the hand of Mr. Greeley: 'Ah, Margaret, the world grows dark with us! You grieve, for Rome is fallen —I mourn, for Pickie is dead.'

"I have shed rivers of tears over the inexpressibly affecting letter thus begun. One would think I might have become familiar enough with the images of death and destruction; yet somehow, the image of Pickie's little dancing figure, lying stiff and stark, between his parents, has made me weep more than all else. There was little hope he could do justice to himself or lead a happy life in so perplexed a world; but never was a character of richer capacity—never a more charming child. To me he was most dear, and would always have been so.... The three children I have seen who were fairest in my eyes and gave most promise of the future were Waldo, Pickie, Hermann Clarke—all nipped in the bud. Endless thoughts this has given me, and a resolve to seek the realization of all hopes and plans elsewhere, which resolve will weigh with me as much as it can weigh before the silver cord is finally loosed. Till then, Earth our mother, always finds strange, unexpected ways to draw us back to her bosom—to make us seek anew a nutriment which has never failed to cause us frequent sickness.

"This brings me to the main object of my present letter— a piece of intelligence about myself, which I had hoped I might be able to communicate in such a way as to give you *pleasure*. That I cannot—after suffering much in silence with that hope—is like the rest of my earthly destiny.

"The first moment it may cause you a pang to know that your eldest child might long ago have been addressed by another name than yours, and has a little son a year old.

"But, beloved mother, do not feel this long. I do assure you, that it was only great love for you that kept me silent. I have abstained a hundred times, when your sympathy, your counsel would have been most precious, from a wish not to harass you with anxiety. Even now I would abstain, but it has become necessary, on account of the child, for us to live publicly and permanently together; and we have no hope, in the present state of Italian affairs, that we can do it at any better advantage, for several years, than now.

"My husband is a Roman, of a noble but now impoverished house. His mother died when he was an infant, his father is dead since we met, leaving some property but encumbered with debts, and in the present state of Rome, hardly available except by living there. He has three older brothers, all provided for in the Papal Service—one as Secretary of the Privy Chamber, the other two as members of the Guard Noble. A similar career would have been opened to him, but he embraced liberal principles, and with the fall of the Republic has lost all, as well as the favor of his family, who all sided with the Pope. Meanwhile, having been an officer in the Republican service, it was best for him to leave Rome. He has taken what little money he had and we plan to live in Florence for the winter. If he or I can get the means, we shall come together to the United States in the summer— earlier we could not, on account of the child.

"He is not in any respect such a person as people in general would expect to find with me. He had no instructor except an old priest, who entirely neglected his education; and of all that is contained in books he is absolutely ignorant, and he has no enthusiasm of character. On the other hand, he has excellent practical sense; has been a judicious observer of all that passed before his eyes; has a nice sense of duty, which in its unfailing, minute activity, may put most enthusiasts to shame; a very sweet temper and great native refinement. His love for me has been unswerving and most tender. I have never suffered a pain that he could relieve. His devotion, when I am ill, is to be compared only with yours. His delicacy in trifles, his sweet, domestic graces remind me of Ellen. In him I have found a home, and one that interferes with no tie. Amid many ills and cares, we have had much joy together, in the sympathy with natural beauty—with our child—with all that is innocent and sweet.

"I do not know whether he will always love me so well, for I am the elder, and the difference will become, in a few years, more perceptible than now. But life is so uncertain and it is so necessary to take good things with their limitations, that I have not thought it worth while to calculate too curiously.

"However my other friends may feel, I am sure that *you* will love him very much, and that he will love you no less. Could we all live together on a moderate income, you would find peace with us. Heaven grant that, on returning, I may find means to effect this object. He, of course, can do nothing while we are in the United States, but perhaps I can; and now that my health is better, I shall be able to exert myself, if sure that my child is watched by those who love him, and who are good and pure.

"What shall I say of my child? All might seem hyperbole, even to my dearest mother. In him I find satisfaction for the first time, to the deep wants of my heart. Yet, thinking of those other sweet ones fled, I must look upon him as a treasure only lent. He is a fair child, with blue eyes and light hair, very affectionate, graceful and sportive. He was baptized in the Roman Catholic Church, by the name of Angelo Eugene Philip, for his father, grandfather and my brother. He inherits the title of marquis.

"Write the name of my child in your Bible, Angelo Ossoli, born September 5, 1848. God grant that he may live to see you, and may prove worthy of your love!

"More I do not feel strength to say. You can hardly guess how all attempt to express something about the great struggles and experiences of my European life enfeebles me. When I get home—if ever I do—it will be told without this fatigue and excitement. I trust there will be a little repose, before entering anew on this wearisome conflict.

"I had addressed you twice—once under the impression that I should not survive the birth of my child; again during the siege of Rome, the father and I being both in danger. . . ."

She wrote also to her sister Ellen Channing:

"About Ossoli, I do not like to say much, as he is an exceedingly delicate person. He is not precisely reserved, but it is not natural for him to talk about the objects of strong affection. I am sure he will not try to describe me to his sister, but would rather she would take her own impression of me; and, as much as possible, I wish to do the same by him. I presume that to many of my friends, he will be nothing, and they will not understand that I should have life in common with him. But I do not think he will care—he has not the slightest tinge of self-love. He has, throughout our intercourse, been used to my having many such ties. He has no wish to be anything to persons with whom he does not feel spontaneously bound, and when I am occupied, is happy in himself. But some of my friends and my family, who will see him in the details of practical life, cannot fail to prize the purity and simple strength of his character; and should he continue to love me as he has done, his companionship will be an inestimable blessing to me. I say *if,* because all human affections are frail, and I have experienced too great revulsions in my own not to know it. Yet I feel great confidence in the permanence of his love. It has been unblemished so far, under many trials; especially as I have been more desponding and unreasonable in many ways, than I ever was before, and more so, I hope, than I ever shall be again. But at all such times, he never had a thought except to sustain and cheer me. He is capable of the sacred love—the love passing that of woman. He showed it to his father, to Rome, to me. Now he loves his child in the same way. I think he will be an excellent father. . . .

"Our meeting was singular, fateful, I may say. Very soon he offered me his hand through life, but I never dreamed I should take it. I loved him and felt very unhappy to leave him; but the connection seemed so every way fit, I did not hesitate a moment. He, however, thought I should return to him, as I did. I acted upon a strong impulse and could not analyze at all what passed in my mind. I neither rejoice nor grieve—for bad or for good, I acted out my character. Had I never connected myself with any one, my path was clear; now it is all hid; but in that case, my development must have been partial. As to marriage, I think the intercourse of heart and mind may be fully enjoyed without entering into this partnership of daily life. Still, I do not find it burdensome. The friction that I have seen mar so much the domestic happiness of others does not occur with us, or, at least, has not occurred. Then, there is the pleasure of always being at hand to help one another.

"Still, the great novelty, the immense gain to me is my relation with my child. I thought the mother's heart lived in me before, but it did not—I knew nothing about it. Yet, before the birth, I dreaded it. I thought I should not survive; but if I did, and my child did, was I not cruel to bring another into this terrible world? I could not, at that time, get any other view. When he was born, that deep melancholy changed at once into rapture; but it did not last long. Then came the prudential motherhood. I grew a coward, a caretaker, not only for the morrow, but, impiously faithless, for twenty or thirty years ahead. It seemed very wicked to have brought the little tender thing into the midst of cares and perplexities we had not feared in the least for ourselves. . . .

"During the siege of Rome, I could not see my little boy. What I endured at that time, in various ways, not many would survive. In the burning sun, I went, every day, to wait in the crowd for letters about him. Often they did not come. I saw blood that had streamed on the wall where Ossoli was. I have a piece of the bomb that burst close to him. I sought solace in tending the suffering men; but when I beheld the beautiful, fair young men bleeding to death, or mutilated for life, I felt the woe of all the mothers who had nursed each to that full flower, to see them thus cut down. I thought even if he (Angelo) lives, if he comes into the world at this great, troubled time, it may be to die thus in twenty years, one of a glorious hecatomb, indeed, but still a sacrifice. It seemed then I was willing he should die.

"I intend to write all that relates to the birth of Angelino, in a little book, which I shall, I hope, show you sometime. I have begun it, and then stopped—it seemed to me he would die. If he lives, I shall finish it before the details are all faded from my mind. . . ."

She had many thoughts about the constancy of Ossoli's love. As she looked down the pathway of the years, she saw herself aging and Ossoli in full vigor, would grow haggard from the unceasing worry about money; the burden of domestic details would rob her of her lightness. Often, too, she feared that, one day, friction might come. She remembered very well how Nathan's ardor had changed to irritability, then to indifference. Ossoli was not Nathan, but he was a man; and he was nine years younger than she. It would be natural for him to be attracted by some one his own age....

She banished such thoughts. She was alive; was not that enough? She was alive and the earth was beautiful. There were the Tuscan vineyards, the glittering fountains, the white statues gleaming against dark leaves.

If only they might go somewhere together and find peace—she and Angelino and Ossoli! Perhaps Ossoli could get some money from his family, now that the revolution was over and the Pope reinstated.

She looked at Angelino. Her heart warmed. She felt that all the secrecy, all the suffering, all her anguish during the siege of Rome, were amply compensated. She knew that there would be questionings, there would be smiles and shrugs and insinuations, when her news was known. But what matter? She had Angelino. She was a mother more than she was a wife.

There *were* questionings and shrugs and insinuations; there was astonishment in New England. And how the tongues rattled! Margaret heard all this from Mrs. Story, and answered her: "I feel confident you will say that what I have done has been in a good spirit and not contrary to *my* ideas of right. For the rest, you will not admit for me as I do not for myself, the rights of the social inquisition of the United States, to know all the details of my affairs. If my mother is content, if Ossoli and I are content, if our child when grown up shall be content, that is enough. You and I know enough of the United States to be sure that many persons there will blame what is peculiar.... But I think there will remain for me a sufficient number of friends to keep my heart warm and to help me earn my bread; that is all that is of any consequence."

Her mother was content. She wrote Margaret the most beautiful letter she had ever written her, in which she said that she rejoiced that she would not die feeling that there was no one left to love Margaret with the devotion she needed.

She offered to share whatever she had with Margaret and her little family.

At the end of September Margaret gathered that little family together and took them off to Florence. The Brownings were there—also with a small son seven months old; Madame Arconati was there, and Powers and Greenough and the Moshiers—a friendly coterie.

But Margaret was not welcome. The authorities were well aware of her republican sentiments, and the police had instructions to keep an eye on her. They kept many eyes on her and made her feel very uncomfortable. Ossoli too was watched. When he came out of church after vespers, which he attended regularly, he saw a policeman hanging around the door. This important functionary followed him till he disappeared into his lodgings.

Horatio Greenough used his influence, but with only meager success. Then Margaret appealed to Lewis Cass. The intervention of the American chargé d'affaires was much more effective. Almost immediately the little family of exiles was left in peace.

Ossoli had managed to get some money from his family; Margaret's friends in the United States sent wedding-presents in the form of checks. Caroline Sturgis, who was now married and a mother, wrote feelingly.

Margaret was happy, happier than she had ever been. She was living in rooms whose windows looked out on the graceful Campanile; her husband and child were with her; she had friends in Florence.

She bathed and dressed Angelo herself. And now her letters are a series of ecstatic eulogies: "He is full of all manner of tricks that I think girls never dream of." "I feel so refreshed by his young life." "I play with him, my ever-growing mystery."

Ossoli continued to be the perfect lover: "He diffuses such power and sweetness over every day that I cannot endure to think yet of our future.... I suppose that very soon now I must do something.... I hope I shall feel able when the time comes. I do not yet...."

She cannot escape the feeling of some approaching catastrophe: "This much I do hope, in life or death not to be separated from Angelino...." "Should I live, I don't know whether I should wish him to be an Italian or American citizen. But should he die, the person to whom he would naturally fall, is a sister of his father, a person of great elegance and sweetness, but entirely limited in mind.... I should not like that."

Mrs. Story assured her that, should the necessity arise, she would take care of Angelo. This was comforting.

Details of her friends' reactions to her marriage began to reach her. The lack of understanding, the curiosity, the meddling questions were all repellent to Margaret. To Caroline Sturgis she wrote: "It is so different here. When I made my appearance with a husband and a child of a year old, nobody did the least thing to annoy me. All were most cordial, none asked or implied questions." And she mentioned one woman in particular, "who might be qualified in the Court Journal as one of the highest rank," who wrote her immediately on hearing of her secret and said, "What difference can it make except that I shall love you more now that we can sympathize as mothers?" This was Madame Arconati.

The reason why Margaret knew nothing of the surprise her marriage had caused among the Americans in Italy was that they concealed it better than did those at home. That there was surprise, that there were questionings in Italy as well as in New England, there can be no doubt. Elizabeth Barrett Browning, whom Margaret met shortly after arriving in Florence, wrote to Miss Mitford, the English author: "The American authoress Miss Fuller ... has taken us by surprise at Florence, retiring from the Roman field with a husband and a child above a year old. Nobody had even suspected a word of this underplot, and her American friends stood in mute astonishment before this apparition of them here. The husband is a Roman marquis, appearing amiable and gentlemanly, but with no pretension to cope with his wife on any ground appertaining to the intellect. She talks, he listens."

A fragment of an undated letter to Mrs. Story says:

"The society of the Brownings affords me great entertainment and pleasure, but I fancy I make but little return. I do not feel drawn out, but like to hear them, especially Browning. When he comes here for an hour, I feel exhilarated by his full tide of talk—fine talk it is, he tells so many things I want to know, and his generous, loyal nature warms one so truly, the while. He is like one of the best American men; I find nothing of the modern Englishman about him; genuine Saxon."

Margaret devoted her mornings to writing the history of the revolution. Ossoli busied himself with trifling tasks; he was largely self-sufficient, and did not mind being alone. He wore his old brown uniform for which he had great affection. Little Angelo had his nurse to keep an eye on him; she was the only servant Margaret had, with the exception of the porter's wife, who helped occasionally with the heavier work.

Margaret had a pupil, Isabella Moshier, the daughter of the Ohio merchant who had become a sculptor. The proceeds from her teaching helped her, she said, "to eke out bread and salt and coffee."

Ossoli was endeavoring to learn English from Horace Sumner, the youngest son of Charles Sumner, who came in in the evenings and read to him. In return, Ossoli sometimes read Italian to him. Margaret sat looking on, a bit of sewing in her hands. More often she went to see the Brownings or called at other English-speaking houses. She and the Brownings became friends immediately. "A very interesting person she is, far better than her writings—thoughtful, spiritual in her habitual mode of mind; not only exalted but *exaltée* in her opinions, and yet calm in manner." Thus Elizabeth Browning in another letter to Miss Mitford.

The English-speaking colony met once a week. They talked of many things. Elizabeth Browning was especially interested in the new book *Shirley* by the author of the sensational success *Jane Eyre*, which had taken London by storm two years previously. *Shirley* was not so much of a success, but Miss Mitford considered it a better book, Elizabeth said. She herself had not yet read it. Tennyson's *Princess* was the latest success. Three editions had been sold. And Tennyson had taken rooms in Lincoln's Inn Fields and was about to become a Londoner. Another bit of news which interested Margaret was that George Sand was waving banners for the Reds....

Very stimulating evenings they were. "Mr. Browning enriches every hour I pass with him," Margaret wrote. Elizabeth she loved; and felt an additional bond with her because their children were both so young and because they were both middle-aged mothers.

The good weather held till the middle of December, then came cold winds and raw rains. Margaret and Ossoli were ill from the cold and little Angelo suffered from chilblains. He could walk now. "I take much pleasure in watching his little foolish legs," the mother wrote to Caroline Sturgis. And many more things she wrote about this, "her mystery and the miracle of her life." Gone was all her pedantic turn of phrase, gone the stilted sentences which sometimes made her letters sound prim. All life now revolved around Angelo; Christmas took on a new meaning for Margaret, for now she saw Christmas through his eyes. She spent hours watching him playing with his toys. "It almost made me cry to see the kind of fearful rapture with which he regarded them." She saw in him characteristics and virtues which no one else saw, just as every mother always sees in her children superior qualities which others may regard as something entirely different. . . .

Spring came back at last and crept into the olive groves; days of long sunshine followed days of long gloom. One walked among anemones, cowslips and daffodils, the old walls became alive with tender, lissome vines, the old ruins were festooned as if for some great occasion. Margaret said over and over, "I never felt as happy as now."

But it was not alone the spring which made her so happy. "Nothing but a child can take the worst bitterness out of life and break the spell of loneliness. I shall not be alone in other worlds, whenever Eternity may call me." And now she knew deep, transcendent peace.

She was eager to return to America. Her history of the revolution was finished, she must find a publisher as soon as possible. She knew that she would receive a much more advantageous contract in her own country than in Europe. There were too other reasons for her eagerness to return —a long heart-hunger for her own people, her family and her friends.

She looked up sailings, made reckonings. Everything was very expensive. She could not make up her mind about a passage. "I am suffering as never before from the horrors of indecision." She could not overcome a lingering feeling of anxiety about her reception: cold, appraising looks at Ossoli, conscious efforts to speak casually, which reveal much; compressed lips and calculating eyes. She constantly tried to reassure herself in such fashion as this—a letter to the Springs, who were now back in New York: "People, when they see me, will not generally be inclined to injure me, for they will see the expressor of a heart bettered by experience, more humble and tender, more anxious to serve its kind than ever before."

The precariousness of the future troubled her; and again she sought to reassure herself: "I think my path will somehow be made plain to me, though I cannot yet see distinctly how."

She thought of returning home by way of France, taking the packet ship *Argo* from Havre. One day she took up a paper and read that the *Argo* had been wrecked on its return voyage from America. Her eyes strayed across the page. She read of the wreck of the *Royal Adelaide,* an English craft believed very seaworthy; and of the *John Skiddy,* a fine American vessel....

She wrote to Madame Arconati, "I am absolutely fearful about this voyage. Various little omens have combined to give me a dark feeling...."

Ossoli told her that it had been prophesied that he would die by drowning. She tried to make light of this, but a great bird seemed to hover over her, with darkening wings....

XII
"'NO MORE GRIEF AND 'NO MORE SEA'"

SHE DECIDED TO SAIL ON THE "ELIZABETH," a merchant vessel which would leave Leghorn on May 17th. To obtain the necessary funds, she borrowed money from the bank, giving Marcus Spring as security for a hundred-day note for $336. She wrote at once to Mr. Spring, telling him how she intended to repay the sum—by royalties from her book on the revolution, or by money she would earn in other fashion.... But there was always uncertainty about a sea voyage....

"Should I perish at sea, I know you will not see it (the note) dishonored. Mrs. Farrer writes that she has $100 for me, Mother that she has placed $100 at Barings for me. For the rest, the means I proposed to raise it by would go to the bottom with me, but Mother or my brothers in such a case would raise it, I am sure. I sail on the *Elizabeth*—Captain Hasty—for New York. We expect to sail to-morrow. Dear Marcus, Rebecca and Eddie, farewell. God bless you, from Margaret."

The *Elizabeth* was a new vessel; this fact recommended it. But Margaret wanted to have a look at it before trusting her beloved family to it. So she went one day with Mrs. Moshier to look it over. She met the Captain and his wife and was pleased with them. Captain Hasty was a ruddy, jovial New England sailor, his wife was a gentle soul. They returned to Florence with Margaret and Mrs. Moshier who invited them to spend the remaining days at her house.

Those remaining days were days of anguish for Margaret. She was so restless she could not sleep at night; during the day she could not remain still. "I am absurdly fearful ... it seems to me that my future on earth will soon close."

All her remaining evenings she spent with the Brownings. One evening she mentioned the prophecy which had been made about Ossoli—that he would die by drowning. This seemed to be constantly in her mind. In the endeavor to calm her mounting fears, she said with a smile to Mrs. Browning, "But our ship is called the *Elizabeth,* and I accept the omen."

But her fears were not calmed. All through that night they stalked through her restless sleep: She heard Angelo calling to her; he was in great trouble. She tried to go to him but could not move....

The next morning she wrote in her journal, "I have a vague expectation of some crisis, I know not what."

Ossoli slipped out of the house and went to church to pray.

The nurse took Angelo into the sun; he listened to the birds which filled all the high places; he gurgled, kicked and clapped his hands. He was a dimpled baby now and very intelligent. Margaret had no doubt that he would become a brilliant man. Had she not read only the best books and guided her thoughts carefully during those somber months of his creation? She wanted him to have her intellect and Ossoli's sweetness of disposition....

The last day. Margaret left her lodgings to wander among the most loved places. The air was soft and full of fragrances; the wind felt its way down from the white-capped Apennines. Peace was all around her, in the flaming gardens, in the ruins, in the trees. But peace in her own soul there was not. She thought how she had always set aside the year 1850— that year—as one in which she would reach some crisis— "where I should stand on a plateau in the ascent of life, where I should be allowed to pause for a while and take more clear and commanding views than ever before." In less than a week she would be forty years old.... And the future was murky.

She had said good-by to the Brownings, had done all the errands for friends in Boston, who seemed to have a craze for cameos just then. She had joked with Hiram Powers who was sending his marble statue of Calhoun home in the hold of the *Elizabeth*. It was a heavy thing; perhaps she had certain fears about it....

The trunks were packed, Angelo was dressed in warm clothes, Ossoli had at last put off his old brown uniform. The porter's wife kept jumping around, darting here and there and not forgetting to poke the corner of her apron into her eyes every little while. A young Italian girl, Celeste Paolini, who was going to America to find a fortune, undertook to look after Angelo on the voyage.

At last they were all on their way to Leghorn. And there

was the harbor with its orange and tawny sails fluttering and its red-shirted stevedores running back and forth. The *Elizabeth* sat calmly waiting for her company.

After a while they went on board. What a lifelessness there seemed to be everywhere! No bustle, no excitement, no sense of anticipation that makes an outgoing ship so mysterious a thing. One would have thought that the *Elizabeth* were contemplating retirement from service rather than a sixty-day voyage.

She was not to sail for two days. This, of course, explained everything.

But it brought back all of Margaret's fears. Perhaps it meant that she should not set sail; perhaps her Fates were giving her a chance to save herself....

She hurried from the *Elizabeth*. "Let us go back at once to Florence!"

On the way back, she felt that she could never return to Leghorn, could never screw her courage up sufficiently to go on board. The whole thing was very strange to her, she could not fathom it. She looked at Angelo, so happy, so irresistible; she looked at Ossoli, so sweet and trusting, so entirely dependent on her. And she prayed, "O Heavenly Father, if we are to die, let us, I pray Thee, all die together."

She wanted to spend the remaining time with the Brownings. It was her desire to see them again that made her return to Florence instead of spending the two last days in Leghorn. Thinking of them on her way back, that day, she had a sudden longing to cancel her passage to America and remain in Florence so that she might be always near them. They strengthened her and soothed her as no one else could do. But they were to leave. Within a few weeks they were going to Venice and afterwards to France. She could not keep journeying around after them....

On arriving in Florence, Margaret went at once to their house. She was in deep gloom and full of "sad presentiment."

Elizabeth Browning, looking at her, thought, "Has she ever been happy in anything? She told me once that she never had." Elizabeth felt more drawn to her that day than she ever had. What pure aspiration she had! What tenderness! What courage!

Before Margaret left, she gave Elizabeth a Bible for her child Robert. It was a parting gift from Angelo, she said. Opening it, Elizabeth saw written, "In memory of Angelo Eugene Ossoli." Strange, prophetic inscription!

That night, Elizabeth could think of nothing but Margaret's melancholy and the apprehension which showed so clearly in her eyes. For days she could think of nothing but this. And she thanked heaven for the warm sunshine and the fair winds and visualized the bark—her namesake—gracefully borne across calm waters toward Margaret's home, where there was to be a family reunion in July....

For several days the *Elizabeth* gave herself gracefully to the soft Mediterranean breeze; for several days the sun shone and the skies were blue. It seemed at last that fear had lost a footing in the world; or that it had been left on shore. There was more laughter aboard than there were sighs. Angelo sat gurgling at his toys, his father and mother went arm in arm around the deck. Celeste Paolini stared with big eyes at the sea and thanked the Blessed Virgin that things had started off so well. Horace Sumner was the only other passenger. He marched up and down, his hands in his pockets, a frown on his forehead—a singularly old and serious young man. Captain Hasty took a great fancy to Angelo and carried him around and showed him the mysteries of the ship. A happy and harmonious party!

Thus passed ten days. The next day the Captain did not appear and the mate assumed command. Margaret went to the captain's cabin to see what was wrong. Hasty was lying on the sofa, feverish and distressed. His wife was very anxious; she could not find anything which gave him any relief.

Margaret brought Angelo to him, to cheer him. The Captain smiled.

Each day Margaret did this; and each day the Captain smiled with more of an effort. His wife was beside herself with anxiety. Margaret tried to comfort her. "We shall soon be at Gibraltar; there we can have the advice of a doctor."

On the night before Sunday, June 2nd, the tall ramparts of Gibraltar rose up against the horizon; by midnight the *Elizabeth* was anchored alongside.

"Courage!" Margaret repeated, "very soon we shall have a doctor."

Through the remaining hours of the night they waited. Before sunrise a steward was sent on shore for a doctor. He returned in an hour, alone. The authorities, fearing that the Captain might be suffering from a contagious disease, would not allow him to land.

At eight o'clock there was no need of a doctor....

Margaret wrote to Marcus Spring: "... the last days were truly terrible. He died, we suppose (no physician has been allowed to come on board to see the body), of confluent smallpox.... I have seen great suffering, but nothing physical to be compared to this.... He died yesterday and was buried in deep water, the American consul's barge towing out one from the ship which bore the body. It was Sunday and divinely calm. You cannot think how beautiful the whole thing was, the decent array and sad reverence of the sailors, the many ships with their banners flying....

"Yes, it was beautiful, but how dear a price we pay for the poems of this world! We shall be now in quarantine a week....

"Should all end well, you see we shall be in New York later than we expected. But keep a lookout. Should we arrive safe, I should like to see a friendly face."

That week in quarantine was one of anxious waiting. Narrowly Margaret watched Angelo, who had been much in the Captain's cabin. If he were taken ill, she might arrange to have him removed to some hospital, where she and Ossoli would accompany him.... The voyage became again a dreadful thing; fear and apprehension came back with all their torments.... Her belief in omens was strong upon her. Perhaps they should give up the voyage. If Angelo fell ill, she would know that this was so; if he did not, they might continue safely.... Narrowly she watched the child....

On the 9th of June, the *Elizabeth* once more gave herself to the winds. "Now all speed forward," Margaret prayed. "Let us get to America as soon as possible." The sun shone and the skies were blue.

The very next day Angelo looked feverish. Margaret brought his toys to him; he scarcely noticed them. She talked to him; she made a cat do silly antics. He scarcely smiled.

So, it had happened! How Margaret hovered over him! She coaxed him to take cooling drinks, she soothed his little burning body with cold cloths.

For days she watched him suffer. His face was atrociously swollen, his body was covered with sores. Margaret did not dare to think that at any moment she might have to give him to the waves. She prayed constantly and tried to add this to her prayers: "If it be Thy will, O God!" But that was difficult. Much more natural to cry out against the injustice of a Power which created human lives apparently to torture them....

At length Angelo smiled....

Once more life resumed its natural course, once more the baby gurgled at his toys. Margaret got out her manuscript and put a few last finishing touches to her book. Horace Sumner sat in a sheltered corner of the deck and read to Ossoli.... The Captain's widow alone remained restless and inconsolable....

But as the *Elizabeth* drew nearer to a friendly shore, even Mrs. Hasty took heart. Four thousand miles had now been crossed; now dark outlines broke the crescent of the Western horizon.

Margaret thought of the gentle woods near Concord, of the birches and the weeping willows which drooped languidly over the Charles, of the quiet paths in Mount Auburn Cemetery, where she had walked so often with Richard. She would be late for the reunion, but what matter? Her family had waited four years for her . . . a few days more would be nothing. . . . She thought of Angelo growing up in America. Would he become a great writer? Would all her shattered dreams be pieced together and made whole in him? O, she must shield him from the early cares which corrode the spirit! He must be a free channel for the spirit of God to work through. . . .

On July 15th, the officer in command of the *Elizabeth* announced that they would be in New York at cockcrow. Joyous news!

And now papers are all gathered up and trunks are packed; only the few necessities for the night remain in the cabins.

The sun did not come out that day; a stiff wind blew from the Southeast. But just over there was the friendly shore of New Jersey. In the afternoon a fog rode over the sea. Night came on. The fog thickened. But the *Elizabeth* was a new vessel and as strong as steel.

By nine o'clock the wind was a howling monster. The officer in command gave orders for the sails to be close-reefed. The little group of passengers went to their staterooms, undressed, went to bed. Celeste Paolini prayed fervently that night, to her Blessed Virgin. Margaret prayed too, and listened to Angelo tossing restlessly in his berth.

Only a few more hours. . . .

By midnight the *Elizabeth* was in the jaws of a hurricane. All night the chief officer stood at his post, looking into the darkness. He knew that to the Northwest were sandbars. . . .

At the hour when the dawn was rising over New England roofs, there was a sudden jolt. The passengers started up in their berths, tried to strike lights. The roar of the sea was everywhere. Against it struck the voice of the chief officer: "Down with the mizzen!" "Cut away the mainmast!"

The chief officer ran down to the hold. Water was pouring in through a great gash in the bottom of the ship. The heavy marble statue of Hiram Powers' *Calhoun* was lying half in the vessel, half in the sands of Fire Island beach! Deep into the sand sank the bow of the *Elizabeth*, the stern was whipped about by the waves.

The passengers heard the sound of falling timbers. One long wail came from Margaret's cabin. . . .

Quickly the sea rushed over the deck, tore open cabin doors, smashed the skylight. Margaret grasped Angelo and wrapped him in a blanket. He began to weep. She soothed him, holding him against her breast and singing to him. Soon he fell asleep.

Celeste Paolini ran back and forth, wringing her hands, trying to mumble a prayer. Ossoli took her by the arm. Together they prayed to their Blessed Virgin to give them strength and courage for what they were about to face. . . .

There was a call for lifeboats. No one answered. Nothing but the roar of the sea and the heavy thud of falling timbers. The passengers thought that they were left alone, that the crew had taken the boats and attempted to go ashore. . . .

Three hours passed. Angelo slept on Margaret's breast, Ossoli comforted Celeste Paolini, Horace Sumner remained with Mrs. Hasty. They knew that at any moment, the large cabin might break up.

Mrs. Hasty went to the door and looked out. She saw a figure standing by the foremast, his face turned shorewards. She called to him. Her voice was lost. She remained standing there, calling and making signs.

The chief officer caught sight of her from the door of the forecastle and gave orders for a man to go to her. No one moved.

He went himself—a perilous journey—and reached the cabin safely. Then two sailors followed. "We must get you all to the forecastle," the chief officer said. "This cabin is likely to be smashed up at any moment."

Margaret looked down at Angelo, Celeste Paolini clung to Ossoli. After a long silence Mrs. Hasty volunteered to venture first to the forecastle.... With her went the officer and the two sailors, clinging to the rail, clinging to the bulwarks. They had not gone half a dozen steps when a wave broke over Mrs. Hasty and threw her into the hatchway. The officer caught her long hair in his teeth as she floated past him.... Thus he made his way, and thus they reached the forecastle in safety.

One by one, the others left the cabin, Angelo in a canvas bag slung around a sailor's neck....

Another hour passed.... Day came on and gave the huddled group a sight of the New Jersey shore—a stretch of barren sand dunes, only a few hundred yards away. It gave them a sight of one human being standing among those sand dunes, his face turned helplessly toward them. Between him and them raged the infuriated sea.

Suddenly some one said, "There is no use in our dying here like rats in a trap. We must swim." Some one else mentioned lifeboats—Mrs. Hasty perhaps. Lifeboats! They were long since taken by the sea.

A sailor tied a life preserver around his waist and jumped. All watched him but Margaret. She turned her face away. He rose and fell, he disappeared and reappeared. Eventually he stood beside the other human being on the shore.

A second sailor followed, and succeeded in reaching land.

Then Horace Sumner jumped. They saw him fall into the raging trough.... But he did not rise again....

For a time no one else ventured. They sat huddling together, their eyes on the stretch of sand dunes. Several figures were moving about now, and several carts. The figures were picking up bits of wreckage and throwing them into the carts.

Margaret murmured, "There still remains something which, if I live, will be of more value to me than anything." She sat with her head bowed and she thought of her months of work on the book which told the story of the siege of Rome....

Mrs. Hasty and the mate went next, and reached the shore.

It was Margaret's turn. She clasped Angelo closer and shook her head. "In life or death let us not be separated." Ossoli and Celeste Paolini remained by her side.

The chief officer tried to persuade her. She would not be persuaded. Her mind was heavy with the thought, "It is my demon, or it is my fate. I shall make no effort...."

A sailor on the lookout reported that he saw a lifeboat on the shore. Hope flamed up, but quickly died. It was impossible to man a boat in such a sea.

The chief officer said that he would take Angelo and that the sailors would help Margaret, Ossoli and Celeste Paolini. Margaret shook her head. Her long, brown hair streamed down over her shoulders and fell upon the face of Angelo asleep on her breast....

The chief officer gave the order, "Save yourselves!" Then he jumped. The Ossoli family and poor, fear-frenzied Celeste Paolini remained....

Noon came; mid-afternoon followed. The storm still raged. The cabin was now tumbling about in the sea and waves were running into the forecastle. The little group went out on deck and huddled around the foremast. But only for a moment. The waves wrenched this loose and tossed it into the sea. The four sailors who remained again urged Margaret to try to save herself—to go with them on a plank.... She shook her head.

The steward took Angelo from her. "I will save him or die, madam." Margaret started forward. A great wave rolled up and struck the forecastle. The mast fell, the deck swerved, the little group disappeared....

Margaret and Ossoli were never found. The little body of Angelo and the body of the steward were tossed up on the shore some twenty minutes afterwards. The story of the Siege of Rome remained among the strange company which haunts the depths of the sea.

Elizabeth Browning wrote: "Now she is where there is no more grief and 'no more sea'; and none of the restless in this world, none of the shipwrecked in heart ever seemed to me to want peace more than she did."